The Charlottesville, Lee Lynchburg and Johnson's Bedford Artillery

1st Edition

This series is dedicated to the men who served in Virginia Units during the War Between the States. It is the purpose of this series to preserve, as a part of our heritage, the deeds and sacrifices of these men. Your support of this project is greatly appreciated.

Number *461* of 1,000

Robert H. Moore, II

Manufactured in the United States by
H. E. Howard, Inc., Lynchburg, Virginia

Printed by H. E. Howard, Inc.

ISBN-1-56190-008-7

The Charlottesville, Lee Lynchburg and Johnson's Bedford Artillery

The Virginia Regimental Histories Series

VIRGINIA

SIC SEMPER TYRANNIS

1st Edition

Robert H. Moore II

DEDICATION

Dedicated to my wonderful wife and children for unequalled understanding and support without which this book would not have been possible.

Also to the men who served the guns
and truly gave their last full measure

Acknowledgements

First and foremost I need to give a well deserved recognition to my wife, Robin, my son, Tripp, and my daughter, Sarah, for giving me support, love, understanding, and most of all for putting up with every new story I found interesting.

An instrumental help in this book were the memoirs and papers of Wilbur Fisk Davis. For them, a great note of thanks is extended to Mr. J. Harvey Bailey of Charlottesville.

Another key contributor to be duly recognized is Lieutenant Colonel John P. Agnew, Ret., for the papers of John Herndon Gibson.

Others who played a considerable role in preparation of this book are Harold E. Howard (of course) for making this series possible, Ervin L. Jordan, Jr., of Alderman Library at the University of Virginia; and Patricia Wohlrab of the Preston Library at Virginia Military Institute. Thanks are also in order for those who helped at Fredericksburg and Spotsylvania National Military Park, Duke University, Furman University, the Albemarle Historical Society, Washington and Lee University, and the Tennessee State Library and Archives.

Thank you Mom and Dad for kindling the interest of a little boy, and allowing it to grow as I did.

A humorous note of thanks needs to be given to Joyce, Myrna, and Toni in Contract Administration for tolerating the "occasional" sound of the lone but loud printer from my 19-century cubicle.

I thank God as well, for seeing me through all times, whether troubled or good.

Havelock, N.C.
June, 1990

THE CHARLOTTESVILLE ARTILLERY
"They seemed to know how to use canister."
1862

Looking out upon the action, a young member of General John B. Floyd's staff could not help but take notice of Captain Guy's Goochland battery to his front. Its precision and clockwork motions stirred his enthusiasm as well as sparking an interest in somehow getting himself in on this fascinating branch of the service. The well educated and well bred young man was James McDowell Carrington, and the place that he witnessed the affair was Carnifix Ferry. Thus was the idea for the Charlottesville Artillery born.

Carrington, as well as being a nephew of General Floyd, was descended from a long line of generals, judges, and politicians who had played vital roles in Virginia's early history. Having attended the University of Virginia, at the time of John Brown's insurrection, Carrington like many others at the University joined the Southern Guards. The company went to Harpers Ferry "to see that fanatic," as Carrington recollected, "hung like every other violator of the laws of God and man should be." Later, at the outbreak of the war, he went to the Virginia Military Institute and attended its Military Science course of instruction for about six weeks, giving him a more firm military background before going to the field. Ironically, James's brother Edward had attended the Institute years before, and now held a commission in the opposing army. Once secured as a "sort of member" of his general/uncle's staff, the enthusiastic Virginian set off for the war and whatever fortunes it might bring. Following the battle of Carnifix Ferry, he received permission from General Floyd to return to Charlottesville and recruit his proposed artillery company.

Once in Charlottesville, Carrington called a meeting of interested individuals to meet at the armory, which was then situated in the courthouse yard, just in the rear of the building. The evening drew a larger crowd than anticipated. Politics filled the room in the efforts of some to gain positions within the proposed company. Carrington noted the competition seemed sharp, as there were several West Pointers and regular army officers attempting to gain the title of captain; but, he later wrote, "to my surprise, however and I confess some alarm, I was chosen for that position. I say alarm because at the time I had hardly attained my maturity and had no experience in the artillery service, and very little in the discipline of men."

With the elections complete and approximately 152 men organized into the new company, the command structure stood as follows: Captain Carrington, 1st Lieutenant James L. Dinwiddie, 2nd Lieutenant John H. Timberlake, 3rd Lieutenant Alexander B. Cochran, 4th Lieutenant "French" S. Bibb, 1st Sgt. Herbert H. Harris, 2nd Sgt. Kenneth McCoy, 3rd Sgt. John Hunter, 4th Sgt. Samuel J. Coffman, 5th Sgt. Thomas C. Wills, 6th Sgt. Waller Holladay, 7th Sgt. George Carrington, Quartermaster Sgt. Charles Harman, Bugler Nat Terrell, 1st Cpl. John Spooner, 2nd Cpl. Thomas L. P. Preston, 3rd Cpl. Francis M. Swoope, 4th Cpl. William Wills, 5th Cpl. Herndon Fife, 6th Cpl. D. Rodes Massie, 7th Cpl. Jere M. Harris, 8th Cpl. Charles P. Estill, 9th Cpl. Robert F. Maupin, 10th Cpl. Patrick Martin, 11th Cpl. John B. Brooks, and 12th Cpl. Elwood Brooks.

The essence of the company was drawn from some of Charlottesville's and the University's finest. Indeed, every officer and almost every sergeant had attended the University of Virginia. Many officers as well had attended VMI's Military Studies course of instruction. Others had also attended, either in combination with the University of Virginia or not, Washington College or Richmond.

Several of the new recruits were mere school boys, having held back (or been held back) from enlisting for some time. John G. Herndon had attemped to continue his education, but a definite fear struck him over the stories of recent Federal cavalry raids. Feeling threatened, the youth finally made up his mind to serve and made preparations to leave on March 13. After bidding a tearful farewell to his family he mounted his father's finest horse and, before riding off, made his vow never to disgrace the family name by cowardice or unfaithfulness. His timing and route were perfect; he enrolled in the Charlottesville Artillery's rolls on March 20.

After organizing, the company took up lodgings in the dormitories around Dawson's Row and the Monroe House on the grounds of the University. (Only one of the structures from the time still stands, the Luther P. Jackson House on Dawson's Row.) Many of the men, being so close to their homes, stayed with their families and showed up for musters and the occasional drilling. Though living a life of relative leisure, desertions and sickness did not take a holiday and spare the new company. The first casualty of the two menaces was Robert Draper, who died while residing at the barracks on April 10. Two more fell to desertion, Fleming Ford on April 23, and James Baber on May 5; neither were heard from again.

The kindess of the local ladies was exhibited in May through their generosity in supplying the company with "elegant uniforms." As Carrington remembered, the uniforms were "too elegant, in fact, for the use to which it was soon put." (Later in the accounts of Port Republic, it is suggested that these uniforms were either blue or gave such an appearance.)

The ladies also provided the men with "many other conveniences and luxuries which only their patriotism and thoughtfulness could suggest."

The only concern of the company during its life of ease was that it was taking an incredibly long time to be supplied with cannons and equippage. If something was not soon delivered, there loomed the ominous threat of being converted into the service of the dreaded infantry. Turning to his mother, Carrington relied on her "blood" influences. In a short time his mother's efforts proved effective. The authorities were finally induced to supply the company with what it needed. By late April there arrived four guns from the Tredegar Iron Works at Richmond: two three-inch rifles and two six-pound smoothbores. Two more were promised for delivery sometime in May. Carrington referred to them as "hard specimens even at that time, . . . but they did pretty good service."

By May 15, two ten-pound iron howitzers arrived with ammunition and the company, including 104 horses, was ready for the field. As anticipated, that same day orders arrived for the battery to move immediately into the Shenandoah Valley to join Major General Richard S. Ewell's forces near Front Royal. The caissons were filled, two days of rations prepared, and sorrowful goodbyes finally delivered.

Saturday, May 17, dawned soon enough for the green battery. Setting off by midday the battery found, as Wilbur Davis recalled, "the whole town agog and we found it hard to get off." Finally leaving the environs of Charlottesville, the battery moved the first day about eight to ten miles toward Standardsville, finally halting for the night and for the first time bivouacking as a company.

The next day the battery pressed on through Standardsville, Wolftown, and Madison Court House. The unit camped on the 19th on Dr. Early's farm; on the 20th on the Gibbon Conway farm; and on the 21st on Robertson River, where Joseph Cheeny slipped away as another deserter. About noon on the 22nd the battery once more set out, with the goal of crossing the Blue Ridge at Milam's Gap.

As the company trudged up the mountain, the "gap" seemed to defy its definition, and certainly was not as easy to cross as anticipated. Wilbur Davis referred to it as no more than a "slight depression." For what seemed a distance of seven miles the sun was unmerciful; but to the men's delight, every few hundred yards or so they encountered "sparkling cold mountain streams." Resting but a few seconds at each "oasis" the men moved on, having been revitalized at every stop. The descent passed much more quickly, covering about half the distance of the ascent. Upon reaching the base, the company set up bivouac in Page County.

The following morning the battery resumed its march toward the pleasant town of Luray, where they camped overnight. At about 5 p.m. on the 24th the men moved toward Front Royal, camping again just four miles from Luray. En route, they could hear guns in the distance, causing their pulses to race wildly. Again on the road first thing in the morning, the battery passed through Front Royal, camping four miles beyond that night. On the 26th they moved through Winchester, camping four miles out toward Harpers Ferry. Young Private Herndon recollected:

> We wanted if possible to get in on the capture or death of the in-
> vaders, but the valley pike being in good order and Banks men
> fleet of feet, our battery failed to get a shot. We however saw
> some of the aftermath along the road near Kernstown, some
> few dead yanks and deserted guns and cannon. I can never
> forget the face and form of one warworn young man who had
> been killed near a cluster of bramble briars on the road and
> evidently had been overlooked. That was the first real forceful
> lesson taught me of the horrors of war.

Upon reaching the camp near Bunker Hill, Captain Carrington reported to General Ewell. The battery joined "Stonewall" Jackson's com- mand and unofficially was assigned to General Dick Taylor's Louisiana Brigade.

Jackson was no stranger to Carrington. He often had seen Carring- ton while he attended Washington College and while residing at his uncle's house, Governor James McDowell. At one of his uncle's affairs Carrington first met Jackson, then a professor at VMI. Of him, Carring- ton said:

> [I] frequently saw General Jackson those days, but never an-
> ticipated his immortal fame. He was exceedingly eccentric, so
> much that it was a subject of general comment. . . .

Following a brief rest at Bunker Hill, the battery moved with Jackson's army at high speed back up the valley to avoid being pinned by Generals Fremont and Shields, both fast approaching. The battery had to leave six of its sick behind in a Winchester hospital, all of whom were cap- tured and later exchanged; only four of them returned to the company for further service.

Being placed among the reserves and wagons in the marching order, the Charlottesville Artillery reached Strasburg on May 31. For the rest of the day the battery camped on the hills overlooking the river. About mid- night orders came to move again, but to leave some men behind to keep the fires buring to deceive the enemy.

Forcing their jaded and tired horses onward, Carrington's battery continued through Edinburg and Mt. Jackson. During one overnight stop on this march the men were forced to make do with whatever shelter they could find in the driving rain. While Wilbur Davis made his shelter "with no protection but a blanket wrapped around me on rails," Private Leroy Cox along with another comrade, found some shelter on the front porch of a small cottage. Cox reminisced:

> The cottage had a long porch and we decided to sleep there. While asleep General Jackson and his staff came up and camped on the same porch. We later learned that some of his staff wanted to move us, but he said, "No let them stay here." When we woke up the next morning I found to my surprise that I had some of General Jackson's cover on me. . . .

Moving on through Harrisonburg at around 4 p.m. on June 5, the company settled into camp four miles toward Port Republic. During their trip from Mt. Jackson, the company suffered three more desertions: Charles Creedon, B. J. Wheeler, and John Yochum.

The evening of the 6th found the Charlottesville men caught in another heavy downpour. To protect themselves, Davis remembered, they "used the large tarpaulins, covers for the guns, to protect ourselves. . . spreading over rails in fence corners. It was while lying under one of these we learned of the death of General Ashby."

The following day the battery moved, along with the ordnance and baggage trains, under a warm sun for some distance before finally crossing the bridge at Port Republic, passing through the village, and settling in a depression behind the Kemper house southwest of town. After setting up camp, several of the men took advantage of the pleasant June afternoon by bathing in the river. Others visited nearby Weyer's Cave.

Sunday, June 8, dawned bright and calm. The general consensus in the camp, however, was that it would not be so peaceful later in the day, despite Jackson's preference to keep the Sabbath holy. Young Cox decided that he would enjoy a short trip over to the river, and asked John Risk if he could borrow his horse and water him while there. Risk accepted the offer, and Cox mounted the grey-dapple horse and rode away.

Captain Carrington stepped out of his tent into the beautiful morning and began putting on a clean shirt. Breaking the morning calm came the hard hoofbeats of the horse of Charles Harman, the Quartermaster Sergeant, who had been sent out to find forage before dawn. Pulling hard on the reins, the sergeant in a nervous rush blurted out that the Yankees were on their way from the direction of the South Fork of the river. Skeptical of Harman's hasty report, Carrington looked over at the porch of the two-story house (still standing today), and saw that Jackson's headquarters people seemed, as Carrington evaluated it, to be "sitting unconcerned." Turning to his Quartermaster Sergeant, Carrington replied to the effect that his report could not be true, and sent him off to continue foraging.

A short time later Harman returned, only to be sent off in much the same fashion as before. Harman soon appealed yet again to Carrington to take heed. Carrington again glanced over to the Kemper house, and this time saw the general and his staff moving hurriedly about. Jackson soon after bounded off on foot in the direction of the bridge. Cox had returned from the river just in time to witness the beginning of the scamper.

Suspecting that the sergeant was right after all, Captain Carrington called upon Nat Terrell to blow the alarm. Once the lieutenants were made aware, the horses and guns were ordered hitched and made ready to move.

Total chaos quickly affected the Confederates in the little village. So much stood at stake; perhaps the very loss of the Valley could result. Jackson and his staff, and just beyond the camp of the Charlottesville Artillery, and the army's entire supply train (with its bright white covers recently supplied by the Federal army) were vulnerable to capture. To add the "worse upon the bad," the bridge that led from Cross Keys to this village was vital; all of the other bridges on the Shenandoah had been burned, and with the Shenandoah so swollen from recent rains, an attempt to ford the river at any point would be in vain. Therefore, if the Port Republic bridge was destroyed, Jackson would be dangerously cut off from communications with a large portion of his army. All that stood between the enemy and the potential "harvest" was the one six-gun battery, a cavalry troop under Captain J. J. Chipley, and a small complement of infantry (three officers and twenty-two men) from Co. I, 2nd Virginia Infantry, under Captain Samuel J. C. Moore. The stage was set for a huge Confederate disaster.

The oncoming threat was lead by Colonel Samuel Sprigg Carroll of the 8th Ohio Infantry, followed by a band of about 150 horsemen of the 1st Virginia (Federal) Cavalry and Battery L of the 1st Ohio Artillery. At first the colonel ordered the cavalry, under Major Benjamin F. Chamberlain, to seize the bridge. The major fell from his horse in the advance, however, resulting in general confusion, and the cavalry returned to Carroll's position. While minutes were lost, Carroll attempted to reevaluate the situation, and ordered Captain Lucius Robinson to open his battery while Captain Earle S. Goodrich took the cavalry forward a second time. Once the bridge was secured, the bluecoat Virginians turned their horses up the main street toward the Kemper house and all lying beyond it. The cavalry pickets fled fast before them.

Carrington had first sight of the enemy "just as some cavalry (Confederate) reached the fence around Kemper's yard where the street turns at right angles into the Staunton Road. Some Confederate officer, whose name I have never found out, had the presence of mind to ride by me and a loud voice halloo, 'Bring up the artillery,' in response to this it will be

6

remembered by some members of the company, that we did roll by hand one piece (from Timberlake's section) in sight so as to command the road from the angle. . .Near us were a few infantry under the command, I think of Lieutenant Preston."

As the group of Confederate cavalrymen turned the corner off the main street they saw the piece, along with the infantry and temporarily drew up in a line in front of it. The cavalry fire was wild and ineffective. Running up to one of them, Cox pleaded for one of the cavalrymen's pistols, as he was sure he would make every shot count. As this was going on the group fired into the galloping enemy and temporarily dispersed them. The Confederate horsemen then drew up and raced away, leaving Cox without his opportunity.

Minutes seemed like hours as all of this transpired. The battery's camp was in an utter state of confusion and panic. Davis remembered that "some were ordering one thing. . .some another." This was probably true, as in a postwar account Carrington claimed to have ordered one section to remain with him at the camp, while the other two sections under Lieutenants Dinwiddie and Timberlake were ordered up two hundred and four hundred yards respectively. Cox recollected the opposite. He remembered that the orders had been to "hitch up and fall back up the Valley as rapidly as possible." As the following seconds showed, whether due to misinterpretation or due to the will to run itself Dinwiddie's and Timberlake's sections began to flee.

Davis later wrote: "In short order the drivers harnessed and hitched the horses and were ordered to limber up and dash up the road in retreat. . . .[on] the road to Waynesboro which many of the cavalry picket had already taken in panic flight."

Drivers urged the hitched horses of the battery onward, out of the village. With perhaps an overdramatic account of the situation, Cox recollected:

I, a mere boy, rushed up to Lieutenant Timberlake and said, "for God's sake, don't let us run without firing a shot." He was sitting on his horse and looked more a general than a lieutenant, his eyes lit up as only a gallant soldier's will flash when all of his faculties are in play and taking the wonderful responsiblity upon himself, being only third officer in command, he at once drew his sword and seemed to grow in stature as he stood high in his stirrups and said, "I will stand with my two pieces if they are captured!" He at once darted off after one piece, sword in hand, to stop it and I heard him appealing and ordering them to stop it and bring it back. The driver of the head horse, Doc Gardner, turned his horse toward the advancing column, while the driver of the big wheel horse, the Irishman substitute Brown jumped and fled. In his place, a colored man, Edmund Drew. . . .

With the piece soon effectively overtaken, Timberlake brought it back into position in the Kemper lawn, a few feet behind the stake and rail fence. "The question," remembered Carrington, "was whether we should open on them with canister. We were afraid that Jackson and his staff had been captured, and were with this cavalry and might be killed. We hesitated but then the order was given by the Yankee Colonel to charge, and hearing this, the Confederate artillery opened on them, aided by Moore's infantry. . . ."

Private Cox, acting number one at this twelve-pound howitzer yelled back to Sam Shrieve for a double charge of canister. Shrieve replied. "there is none." Cox blurted back, "Then bring me anything!" Julius Goodwin, also at the gun, loaded the powder and shell. Cox rammed it home and ran around to pull the lanyard. To the gunner's disgust, they had forgotten to elevate the piece and the shot blasted the fence in front of them, sending splinters and fragments of wood along the way. The shot still proved effective, and the enemy halted their advance.

Davis remembered of Lieutenant Dinwiddie's section, to which he was attached: "Off we dashed, the drivers whipping their horses to a rapid trot and we went running alongside. . ." Having gotten over a hundred yards, Lieutenant Dinwiddie struck out after his crew and pursued them until he overtook them at gallop. The lieutenant finally had to draw "a pistol on some of the drivers to enforce his commands. . . ." Once he gained control of the section, the lieutenant led it back to the Kemper yard.

As Dinwiddie's section returned, Captain Carrington noticed that "Dr. Dabney appeared upon the scene and after some conversation with him as to what could be done with the artillery, the Doctor rode with me (along with Dinwiddie's section) directing me through a lane which led in front of the Kemper house. I unlimbered the section there. . . ."

Davis commented on events at about this time:

The first (no. 1) gun to which I belonged was the one of these on the left. I was no. 4 and my duty consisted in using the lanyard . . . . however, when we came to look in the box in which the lanyard is carried on the gun, lo and behold, it had been carelessly jostled out and lost, nothing there in place of it. By the time the gun was loaded, however, a driver handed me his whip to use as a lanyard. Tying each friction primer in succession to the end of the lash, I managed in the first fight of our battery, to make it answer the purpose. After loading and standing ready to fire, Major Dabney ordered us to hold our fire.

For the second time that day there was some concern whether or not

8

the gun should open. The uncertainty this time was to whether or not the troops to their front were friend or foe. The wait was short, for in a seconds the answer came from an enemy gun posted at the far end of the main street. Davis saw "a puff of smoke from a cannon, and a shell crashing through a frame building just in our left front, not 20 yards off, but considerably above our heads." Dinwiddie's crews, and Timberlake's just above the rise to the left, responded to the Ohio gun at a range of about 400 yards, with loads of canister.

Davis's crew found matters worse after the first shot. The lanyard was not their only problem. The rammer had its sponge broken off earlier by being run over. With each discharge of the gun, Marshall Burgoyne, no. 1 at the piece, had his fears heightened in anticipation of a premature discharge. After about three shots he could take no more and hesitated in loading the un-spounged gun. Hanson Boyden, seeing the fear in the big Irishman's eyes, "sprang forward and volunteered," as Davis recalled, "in each exercise of ramming. . . .trying to manage to lose as little as possible of his arms if the gun should go off while he was at it."

Minutes later Confederate artillery from the opposite side of the bridge caught the enemy in tight fix, and encouraged a general withdraw of the enemy from the village. A charge by the 37th Virginia Infantry across the bridge sealed the fate of the Federals. The enemy left in their wake two cannon with caissons and at least fourteen dead horses. Carrington rode up later and viewed the prizes and carnage that his battery had assisted in executing. Jackson, his staff, and the supply train had been saved. Cox took particular delight in the general's reaction: "Jackson later came up and said, when he saw where we had shot canister through the plank fence, 'If it was a lot of green men, they seemed to know how to use canister.' "

The only casualty suffered by the battery was Henry Clay Page, The wound, though unspecified, was bad enough to have him discharged several weeks later. Daniel Brown, having run during the fight, deserted and never returned.

The Charlottesville boys had played an indirect role earlier, when Captain Poague's Rockbridge Artillery stood ready atop the banks of the river opposite the village. "Stonewall" spied a single field piece manned by blueclad gunners moving in the direction of the opposite end of the bridge. Naturally the general suspected that it was an enemy gun and turned to Poague. "Fire on that gun!" barked the chieftain to the captain. Poague replied, "General those are our men!" Again Old Jack repeated the order, to which Poague protested once more. After Poague explained that he had seen Carrington's new battery earlier at the Kemper place, and that it was clad in uniforms similar to the men at the bridge, Jackson paused. Riding up a little way, Jackson shouted, "Bring that gun up here!"

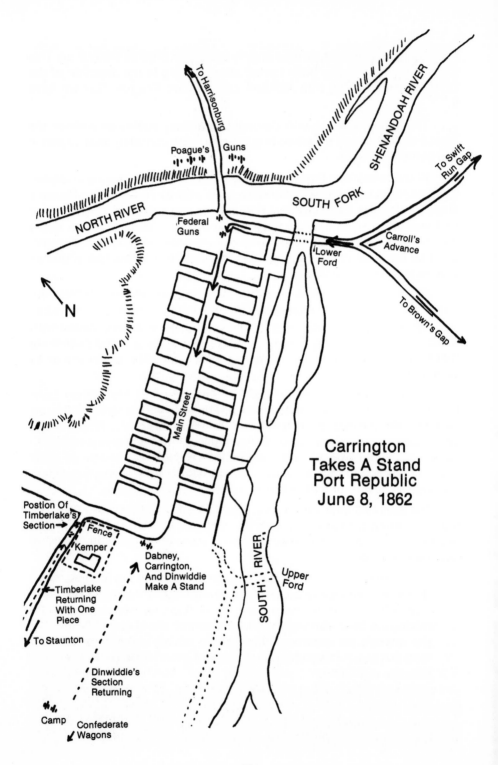

To Harrisonburg

Poague's Guns

SHENANDOAH RIVER

To Swift
Run Gap

SOUTH FORK

NORTH RIVER

Federal
Guns

Carroll's
Advance

N

Lower
Ford

To Brown's Gap

Main Street

Carrington
Takes A Stand
Port Republic
June 8, 1862

Postion Of
Timberlake's
Section

Fence

Kemper

Dabney,
Carrington,
And Dinwiddie
Make A Stand

SOUTH RIVER

Upper
Ford

Timberlake
Returning
With One
Piece

To Staunton

Dinwiddie's
Section
Returning

Camp   Confederate
Wagons

Receiving no response, he rose angrily and again ordered the gun up. This time, the gun opposite them turned about aiming in the direction of the Confederates. Seeing this Jackson commanded Poague: "Let'em have it."

The following day found Carrington's battery posted on a hill on the west side of the river, commanding the fords. The company took no part in the battle of June 9.

With the battle of Port Republic won and the enemy reeling in retreat, the Charlottesville Artillery withdrew with Jackson's army into Brown's Gap, burning the bridge at Port Republic to prevent pursuit. A deserved rest was afforded in the few days that followed. During the time, many men from the company fell ill and returned to Albemarle County. The only one that never returned and was later dropped from the company rolls as a deserter was Caleb Goode.

At the expiration of its "vacation from the war" at Brown's Gap, the Valley army moved into Albemarle County, and then back into the valley near Rockfish Gap. In the days that followed, trains arrived loaded with reinforcements, causing rumors to fly about the camp of the possibility that they might be going back down the valley, or by Manassas and on to Washington.

Wilbur Davis took one of these trains ahead of his battery from Mechum's River to Charlottesville to have time to visit his family. En route he witnessed the evident fatigue that had befallen Jackson. Riding in the same car as the General, Davis looked back at him, "3 or 4 seats back. . . He sat barehead with his eyes sometimes closed — sometimes wide open — looking steadily forward — with a faraway unspeakably calm expression — not turning his head or saying a word to anyone."

The battery continued on past Charlottesville, with no help from the trains, passing through Gordonsville, Louisa Court House, and finally reached Ashland, where the company went into camp at the old racetrack. Herndon wrote:

> . . .so exhausted from the day and night marching, we dropped down and fell asleep soundly for several hours. having in our haversacks some fat bacon and loose flour, we commenced mixing the flour with water from canteens on the stumps (using the stumps as kneeding boards) and taking the dough we wound it around well sharpened sticks, turning them every few minutes until done.

Attached officially now to Taylor's Louisiana Brigade, the Charlottesville Artillery set out from Ashland on June 26, as Herndon remembered "with orders not to sound a drum or fife or fire a shot." Davis recalled having crossed "the C&O at or near Atlee's — Had to move slowly by crossroads, going continually farther and farther east around Richmond — crossing road after road as they converge toward the city."

Continuing along with Dick Ewell's division, the march took them past the Lebanon, near Merry Oaks, and Shady Grove Churches. Finally, a little after 5 p.m., they reached a position on Jackson's right. The day was hot and the march miserable, men having occasionally fallen out to obtain water from a nearby stream. Gratefully the men of the battery stopped and bivouacked for the night.

The following morning the battery was again on the road with its brigade now under the command of Colonel Isaac G. Seymour. Due to being misled by a guide, Jackson's men lost valuable time. Finally reaching Old Cold Harbor, the artillery slowly massed on the left of the Confederate line upon the battlefield. The Charlottesville company did not reach the site until late in the afternoon.

The distance travelled along the way was rough, the roads being poor and narrow, and the ambulances and wagons crowding the batteries out and preventing their passage to the front. Davis recalled upon nearing the battlefield that "the musketry firing was the most continuous — overwhelming and prolonged I ever heard. It must have lasted from about 3 p.m. til 8. We could see nothing of it for the woods — though frequently somewhat under fire. . . ."

With the batteries strung out all along the road, Davis did recollect seeing one deploy (Pelham's) not far to their front and open on the Federal batteries. Though Davis recollected not becoming engaged, reports indicate that at least one section was, deploying with Brockenbrough's and Courtney's near the left of the line. The casualties of the day included Dallas Rhodes and J. W. West wounded and one caisson from Carrington's battery hit by a shot from the enemy. "It all came to a stop," declared the Tarheel-born author, "with the yelling charge which captured the [enemy] battery."

After a gruesome breakfast the following morning (of recently captured crackers, meat, and coffee) amongst large numbers of Federal dead, the battery resumed its place in the line of march with Ewell's division.

The trek on that hot summer day led Carrington's Battery down the north side of the Chickahominy River to the York River Railroad. After staying at that place "all Sunday," they were ordered across the Chickahominy at Bottom's Bridge, crossing there around dusk, finally halting and pitching camp in a heavy rain in the already marshy bottomland. While Davis made his bed atop a caisson, most of the others lay "down in the corn rows, and actually in the water."

The following morning, June 30, the soaked men marched again with

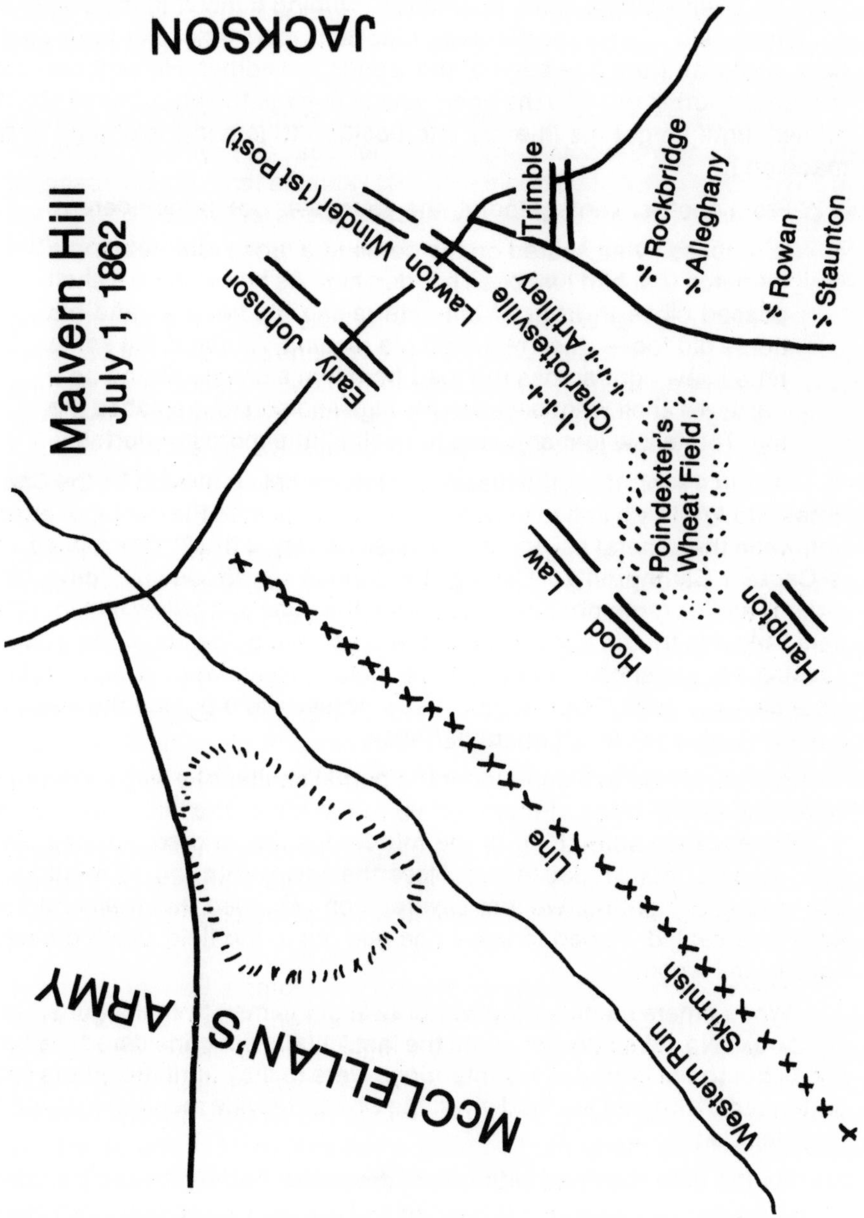

Malvern Hill
July 1, 1862

JACKSON

Rockbridge

Alleghany

Rowan

Staunton

Trimble

Lawton Winder (1st Post)

'Charlottesville' Artillery

Early Johnson

Poindexter's Wheat Field.

Law

Hood

Hampton

Line

Skirmish

Western Run

McCLELLAN'S ARMY

13

the division to Savage Station and White Oak Swamp, not becoming engaged before bivouacking again for the night.

Up and moving again on the morning of July 1, Carrington's Battery reached the action at Malvern Hill between 2 and 3 p.m. Once there the company took shelter in a wooded area and out of sight of the enemy. Even so, enemy shells came in on them. Finding himself in the presence of "Stonewall," Davis recollected: "Jackson rode time and time again back and forth from one edge of the woods to another. He sent one battery after another out into the open field to engage the attention of McC's artillery until he got his infantry into position to join in the charge to be made on it."

From another vantage point, the youngster Cox remembered:

> . . .Jackson was seated on his horse at a cross road reading a dispatch that had just been handed him. As he sat there a shell passed close in front of him. He raised his head — and his horse did too — then resumed his reading. At about the same time I saw right across the road from him a private sitting on a log and a shell went between his legs and sort of displaced the log. The fellow just adjusted himself a little more comfortably.

Within a short time, the dispatch Jackson held proved to be the Charlottesville Artillery's call to service. Again Cox claimed the center of attention when the general asked him, "Whose battery is this?" Cox replied, "It is Captain Carrington's." Calling the captain up, Stonewall "gave him orders" as Cox remembered "to unlimber the guns and follow him into the field." Moving the six guns by hand the crews struggled out of the woods, passing by batteries coming off the field. "There were a great many wounded and dead," Cox wrote. "I saw horses there pulling the wagons out with two legs cut off about half way."

Having been led to a spot under the partial shelter of a slope, the guns were loaded and three of them run up to the top of the hill. Davis wrote: ". . .We escaped something of the murderous fire, and so suffered less than some of our predecessors. Nevertheless, within the 15 minutes, I conjecture, of fighting, we lost several men wounded and many horses were so disabled we had to leave one gun out in the field, when ordered back to the woods."

When orders came for the withdrawal of the men from the guns, Cox cried out, "No, let's stay here until the last." Listeners considered the boy brave, but to the contrary, his intentions were to stay until the others had gotten out of the way and had given the Charlottesville men a clear path if they decided to run.

By the time they had withdrawn, the actual battery losses included one killed and two wounded (I. Iseman and Addison Roler wounded) more than a dozen horses killed or disabled. The gun left in the field was later recovered when some men volunteered to drag it back.

The following day, the company went out into camp three miles west of the battlefield. It moved again on July 3, one mile nearer to Richmond. The unit stayed for a couple of weeks, Davis recalled, "the whole time never free from stench of decaying horses."

On July 14 the company was ordered to General W. N. Pendleton, who assigned it to Major William Nelson's Battalion of Reserve Artillery. The battery moved four miles east of the capital near Nine Mile Road. The Charlottesville Battery was joined by Huckstep's Fluvanna, Kirkpatrick's Amherst, and R. C. M. Page's Morris Artillery.

The weeks that followed found the new battalion moving about Richmond: on the 16th, four miles up the York River Railroad; and on the 17th around Richmond, crossing the Mechanicsville Turnpike and camping on the Virginia Central Railroad. During their travels, an election was held and John Hunter was promoted to 1st Sergeant; McCoy to 2nd Sergeant; Thomas Wills to 3rd Sergeant; Waller Holladay to 7th Sergeant; and Swoope to Corporal. Desertion also struck again when on July 13, Patrick Shannon, a transfer from the 19th Virginia Infantry, slipped away. On the 16th James Lewis found his way out. Lewis was later discharged, however, due to having enlisted without parental consent.

The lull of moving about and drilling was broken when on August 6 the battery marched down the Charles City Road to the vicinity of Mechanicsville, then ordered to rejoin Jackson at Gordonsville, finally arriving there on the 12th. En route, at a camp near Louisa Court House, several men of the company took note of the booming of guns some miles away at Cedar Mountain, which had at first been mistaken for distant thunder.

At Gordonsville, the Charlottesville Artillery resumed its daily drilling and tried to make due with whatever was available to shelter themselves from the heat and summer storms. While drilling one day the newly elected 2nd Sergeant McCoy was run over by a caisson, sending him to a hospital and crippling him temporarily.

Remaining near the quaint little town and missing both Manassas and Sharpsburg, the Charlottesville Artillery was finally ordered to rejoin the army in the Shenandoah Valley on September 21. After five days, the battery reached Bunker Hill and was assigned once again to the Louisiana Brigade, D'Aquin's Louisiana Guard Artillery already being attached to Hays.

The Virginians tried to get along among the Louisianans. Harmony did reign for the most part; however, many of the Charlottesville men felt disappointment when their own battery was so often during that fall referred to as the Louisiana battery. The title apparently not entirely incorrect, for on October 4 artillerist Marshall Burgoyne was found to have been a deserter from the 8th Louisiana. Though he was returned to his regiment, the Charlottesville Artillery had not seen the last of this big Irishman.

Early on the morning of October 17, Carrington's Battery left its modest bivouac and set out on the road again toward Martinsburg, finally reaching that place with the brigade at about 2 p.m. on the 18th. The following day the artillerists moved with the brigade up to the Baltimore and Ohio tracks. As the Louisiana infantrymen descended upon the railroad, the artillerists lounged about their guns and gazed in awe at the amazing work before them, of which Davis wrote: "...the infantry did it — burning the ties in great piles, and laying the iron rails across. After the rails got hot enough in the middle, they were bent so as to be useless."

The following afternoon the battery returned with its brigade to camp near Martinsburg, and then on the next morning through the town to the railroad east of it, camping again. On October 23 at 6 a.m. the brigade passed back through Martinsburg, and to within one and a half miles of the Bunker Hill encampment.

Upon returning to their camp, Carrington's men relaxed in the splendor of the Valley's magnificent fall foliage. Of the company's time there, Davis recalled:

> What a glorious fall that was! and what a magnificent country that was! I have never seen elsewhere such grand forests, or such gorgeous coloring on the hickory, poplar, sugar maple, and other trees. How we revelled in the bracing air and enjoyed the fires. In the latter we often burned whole tree trunks, laying flat on the ground after trimming huge hickory and sugar maple often from 2 to 3 or 4 feet in diameter, burning their whole length, and we sleeping in solid ranks, feet to fire. This happened only a few times of course.

That fall Lieutenant Dinwiddie left the company. He later held a position in the Ordnance Department and reached the rank of major.

On November 2, the period of rest and relaxation was broken when skirmishing was reported at Snicker's Gap and the battery received orders at 4 p.m. to prepare to move. The following morning at about 6, the company set out for Berryville, and then on to Millwood, reaching the latter place at 4 p.m. Twenty four hours later the battery pressed on again until it reached a point outside of Front Royal and camped on a Mr. Mitchell's farm.

Carrington's men again hitched their horses and moved the following day toward the Shenandoah River. By the 7th matters worsened as snow began to fall.

At 3:30 on November 15 the column came to a halt as another railroad-destruction effort began. The battery posted itself in camp next to the Courtney Artillery, and looked on as the infantry tore up tracks.

On November 17, the battery with its contingent recrossed the mountain and spent the next several days under a heavy cold rain.

When the rain subsided, and at light on the 21st, the battery moved with the Louisianans to White Post, through Front Royal, along the Valley Pike, then on to Newtown, Shepherdstown, and finally into camp one mile beyond. The following three days, the men of Charlottesville found matters no easier, rising at light every day and marching through Woodstock, Edinburg, and Mt. Jackson on the 22nd; New Market and across the Massanutten on the 23rd; and on the 24th across the Blue Ridge at Fisher's Gap.

Davis wrote of the crossing:

...took whole day to pass the gap ... about 12 miles — 5 up from the valley and 7 down. We got over to a bare rocky desolated region, without wood of any kind — except rails. Jerry Harris, seeing we were soon to go into camp, picked up a good turn of rails to cook with, and he was a stout stalwart six footer. He had hardly got them well up when old Jube Early, our Division Commander, came riding up and with an oath ordered, "Drop those rails." Jerry promptly obeyed, but stood right in the same tracks till old Jube got out of sight and then picked those rails back up again and went on to camp. Old Jube himself, I don't doubt sat by a rail fire that night, for there was no other wood to be got as far as I could see.

At about 7:30 a.m. on November 25, the army was well on its way to deal with the oncoming threat of Burnside's Army of the Potomac. The Charlottesville battery over the next five days travelled through Madison, Liberty Mills, Orange Court House, and on November 30 by 3 p.m. reached Chancellorsville.

The following day the battery struck out early and on December 2, after a night of rest, arrived at about 9:30 a.m. just six miles from Guiney Station.

On December 4 the battery was sent out with a Whitworth of Hurt's Alabama battery to Port Royal, where, Herndon wrote, they were to "watch the gunboats in case they attempted a trip up the river." After some days of staring at each other and some firing back and forth, Herndon felt that "They failed to attempt, thinking perhaps prudence would be the batter part of valor."

The picket position was relieved on December 12, and the Charlottesville Artillery was ordered back to join the army at Fredericksburg, getting within four miles of there by midnight. After a short rest the battery rose early the next morning and reached Hamilton's Crossing after the action had already opened. Parking in a sheltered spot behind a range of hills, the battery awaited orders to go forward. Davis wrote of the day:

> There we spent the day, on the south slope of the hill just west of the railroad, and protected it, tho the shells from across the river and from nearby were flying over and sometimes seeming to skim the ground. We lay down very close to the ground — not called into action at all — tho very fierce fighting and looking for orders to go in. Ned Massie, who had been promoted from our battery to a lieutenancy in the infantry (elected) came by us with a flesh wound thro. the leg — exulting in the glorious infantry charge he had taken part in, which had driven the Yankees in confusion. "Boys! Boys!' " he cried, "it was worth a wound like mine to be in that charge and see the Yankees run." He told us the infantry fighting wasn't half so scary as artillery, tho he knew it was more dangerous.

Later in the evening, the Charlottesville Artillery moved to A. P. Hill's left and replaced Latimer's and Brown's batteries coming off the line. Here the battery awaited the renewal of battle on the following day and gazed out into the night sky at the haunting Aurora Borealis.

Three-thirty in the morning came awfully soon for Carrington's gunners as they were aroused from their short sleep and ordered out several hundred yards in front of, and to the left of, the Louisiana Brigade in order to confront what was thought to be an advancing column of the enemy. Anticipation was high for the battle to reopen, much as it had the morning before. Colonel Edmund Pendleton, commanding the Louisianans, commented in his post-action reports, however, that the battery was "not to open unless the enemy threatened us with an attack as we would thereby attract. . . crossfire of three enemy batteries, from which ground afforded no protection."

Davis remembered that once the guns reached the woods opposite their destination, the gunners "paused long enough. . . to engage in a prayer led by Sergt. Waller Holladay." Unlimbering his pieces on a wide level plain, Carrington at once detected movement about a mile off, and broke the morning calm with blasts from his rifled pieces. At once, and as Colonel Pendleton had predicted, return fire was delivered quickly and began to inflict damage.

Within minutes the guns were ordered to cease fire, light beginning to show that indeed there were no advancing Federals. The battery held its position throughout the day. Random firing continued, doing less damage than before dawn. In the foray, five men were wounded: Isaiah Iseman, Hugh Patton; William Gillespie and Cpl. William Harding both severely in the shoulder; and Alonzo Wheat, who was run over by a caisson and died in March. Seven horses were also disabled. Davis recalled that in the lull, "At one time, a flag of truce passed and then we could see, perhaps half a mile off or more, the lines of battle — the men, all standing, who had been lying down, for a mile or two, to the right and left over the level plain. That was the last of it — as the enemy withdrew across the river under darkness of night."

Returning to the picket line at Port Royal on December 19, the Charlottesville Artillery, along with a Whitworth detachment, took rest in a thicket of pines and cedars, enjoying life not unlike that of a regular camp. When time and darkness permitted, some men of the battery would find a way to contact the enemy pickets and work out trades, usually taking a party on a small boat and meeting midway in the river. The exchanges were of the common nature often written about, and generally consisted of the Confederates trading tobacco for coffee. Lieutenant Dinwiddie even took advantage of one such meeting and was able to send some letters through the lines. Passing Christmas on the Rappahannock, the men of the company longed for home and family.

On the evening of December 26, the Charlottesville Artillery was relieved and moved with its brigade toward Bowling Green about five miles. Rumors began to fly about the company as to what their disposition would be in the following month. Some heaard of all the artillery forming at Bowling Green for reason of better forage; still there was a disheartening rumor that worried several, having the company go with its brigade back to Louisiana. All fears were dispelled, however, when on the 31st the company marched within two and a half miles of Bowling Green and went into winter quarters.

"...The enemy completely routed...and we standing still."

1863

In their camp just across from the home of Dr. John Baylor the men of Charlottesville wasted little time in building their winter dwellings. Wilbur Davis, the faithful Charlottesville Artillery historian, kept a vivid account of the winter and of his mess companions, Sergeant McCoy, Hanson Boyden, Pendleton Wash, Roler, Sergeant Waller Holladay and his brother Albert, Francis Fitzhugh, and A. L. Marshall. Though cramped, accommodations withstood the winter and proved adequate. The group of men prepared a "large log cabin covered with clapboards, and daubed and chinked with mud." Davis's cabin "had a large fire-place and two tiers of bunks, one above the other on one side."

In their humble abode, Davis wrote, the men "had a jolly time till near the end of April." Only twice was the Charlottesville Artillery village disturbed. One interruption came on January 18 when the battery was ordered with its brigade to a camp near Port Royal. There they spent several days, finally returning to Bowling Green on January 26. The second time was on March 18, when orders came to march to Fredericksburg, only to be countermanded the same day.

The season passed with what entertainment the men could invent, on which Davis commented:

> ...chess was a favorite game — Wash being champion player and W. Holladay, unsuccessfully disputing the palm with him. Wash could beat me, and could give me odds. . . . Holladay would never accept odds from him — tho. he was no better player than I. We read aloud during the long winter nights by the light of the pine knots. Among other things I remember, Sheridan's play The Rivals, Dicken's Pickwick Papers. We had family prayers regularly once a day — all except McCoy and Wash being Christians (McCoy however, later joined in with the revival spirit as did so many others in the army).

Though away from their homes, several of Davis's mess found comfort in the hospitality provided by Dr. Baylor and his family. In an effort to give aid to some of the sons of his old friends, the good doctor requested that Boyden, Wash, and Albert Holladay be detailed as guards to protect his sheep from bands of "rogues." When leave could be obtained, the rest of the mess was warmly received at the doctor's home, "New Market," where they dined and enjoyed several nights of good rest.

When at their cabin, the mess was well tended by Thornton Brown, a slave who had come into the army with Davis. Paying him "10 or 12 dollars a month hire," the mess "could well afford to feed him out of the rations out of the mess, besides the chance he would forage, buy milk and vegetables, etc. for us." Thornton proved often to be a valued and trusted companion to many of the company. The men entrusted him with valuables before going into action, and left him with instructions to return the items home if they were to fall.

Boxes from home were also well appreciated, Davis on one instance being introduced to the sweet and delicious apple butter sent from the Valley to either Swoope or Roler.

The losses of the winter were mild. John McGuire and John Riley deserted on February 5 and April 4 respectively, and Harry Estill, after being promoted to corporal, was transferred and later appointed 1st lieutenant on General Colquitt's staff.

On February 19, an inspection of the company yielded these findings: Two 3-inch Richmond rifles; two 6-pounder and 12-pounder howitzers, all iron; sent 3 caissons and limbers to workshop to be recovered, and 3 carriages to be repaired; horses, 90 serviceable; ammunition and harness good; 2 4-horse and 2 2-horse wagons in good order; 3 officers and 100 men present; 1 officer and 5 men detached; 1 officer and 3 men (absent) with leave; 3 men absent without leave, and 24 sick; 4 unserviceable horses.

During a major reorganization of the artillery in April, the Charlottesville Artillery was assigned to Major Hilary Pollard Jones's Battalion, along with the Staunton Artillery, the Courtney Artillery, and the Chesapeake Artillery of Maryland. Jones was no shining star of the artillery service, but he was well acquainted with the duties of the position and was senior in grade to some of the other officers who might have been selected.

Before coming out of their winter quarters, the Charlottesville Artillery too had some reorganizing within the command. Herbert Harris was promoted by election to sergeant major, Jere Harris and Wilbur Davis to corporal, and James Atkins to 5th corporal.

On April 31 the new battalion set out around 2 p.m. and moved along with the rest of Jackson's Corps in response to a new threat across the Rappahannock in the form of General Joseph Hooker. Trudging along through heavy rains and horribly difficult roads, the battalion reached Hamilton's Crossing at sunrise on May 1. Awaiting an attack, the Charlottesville men stood by their guns and watched enemy balloons for several hours before moving into camp near Massaponax Creek.

The following morning Jones's Battalion marched with Jackson on his incredible flank movement. As Davis remembered:

... it was forced march without halt or rest — at the rate, I think of three miles an hour, and we were until 5 p.m. or later getting into position and making the charge which swept them for over a mile. I remember that but for Captain Carrington's lending me his horse, to get me a rest, for perhaps an hour, I could hardly have kept up. We followed the charge as fast as we could walk, but did not get into the fight that evening. We found the fires lighted and suppers cooking from which the Yankees had been driven — with wounded and dead strewed here and there along the old turnpike and the occasional opening and thin places of woods on each side and went into camp about sunset. Well do I remember the cannonade and musketry that suddenly broke out about 9 p.m. that beautiful moonlit night after we had laid down to sleep.

Early on May 3, Jones once again put his battalion on the move, sending forward most of his Napoleons with the exception of Tanner's Battery. This "demi-battalion" under Captain Carrington and Lieutenant Alexander H. Fultz (commanding the Staunton Artillery), took to the turnpike and then off to the right of it about half a mile. Pausing briefly, Captain Carrington reported to Colonel T. H. Carter. Davis recalled the morning's events:

... after remaining at one point, woods at each side, for what seemed a long time not many hundred yards behind a battery already engaged — one of whose caissons we saw blown up by a shell from the enemy, we were rushed out on an obscure byroad at right angles to our right, perhaps a quarter of a mile or more (the intention being to front fire the enemy works and enfilade the road). There we came upon an open hill with deep ravines in front to our left as we approached another hill behond the ravine filled with Yankees — 500 or 600 yards in a straight line. Each battery was wheeled into position to the left, as it reached the open space, ours being last, passed by the others and took our position on the extreme right of all.

In a short time the crews were rushing about, preparing their guns. Young Leroy Cox remembered that General Stuart and a young artillery officer rode up as they were loading and ordered them to fire into a wooded area where the enemy was located. The fire grew hot and rapid, a good bit being returned by the enemy. Davis, acting caisson corporal, looked about and witnessed several men fall, and within "ten paces" a horse shot through.

After a short while the gunners found a mark that pleased the young artillerist with Stuart, as he cried out to Cox's crew, "You've got it, kid! Give it to them!" Ramming home what he estimated to be fifty shots, Cox watched as the woods soon caught fire. With the enemy position softened up, the batteries were ordered to cease fire while the infantry swept the field. Davis wrote of what followed: "We ran up in front of our guns and saw the charge up the slope of the opposite hill from the right — saw the line of Yankees leave their line of breastworks and dash for their rear preceded by the batteries we had been fighting. We threw up our hats and yelled. In the very act several of our men were wounded."

To the surprise of the artillerists, as they looked out to their front and saw that the tide had somehow temporarily turned. While the guns and crews ceased near the Charlottesville men, other guns to the left continued firing on a column of troops coming down the road from the direction of the Chancellor House to re-enforce those in the works. In the action that followed the Confederate surge, an enemy brigade turned a Confederate brigades flank, exposing the batteries. With this Confederate brigade stalled in front of the guns, the enemy delivered a couple of volleys that lashed both the infantrymen and the artillerists.

In the first round Lieutenant Bibb, standing near to Corporal Davis, fell shot through the upper thigh near the groin. Bleeding and faint, the stalwart lieutenant cheered his men on even while being carried to the rear.

After the enemy had been driven from their front, the batteries were again hitched and ordered down the steep hill in front. Carrington's gunners encouraged the horses onward, crossing a ditch with a stream at the bottom on an improvised bridge and up the slope to the very position from which the enemy batteries had been driven. Cox remembered that along the way "the bullets commenced hitting on our guns." Dropping into the enemy works, the crews hurriedly made ready their guns and renewed the fire in the direction of the Chancellor House. Cox recalled: "We opened up with a double charge of canister and there was a big execution. After firing this double charge of canister, we then changed to single charge of canister and then to shrapnel and then fired second and one-half bullets."

Amongst the Charlottesville guns rode Colonel Carter, boldly remaining on horseback and witnessing the effect on the enemy and the Chancellor House as it burst into flames. Davis remembered the colonel as quite possibly the only man to remain on horseback throughout the fight.

Corporal Davis wrote in later years of an event that "deeply impressed" him at this point during the battle: ". . .being compelled — in order to open the rear and last chest of the three on my caisson, to mount the top to disengage the dray rope. I remember thinking of the caisson I had seen blown up — on entering the fight and how fatal it would be for me if a like

23

thing should occur just then."

Sergeant McCoy would not come out of the battle as fortunate as Davis. Filling the place of number 6 in his gun, the young sergeant not only directed the cannon's shots, but also performed a downed man's duty. In the wounded gunner's place, McCoy continued to receive shells from the caissons with fuses cut at two seconds. As he returned to the gun with one of the shells, it exploded suddenly in his hands, lacerating them, breaking fingers, one fragment passing under a part of one arm, carrying away the flesh to the bone, another striking him in the knee. With his face badly burned, clothes on fire, and eyesight gone, McCoy writhed about in anguish before the fire finally was extinguished.

After exhausting its ammunition, the victorious but battered Charlottesville Battery retired from the field.

Davis helped to take his messmate from the field and wrote of the painful episode: ". . .putting him as gently as we could upon a blanket — four of us took him down a short distance to a spring — around which some dozen wounded — nearly all Yankees, were already lying helplessly. Waiting 2 or 3 hours, the asst. surgeon came with an ambulance."

Captain Carrington recollected, "After the fight I assisted in bearing him from the field, and not withstanding his terrible condition, he spoke calmly and bravely."

Once in the ambulance, McCoy lay supported in the arms of Lieutenant Bibb as they were carried away to Hamilton's Crossing on the Richmond, Fredericksburg and Potomac Railroad. McCoy died in Richmond on May 19, and Bibb expired nine days later on May 28.

Turning to the wounded, friend and foe alike, Davis moved about providing water to the "parched and suffering throats, and still more to put on their wounds — roughly bandaged — in the hot sunshine."

The Charlottesville Artillery also lost Fleming Elliton killed. The other wounded included George M. Cochran, Francis C. Fitzhugh (left thigh), B. F. Gruber (bruise from shell), B. F. Maupin (back of thigh and skull), and G. W. Terrell (left thigh and knee).

Moving back out of Hamilton's Crossing on May 6, the battery took time to mourn their losses and the loss of their beloved "Stonewall." On May 18 the battery moved again to a point six miles below Guiney Station on Telegraph Road.

The beginning of June brought with it elections, to fill gaps from both casualties and transfers. Promotions included Francis Swoope to 2nd lieutenant, Wilbur Davis to sergeant major, and Michael McCarthy to corporal.

The same day that Davis rose in rank, Jones's Battalion got into motion toward Culpeper. The days that followed took them to within three miles of Culpeper on June 5; at Culpeper and camping three miles beyond on the Sperryville Pike on the 8th; beyond Brandy Station on the 9th; through Washington, Chester Gap, Front Royal, Newtown, and finally to the outskirts of Winchester on June 13. Finding the enemy holding, Confederate infantry deployed and engaged in skirmishing. The artillery remained in reserve. While holding in the rear an exploding shell killed one of the Charlottesville Battery's horses.

The following morning the Confederates set out to dislodge General Robert H. Milroy's Federals, who were well fortified around the town. Moving in an effort to flank the enemy, Jones's Battalion, under Captain Carrington, moved with Jube Early's division. By 3 p.m. the division had reached the right rear of the enemy, and had yet to be discovered.

Along with, though only temporarily attached to the Charlottesville Artillery was Robert Stiles. Stiles, a former law student and member of the Richmond Howitzers, had come to the battery in a roundabout way. Stiles had reported to Major General Early in regard to organizing a company of engineers, but the general found Stiles's proposal less than desirable. Stiles still wanted to hold a position in Early's headquarters. Using his college ingenuity, he proposed that he would act as a requisitioner for supplies for the Pioneer Corps, or whatever else would necessitate his presence at the headquarters. Stiles, being a former artillerist, also proposed that when he was not with Early he would fall in with a battery of Jones's Battalion (usually Carrington's) when going into battle. Recognizing the young law student's determination, "Old Jube" consented.

As the infantrymen about them lay down to catch their breath, the guns began to deploy, still under cover of a rise. Twelve guns (four of Jones's Battalion and eight of Brown's under Dance) were placed three-quarters of a mile on the left. Nearer the mass of infantry, from where a better enfilade fire could be provided against the enemy works, eight guns of Jones's Batatlion under Carrington unlimbered just under the crest of the hill and made ready.

As Stiles remembered, the men of the battalion "shoved their guns forward by hand up to and just back of a rock fence. . . . They next removed a few of the stones in front of the muzzle of each gun, taking great care to remain concealed while doing this; and when everything was ready and everyone warned to do his part on the instant, the guns were discharged simultaneously upon the outwork and rapid fire kept up upon it. . . ." The "outwork" Stiles remembered was what was called the flag fort.

Following a short but fierce exchange of artillery, the Louisiana Brigade swept across the field in a grand spectacle. Leaving only Dance's guns to maintain their fire, the other artillery received the orders: "Cease firing, limber to the front, cannoneers mount!" Having just given his horse to a member of the Charlottesville battery, Stiles had to mount himself upon a casson in an awkward way:

I sprang upon a limber chest upon which there were already the full complement of three men, all faced, of course, to the front. I faced to the rear, and bracing my back against the back of the middle man, attempted to hold my position with my feet resting on the "lunette plate". . . . We started at a run and were galloping under fire through a grove, by a wood road the track of which was full of limestone rocks projecting more or less above the ground. It was very difficult to keep my footing, as I had on a pair of stiff and slick-soled English shoes, the nails in which had worn perfectly smooth.

Stiles's team suddenly ran across one of the high limestone outcroppings with dramatic results:

The jar was terrific, and all the men were thrown off, but the others, having firm footing, described arcs which landed them on the turf at the side of the road. My feet, however, slipped, and I went down between the front and rear wheels and directly under the gun. The concussion was so tremendous that I supposed the limber chest had exploded, and distinctly remember thinking to myself, "Then this is the way it feels to be blown, is it? Well, I'll try anyhow to save my arms and legs in case I shouldn't be killed," and with a violent effort I did manage to get them out of the track of the hind wheels, one of which, however, ran directly, or rather, diagonally, across the small of my back on a flat limestock rock.

The crew, now on their feet, stared back in horror, expecting that their part-time comrade had been killed. Dragging Stiles off the road and out of the way of more oncoming caissons, the gunners placed the young man under a tree in the softness of the grass. It was not long after, however, before the bruised and sore law student found his way to his feet and returned to the front to join the battery at its next position.

During the same, or the next, change of position another horrid spectacle was observed by the Charlottesville men when, while following behind Garber's Staunton Artillery, a man received a gruesome wound. Stiles commented:

The farm road we were using led between two heavy old-fashioned gateposts. . . .One of Garber's men, belonging to his rear gun [and at this time on foot], attempted to run abreast of the piece between the gateposts. . . .There was not room enough for him to pass, and the wheel crowded him against the post, the washer hook caught and tore open his abdomen, dragging the poor wretch along by his intestines, which were literally pulled from his body in a long, gory ribbon.

Once returning, to the amusement of his crew, Stiles took his place as number 6 at the limber of his gun.

...at one of the limbers. . . .I several times instinctively clapped down the lid of the ammunition chest as the shell seemed to burst immediately over it. We were at a loss to account for the preternaturally accurate aim of the guns and cutting of the fuses, until someone chanced to observe the practice target of the fort standing between the gun at which I was serving and the one next to it, when, of course, we shifted our position in a twinkling, dashing up still closer to the fort and finding, to our relief, that here the shells passed for the most part over our heads.

At one of the batteries shifting of positions, Sergeant Hunter, while riding upon his little chestnut mare ahead of his gun, was suddenly stunned as his mount gently dropped from under him. Stiles, the best first-hand witness to the Charlottesville Artillery in this day, had been looking in the direction of the sergeant, "when a thirty-pounder Parrott shell passed through her [the horse's] body, just back of the legs of the rider, exploding as it emerged, and spattering me profusely with the blood of the poor animal. Little Madge. . .never knew what hit her, but sank gently down, while Hunter did not even get even as so much as a decent 'shaking up. . . .' When his feet touched the ground. . .he simply disengaged them from the stirrups, turned around, glanced a moment at the bloody horror, and said, "Well, poor little Madge!' "

Ordering the advance to continue, Carrington placed four guns in line very near to the works, where they came under a galling fire. Four guns were quickly emplaced, two of the Louisiana Guard Battery on the right, and two of the Charlottesville Artillery next to them on the left. With Captain C. A. Thompson of the Louisiana battery in command, the batteries returned the enemy fire with marked effect upon the flag fort. Riding about the guns in a brave and bold manner, Thompson cheered on the crews of the four guns. At one point, as darkness came on, he rose up in his stirrups to give the men encouragement, at which moment a shell tore away his bridle arm high up near the shoulder. Stiles wrote respectfully of the brave captain, who "Instantly. . .caught the reins with his right hand and swung his horse's head sharply to the left, thus concealing his wounded side from his men, saying as he did so, 'Keep it up, boys; I'll be back in a moment!' As he started down the hill I saw him reel in the saddle, and even before he reached the limbers the noble fellow fell from his horse — dead."

As night settled on the hazy, gray battlefield, only a spattering of random muskets could be heard. Carrington, seeing that the fight might be reopened on the following day, ordered all of the battalion up and into the enemy works.

The Charlottesville Artillery's losses turned out to be only one killed, John Terrell, and Corporal Michael McCarthy wounded. McCarthy would later desert from the hospital and never return to the battery's service.

Some of the Charlottesville men looked around in the fort that night for some of the remaining goods not already looted by the Louisianans. One of the more important captured supplies, in the eyes of Colonel Jones, was the abundance of artillery sabres, which the commander ordered all of his sergeants to obtain. Sergeant Major Davis took one for himself, but seemed glad that later, after he visited home, he left it there. The more prized booty included better guns, horses, wagons, paper, and an abundance of dried fruit, molasses, poatoes, beans, coffee, and sugar. Other goods issued from the capture of the sutler's stores included candy, cigars, soap, and ink.

The following morning the enemy were found to have abandoned totally any further attempt at holding Winchester. Putting the battalion back in line with Early's division, the artillerists pressed on in the following days through some cloudbursts across the Potomac at Shepherdstown, then through Boonsboro and Cavetown into Pennsylvania by June 22. Camping outside Greenwood on that day, the batalion retraced its steps the next morning to Waynesboro, Pennsylvania.

The battery moved light, from what Davis wrote: "Only one wagon for the men's rations and it carried the few cooking utensils not carried by the men themselves, and one or two tents for the officers. Of course there was at least one or more wagon for the battery to draw, or collect from the fields, corn and long food for our horses."

Though the Charlottesville men found their trek into Pennsylvania greeted with general indifference, their accompanying slaves were particularly harsh in comments about what they found. Sergeant Major Davis commented: "Thornton and Jim were great cronies, marched at their own sweet will, without orders from anybody, but keeping of course along with our commisary wagon. . . passed some villages or settlements of what they called 'free niggers' upon whom they looked down with contempt as they had always been accustomed to do at home, and freely expressed their sentiments."

While en route, Lieutenant Timberlake was forced to retire due to poor health, and Sandy Cochran was elected in his place. Other promotions during the same time included D. Rodes Massie to 2nd lieutenant and John Spooner to 4th sergeant.

On the 27th and 28th, the batteries rolled via Huntersville, New Castle, and Berlin before finally arriving at York. "Passing through the heart of the town, crossing a stream over a stone bridge," Davis recalled, the battery entered the beautiful town at about noon. The artillerists bivouacked on the fairgrounds in the northeast part of the town. Captain Carrington observed that despite General Early's demand for supplies, "In that city we were treated with much kindness by many of its citizens, and there I met friends and acquaintances who were cordial and hospitable."

Davis wrote at length of his experiences that afternoon:

Captain Carrington, Lieut. Swoope, (and Lieut. Rodes Massie, too, I think) and myself took a stroll through town, from Main St. we walked out across street north, which seemed the street of first residences. On the roofless porches or "stoops" and front steps were sitting family groups, chiefly women and girls enjoying the cool of the evening. As we passed one group, some distance on, we heard in low tones to our surprise, "Good evening, gentlemen." Of course we bowed. A little further on some ladies repeated the greeting, "Good evening, gentlemen," adding in whispered tones, "Glad to see you!" We simply took off our hats and passed on. Getting to the end of the street or past the houses mostly, we held a council of war and decided to retrace our steps and get into conversation with that last group, who were so cordial. Accordingly, we do so, and were at once urgently invited to walk into the house. We at first demurred, telling them we feared that if we did, they might suffer for it after we left. Nothing else would do, and so we went in. There we stayed until 10 or 11 p.m. — most hospitably and warmly entertained — cake, tea, coffee, domestic wine offered. Some friends, all ladies, from neighbors were called in. It turned out the family were Virginians, originally, and from the Valley. They told us that the old grandmother could scarcely contain herself when she saw the confederate troops, and their flag floated over York. They had to forceably keep her in doors and perhaps upstairs — to prevent her exulting in the street.

A year later, while several of the Charlottesville men were at Fort Delaware, they wrote to this family, who gave of their hospitality again through boxes of fine edibles.

Before leaving the following morning, several of the Charlottesville men descended upon the stores of York and passed their worthless Confederate bills in exchange for goods.

Moving out of York, Early's column followed the turnpike in the direction of Heidlersburg. Their orders were, as Davis recalled, "to keep close to our places each side of guns and caissons, and were told that we might expect at any time to come upon the enemy, as we had a very small force of cavalry only in our front. . . ."

The captain commented that "after resting that night near the village [Heidlersburg], Early's Division with. . .Jones' Battalion. . . accompanying it, marched toward Gettysburg, which was south of us and near which we could hear the roar of battle."

About the march and the sound of battle, the sergeant major noted:

. . .When at a village we heard the roar of the guns in the fight already begun at Gettysburg. We cannoneers were mounted on the guns at once and driven at a trot for five miles or more perhaps on the level pike. . . We came upon the field from the northeast — rushing into full view of the fight below us on the right and just outside the town — We ourselves being on the brow of a high bluff. Immediately the whole battalion was thrown into battery on that bluff, to the left of the road except our battery.

The three other batteries, positioned in front of Robert F. Hoke's Brigade, went into action immediately, blasting away at the enemy batteries that were wheeling into position across from them on the north side of Rock Creek.

Of the action that followed Captain Carrington maintained a detailed memory and wrote: "While these batteries were thus engaged, I and my men became a little impatient, and General Early passed by towards the front. He paused for a moment, and I playfully stated this to him. He replied to me good naturedly that I need not be impatient, that there would be plenty for me to do after a while."

As the Charlottesville gunners stood by and waited, tension and the cannonade grew more intense. Carrington continued:

He [Early] rode off, and I suppose an interval of ten or fifteen minutes elapsed, when I saw Gordon's men on the southern side of the creek gallantly advancing towards the enemy in the open field. . . .General Gordon in leading them presented a splendid picture of gallantry, there being nothing to obstruct the view. In a few moments an order came to me to move across the bridge in front of me over Rock Creek, and follow up Gordon's men.

Looking out upon the bridge and the task before them, Carrington felt genuine concern because the Federal artillery occasionally dropped a shot very near to the crossing. If just one horse were struck while the battery crossed the bridge, it would create a very difficult situation for the guns following it. Drawing on common sense, the captain preempted the orders and directed the guns to cross one piece at a time, with considerable space between each limber. As Davis's piece rocked forward, he remembered, "We dashed down the hill, still mounted, and across a bridge over a stream. In that hurried drive, I remember distinctly saying to my companion on the limber chest with me, and pointing to the height back of the town, 'If we don't drive them beyond those heights now, they will be fortified by night.' I also remember seeing, for the only time in my life, a cannon ball high up in the air coming towards us."

Once across the creek the battery turned to the right and held up briefly in a field near the southern bank. Met by General Early, Carrington led his battery onward in the direction of Gordon's troops toward the town. Young Robert Stiles too fell in with the company, in charge of a piece.

Captain Carrington, who rode along with Early recalled years later: "Early was silent as we rode together, most of the time his attention being absorbed by what was going on in front. He was perfectly cool, but manifested the deepest interest. Once in the middle of the field, General Early suddenly turned his horse towards me and in quick sharp tones ordered me to prepare my battery for action."

Unlimbered and loaded with canister, the battery stood by and watched Gordon press the enemy further. In anticipation of new orders, Carrington rode up to join the general.

No sooner had the Captain reached Early than a sergeant of the battery caught up with him, and stated that there was a Federal officer lying wounded back near the battery. Carrington returned to his company and found a lieutenant colonel lying between one of the caissons and a gun. The captain wrote:

I got off my horse, told him I was Captain of the battery and wished to know what he wanted. He stated to me in a manly way that he was helpless from the effect of his wound, and asked me to remove him to a place of safety. I immediately said to him, "Certainly, Colonel that shall be done." Four of my men took him up and laid him in the corner of the fence nearby.

Carrington rode over to where the colonel lay, dismounted, and began to engage in some conversation, making the Federal more comfortable to suppress the pain of the wound. Not expecting so much kindness from a Rebel, the colonel expressed his appreciation and offered the captain a "fine pair of field glasses." Captain Carrington declined at first under the provisions of General Lee's orders in regard to such things, but the colonel insisted, expressing the fear that another might later come along and seize the prize in a more abrupt manner. Carrington then accepted the gracious gift, and upon assuring the poor man's comfort, rode back to join the command. Some years later, Carrington found that the man he had been so kind to had gone on to become Ohio's Lieutenant Governor Lee.

Back on line with his guns, Carrington at once made use of his new field glasses and looked on as Hays's Louisianans and Hoke's Tarheels beat back Coster's Federals and captured Heckman's Battery.

Ordered forward again, the Charlottesville Artillery limbered up and raced forward, still unable to engage the enemy that fled before Early's infantry. Sergeant Major Davis later reported:

As we moved into the town to this last position, we met some 3000 or more prisoners coming out and found what were said to be 1200 to 1500 wounded in the town. Those of course had been taken into the houses, and we saw nothing of them. Our guns were just in front of a tall brick house, a residence and at the window of the highest story were ladies peeping out. We admonished them that we were expecting any minute a renewal of the fight and that they would be far safer in the lowest story.

An artillerist with the other guns of the battery remembered:

My gun had come again into battery in the outskirts of the town. No enemy was in sight in our front; but in anticipation of a sudden rush I had the piece loaded and several rounds of canister taken from the ammunition chest and put down hard by the gaping muzzle, ready to sweep the street in case they should turn upon us. At this moment little George Greer, a chubby boy of sixteen, rode on by further into the town. George was General Early's clerk and a favorite with Old Jube. . . .I shouted a caution to him as he passed, but on he went, disappearing in the smoke and dust ahead. In a few moments a cloud of bluecoats appeared in the street in front of us, coming on, too, at a run. I was about to order the detachment to open fire, when beyond and back of the men in blue I noticed little Greer, leaning forward over the neck of his horse, towering above the Federals, who were on foot; and with violent gesticulations and in tones not the gentlest, ordering the "blue devils" to "double quick to the rear of that piece," which they did in the shortest time imaginable. There must have been over fifty of them. . . .The men had thrown away their arms and were cowering in the streets and alleys.

As matters would have it, in Stiles's crew of cannoneers stood old Burgoyne, having left the Louisiana Brigade once again to partake in his preferred artillery service. Stiles described the bold Irishman as "a typical son of the Emerald Isle, over six feet high in his stockings (when he had any), broad-shouldered and muscular, slightly bow-legged, and as springy as a cat; as full of fire and fight and fun as he could hold. . .and never having to be known to get his fill of noise and scrimmage."

Having taken his place among the Virginians earlier, Burgoyne got right to work. Stiles wrote of him later: ". . .[he] seized the sponge-staff and rammed home the charge, and was giving vent to his enthusiasm in screams and bounds that would have done credit to a catamount."

Stiles remembered that all probably would have gone smoothly at the gun had it not been for another Irishman, an arrogant Federal at that. As he stood by and watched the piece as it was being laid, the blue-jacket took note of Burgoyne's brogue and called out: "Hey, ye spalpane! say, where are yez doing in the Ribil army?"

Quick as a flash, Burgoyne retorted: "Be-dad, ain't an Irishman a freeman? Haven't I as good right to fight for the Ribs as ye have to fight for the   Yanks?" "O, yes!" sang out the Federal Irishman, "I know ye, now you've turned your ougly mug to me. I had the plizure of kicking yez out from behind Marye's wall. . . ." "Yer a   liar," shouted our Pat, "and I'll jist knock yer teeth down yer ougly throat for that same lie," and suiting the action to the word he vaulted lightly over the gun, and before we had time to realize the extreme absurdity of the thing, the two had squared off against each other. . . and the first blow had passed, for the Federal Irishman was as good grit as ours. Just as the two giants were about to rush to close quarters. . . I noticed that the right fist of the Federal Gladiator was gory, and the next movement revealed the stumps of two shattered fingers, which he was about to drive full into Burgoyne's face. "Hold!" I cried; "your man's wounded!" On the instant Burgoyne's fists fell. "You're a trump, Pat; give me your well hand," said he. "We'll fight this out some other time. I didn't see ye were hurt."

Back where Davis stood in the town, the guns had remained still for more than twenty minutes. Carrington, seeing Ewell, Early, Gordon, and several other officers gathered nearby, could not resist temptation, and rode over to them.

I could not resist. . .to see what was the matter, and why the battle had so suddenly stopped. I naturally and modestly held my horse a little back from the distinguished group but caught portions of their conversation, but too indistinctly to attempt to repeat it at this late day; but I think I cannot be mistaken when I say that both General Early and General Gordon were urnestly urging an immediate and further advance. I could not hear General Ewell's language, but evidently Ewell's manner in-

33

dicated resistance to their appeal.

The day's fight ended with no loss to the Charlottesville men. Their disappointment in the cessation of the attack was apparent. Davis wrote in frustration: "Not later than 5 p.m., one of the longest days of the year, the sun two and a half hours high, the enemy completely routed, and getting off as fast as possible, and we standing still."

Camping for the night on the left near the town, the battery remained out of any fighting. Their only move within a period of two days took them to a point along the railroad with instructions to guard that place.

On July 3 the battery was stationed in an orchard on the edge of town, ever anticipating the order that would not come. Davis remembered the artillery fire just before Pickett's charge: "...To form some idea of the rapidity of the cannon shots, I counted my pulse and found that tho they beat 70 to the minute, they were not so rapid as the cannon shots."

Later in the afternoon, rumors of orders whisked through the battery that it might be ordered to follow behind Ewell's assault up the heights, leaving the cannon behind, the purpose of the unarmed tag-along being to man the enemy guns if they were captured. Though the men had anxiously awaited orders all day, many remembered that they were glad to find that this order never came.

Before dusk on that hot and costly summer day, Carrington's company was ordered to shift positions again, this time farther to the right to the crest of Seminary Ridge near Lee's headquarters.

On July 4, the Charlottesville Artillery was again ordered to move, this time to spot the men found far less favorable. Though there was no fighting, Stiles, in his last account while with the battery, poignantly explained:

> ...dead bodies of men and horses had lain there putrefying under the summer sun for three days. The sight and smells that assailed us were simply indescribable — corpses swollen to twice their original size, some of them actually burst asunder with the pressure of foul gases and vapors. ...several human or unhuman corpses sat upright against a fence, with arms extended in the air and faces hideous with something very like a fixed leer, as if taking a fiendish pleasure in showing us what we essentially were and might at any moment become. The odors were nauseating, and so deadly that in a short time we all sickened and were lying with our mouths close to the ground, most of us vomiting profusely. We protested against the cruelty and folly of keeping men in such a position. Of course to fight in it was utterly out of the question, and we were soon moved away; but for the rest of that day and late into the night

the fearful odors I had inhaled remained with me and made me loathe myself as if an already rotting corpse.

Not until 9 a.m. on July 5 did the Charlottesville Artillery finally fall into line with the retreating Army of Northern Virginia. Serving as a portion of Early's rear guard, Jones's Battalion had waited until everyone else had moved out. Davis remembered the slow, dismal going, with frequent halts. One such halt occurred near Fairfield,

> . . .the infantry lying at ease and in jovial humor. General Early, it is said, got impatient and called for Colonel Pendleton to put a blank cartridge in one of his guns and fire over that train of wagons to start them up. Just about that very time, one of our men looking back, said he believed the enemy was bringing out a battery on a high hill we had passed. General Early, sitting on his horse near by, took out his field glasses and looked, and then replied in his high pitched whining tones, "No, nothing there but a cow and a horse and a straggler." He had hardly gotten the words out of his mouth when there was a puff of smoke on that aforesaid hill and here come a shell which fell right in the line of infantry lying on the ground and exploded. There was rapid scrambling to get away from that shell, which did no damage. One or two shots followed. . .

Federal fire killed two of the battery's horses and broke the tongue of one piece. Blocking the road until fresh horses were harnessed, Carrington's guns moved out into the field and made ready for action. Gordon's infantry proved effective again, however, and the battery remained in position and unengaged until dark. By the time Carrington's battery moved late that night, two men, Henry Sprouse left behind sick, and William J. Bowen had fallen into enemy hands.

Marching on the 6th to Waynesboro, and on the 7th through Hagerstown, the battalion reached the trenches near the Potomac on July 13. Davis recalled that the company left these lines about dark and the guns moved down approximately nine miles to pontoons across the river at Falling Waters. Rain and the darkness of night seriously impeded their progress.

"Sandy" Cochran had fallen so ill by this time that the sergeant major took charge in his place. he recalled: "We had a lantern here and there along the line at intervals of a hundred yards or more. Sometime in the night, well on towards day, one of my guns got stalled in the stumps and mud, and there it stayed till broad daylight."

A detachment stayed with that gun and limber through the early hours until day, and the piece was finally recovered and put back on its way across the Potomac.

En route south again on the 15th, the battery marched with the battalion until it bivouacked at Darkesville on the following night. They moved across North Mountain and by Hedgesville to Bunker Hill by the 22nd; through Winchester, Cedarville, Newtown, and up the Valley Pike to New Market; across the Massanutten and Blue Ridge to Madison, and finally to Liberty Mills by July 31.

After changing its campsite from Liberty Mills to Colonel Magruder's farm in early August, the battery finally settled to a long term campsite near Gordonsville on September 4. While there, the battery was visited by friends and family. Davis wrote that "some of the young ladies of Cobham neighborhood, Boydens, Lewises, and visitors came down. . .we had quite a picnic. I had ridden up with Boyden, Bob Lewis, Pegram, and Coffee to attend church at Walker's Chapel, and spent the afternoon and night visiting Hopedale. . . ." It was a welcomed and well deserved homecoming.

The battery moved again on September 17 to Somerville Ford on the Rapidan. Peace took the place of war and death for more than a month until Lee found it time to move on the offensive once more. In an effort to flank George Meade's army, the Army of Northern Virginia got under way on October 8. That night Jones's Battalion moved out of its works and crossed the Rapidan at Peyton's Ford on October 9. Behind Early's division, the battalion marched through Madison and Culpeper County, and after crossing the Rappahannock at Warrenton Springs, on to Warrenton and halted on October 13. Up and moving the following morning, the battalion's march continued at daybreak. It was not long into the morning until Early's vanguard encountered the enemy at Auburn.

In their effort to flank the Federals, Early's men were not able to come into position until the bluejackets had almost entirely withdrawn. Their pursuit brought the division to Bristoe Station about 4 p.m. Finding A. P. Hill actively engaged, the Courtney Artillery was deployed with its long-range gun, while the others remained in reserve. Jones's Battalion bivouacked at the station for the next few days before withdrawing to Culpeper on the 18th and reaching Brandy Station on October 19. Sergeant Major Davis recalled the route: "We came back soon along the Southern RR [Orange and Alexandria RR then] through Fauquier, and crossed the Rappahanock on a pontoon bridge at RR crossing. We had to wait an hour or two there for the completion of this bridge — our battery being right there. Here I had the best view of General Lee I ever had. He rode up, dismounted and stood some time right among us, intently watching the bridge building."

At the campsite near Brandy, the battalion remained quietly. Jones took leave of absence on November 3 and left Carrington in command. One day later, as Meade's army pressed forward, Lee was forced to fall

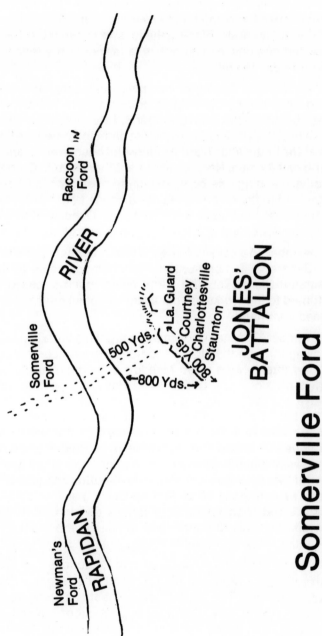

Raccoon
Ford

RIVER

Somerville
Ford

500 Yds.

La. Guard
Courtney
Charlottesville
Staunton

800 Yds.

800 Yds.

JONES'
BATTALION

Newman's
Ford

RAPIDAN

Somerville Ford
September 1863

back upon the old line along the Rapidan. Carrington led the battalion out early on November 4 to camp for the evening near the Major house in the vicinity of Cedar Mountain. Finding the location unsuitable, the battalion, after remaining one day, moved one mile farther to the rear, where it remained until Friday the 6th.

Saturday morning Carrington had his cannoneers harnessing horses and moving back across the Virginia countryside to Brandy, which they reached at about daylight on November 8. After holding a position near Culpeper all day, the artillery fell back that night to Somerville Ford, where it found that the Louisiana Guard Artillery had been overrun and lost all of its guns and half its men. Nervous about another assault, Carrington kept pickets active, sending one company (quite possibly the Charlottesville Artillery) forward to the ford near Halsey's house from the 9th to the 15th. While at this post, four men were captured: Obediah Calvert, George McIntire, Henry Pace, and Michael Morgan (a substitute who deserted).

On November 15 a cavalry force did finally appear opposite Morton's Ford, and General A. L. Long ordered two companies up to the ford at once to support the picket. The alarm being found unbased, the companies returned to the works on that evening. Jones returned on the 23rd and resumed command.

On November 27, Jones once more brought his battalion into a line of march, moving through the night in conjunction with Lee's army to Mine Run. The new threat came when Meade's army crossed the Rappahannock. Early's division, now under Harry Hays, did go into action near Locust Grove, but the terrain and thick overgrowth of trees ruled out any effort on the behalf of the artillery. During that night Hays deployed the division along Mine Run. Two batteries of the battalion were placed near the Rowe house, in support of the Tarheels of Hoke's Brigade. The remaining two were placed elsewhere on the line. Only slight action involved the guns of the battalion and inflicted no reported casualties. The army came out of its line along Mine Run on December 2 to pursue Meade again. Jones's Battalion joined with Early's division as it chased the enemy for ten miles before returning to the line in the evening.

On December 15 the battalion moved thirty miles to what would become its winter home in Louisa County, at Fredericks Hall. Once at the quiet Louisa village, Carrington filed a report of absence without leave against Sandy Cochran. The captain had not heard anything from his sickly lieutenant in a long time. Cochran, in defense of himself, turned to General Long for help, telling him that he "was under the impression that he had been retired." Long recognized the circumstances affecting Cochran and dismissed the the charge against him. Though the lieutenant would be tentatively restored to his post in early January by order of Lieutenant Colonel Jones, Cochran did not return and was retired in May 1864 to the Invalid Corps.

"Good-bye"
1864

The longing for lost comrades and anxiety over the way the year had ended was apparent among many of the messes in the winter of 1863-64. Though spent pleasantly the winter was, Davis recalled, "not as pleasant as the prior."

> We had a little village of huts about three miles out from the depot, south of the RR. Our tent, I was with the Captain and Lieuts. Swoope and Massie, was built of logs, with log chimney, all chinked and daubed with mud, quite large and roomy, but roofed with a large canvas tent. We were in a pleasant neighborhood, refined and intelligent. . . .Lieut. Massie's wife, a bride of a few months, boarded with the latter. We had one or two rude disturbances of our rest after Christmas. By the way our mess indulged Christmas in a dish of "possum and sweet taters" provided and cooked for us by a darkie of the neighborhood. We greatly enjoyed the Irish potatoes we had at times thro. the winter, roasting them in the ashes. . . . We had a rude church here, and a series of services — first by the Rev. L. A. Cutler, and afterwards by Rev. D. P. Wills. We had a violent storm of wind, rain, and lightning which nearly took our tent from over our heads. It was all we could do to hold it — every man in it using all his strength to hold pole, canvas and cords. . . .

The "rude disturbances" referred to by Davis included a march up the Rapidan to counter an attack that never came, and a sortie against Colonel Ulrich Dahlgren's raid in late February. On the morning of Dahlgren's advance Carrington's battery was out drilling when they heard of the advance of a large body of the enemy moving in their direction. Davis recalled: "Col. Jones and several other officers, on a court martial near the depot were captured, and we were told the yankee cavalry might be expected. We did the best we could to meet them — without support of any kind as we were, by forming our batteries in a hollow square, or ring, with guns pointed in every direction. . . ."

As the threat turned toward Richmond, preparations were made for the artillery to join in the pursuit already under way. Carrington noted that . . . "this was done without any stirring event, most returning in the evening."

Jones escaped from his captors and was soon promoted to full colonel and transferred away from the battalion. In his place came Lieutenant Colonel W. E. Cutshaw with Major Robert Stribling as his second.

Another disturbing matter that gave the company some aggravation was a disease which broke out among the horses. Known as the "grease heel," this infection was attributed to the want of long forage. It so baffled the veterinarian surgeon of the battalion that little could be done but to let it pass.

Other Charlottesville Artillery matters for that winter included the promotion of John Hunter to lieutenant and John Lewis to 4th corporal. Returns included Obediah Cavlert from exchange and Ned Massie, after his resignation from the 52nd Virginia Infantry.

At the end of the winter and into the early spring, the Charlottesville men were forced to send their horses off to grazing camps near Liberty Mills. By April 17 the horses were back, in time for the battery to pull out of its winter home. On the following day the company reached a point between Blue Run Church and Charles Graves's house and camped there. On May 3 the battery again moved with the battalion at about 2 p.m. and reached Pisgah Church at 11 that night. The following day Cutshaw's Battalion moved closer to the enemy and arrived at Locust Grove at about 1 p.m. Of what followed in the next few days, Carrington after the war found a quote from Stiles's book appropriate. The "Wilderness was essentially, yes, almost exclusively an infantry fight, and we of the artillery saw in fact, next to nothing of it, but around its edge thrilled and solemnized by the awful roar and swell and reverberation of the musketry and by the procession of wounded men that streamed past."

On May 6 the guns of the battalion quickly moved on line with the infantry just to the right of the Orange Turnpike. Positioning their cannon behind the breastworks, the artillerists remained by their guns and watched as the Federals fell back from their front. "Suddenly," as Herndon Fife remembered, "the enemy came back at us and our fellows, myself with the rest, had run for the breastworks." As the men "tumbled into the works" and manned their guns, the Charlottesville battery soon opened with shell and spherical case. In short order the enemy advance was checked. Fife continued:

> One or two things made an impression on me. A shot struck a small tree that stood near the breastworks cutting it off not more than a yard above your [Carrington's] head. I was impressed with the cool way you took the matter. Another was, that a minnie ball went through the windpipe of Lieutenant Swoope's mare, a very handsome animal he had just brought to camp [Carrington recalled that the matter disturbed Swoope as if it were his own windpipe]. . . .

40

The battery remained in support of Rodes's division as the enemy on May 7 drove in the skirmish line and, as Francis Fitzhugh recalled, "poured volley after volley of musketry into us in the breastworks." With only one man slightly hurt, and an estimated eight to ten horses disabled, Carrington's battery followed with the battalion that night past Shady Grove Church. As the ominous power of Grant's legions attempted to flank Lee's army, the battalion again moved on Sunday, May 8, in the direction of Spotsylvania Court House, going into camp that night within three or four miles of their destination.

On May 10 the Charlottesville Artillery moved to find a position along Lee's line. Garber's and Tanner's batteries were successful in doing so, but Carrington's men found less fortune and returned to their camp for the night. Having just settled into their evening routine, Terrell blew assembly and volunteers were taken to remain with some of the guns from which the 3rd Richmond Howitzers had earlier been driven. A group of thirty-eight (including Fitzhugh and Fife) went out, getting as far as the Harrison house, where they were stopped and told they were not needed. Remaining there until the guns came up on the following day, Lieutenant Massie encountered the crew and sought more volunteers, from which were taken eight privates and a corporal (and once again, the now reluctant Fitzhugh). The mission this time was to take a gun back which belonged to a battery near the Howitzer's position. Once the lot had arrived, the captain there tried to encouraged the men to stay, but they refused and made their way back to find their own battery.

Meanwhile, Carrington's other men had set off to find a position for their guns. Maneuvering "around in the woods that afternoon near McCool's. Fife recalled, ". . .a shot occasionally cutting down a tree near us . . . ." A guide misled the Charlottesville men along an old woods road that ended abruptly. Taking up their axes, the men cut their way through and about nightfall went into a position in the angle of the line. Davis reflected on their predicament:

> The position was an exposed one, offering opportunity for a cross fire from the Federal line. Only the guns and cannoneers were put into the breastworks — the horses and caissons being sent back to camp some distance in rear under charge of Sergt. Hunter. I have a vivid recollection of our position which we all thought a very mean one for us. It was 300 or 400 yds. to the left of the sharp salient in Lee's lines which became famous as the "Bloody Angle." Two of our guns were in the corner of a right angle of open woods — which extended unbroken to our right — enveloping the salient. In front there was an open space, not perhaps much over a hundred yards in width — sloping downward, and shut in by a dense body of wood — into

41

which we could not see many yards. To our left, there was also an open space — within the breastworks as well as without — extending back some distance to a farmhouse and buildings. This was sort of a valley, and on the farther slope of it near and on the top there was woods again. Across the open depression and up the rising ground and into the edge of the woods on the crest, ran our fortifications in a straight line — the same on which our two right guns were placed. It was on that crest beyond the depression — 300 yds. or more to our left, that Grant had carried our lines on the 10th. So the other section of our battery — two guns [one under Herndon Fife] were placed so as to fire over this depression, and enfilade the approach to that line. These two guns, of course were not in the line of breastworks but withdrawn some 30 or 40 yds. perhaps from them and pointed to the left, almost at a right angle. They were also somewhat within the line of woods, for both protection and concealment.

The night was spent strengthening the works, which were oblong pens of logs, filled with earth, and left with openings in front for the cannon. Cold, wet, and dismal the night of May 11 passed. Colonel Cutshaw, riding about to check on his battalion, left Carrington's men before dark, leaving the captain in the anticipation of orders to move to the right before morning. Fitzhugh recalled that during the night fhe Federals played "beautiful music — Star Spangled Banner, etc., etc."

Espionage crossed the minds of the men that night. Their suspicions were aroused by a couple of characters, supposed stragglers, looking for their command. These men had come by earlier and talked to some of the members of the company, and then went from company to company along the line, talking with each along the way. The artillerists, certain that these men were spies, launched a general search for them, but they could not be located.

Finding it difficult to sleep, partly on account of the poor weather, and the rest in anticipation, the camp had a solemn stir about it. Sergeant Major Davis felt certain that there would be a fight the next day and knew that he would be no more than an assistant to the captain in the forthcoming action. Furthermore, knowing that this fight would not be an easy one, Davis asked for and received command of the gun on the far right.

Carrington himself took time to rest, feeling that there was no present danger, only to be awakened around midnight by someone informing him that General Ed Johnson had called for him. Meeting with the general near one of the guns, Carrington recalled that Johnson stated in an "abrupt way, that he did not know what was going on in his front; but he wanted the utmost vigilance." While Johnson made his way "slowly" up

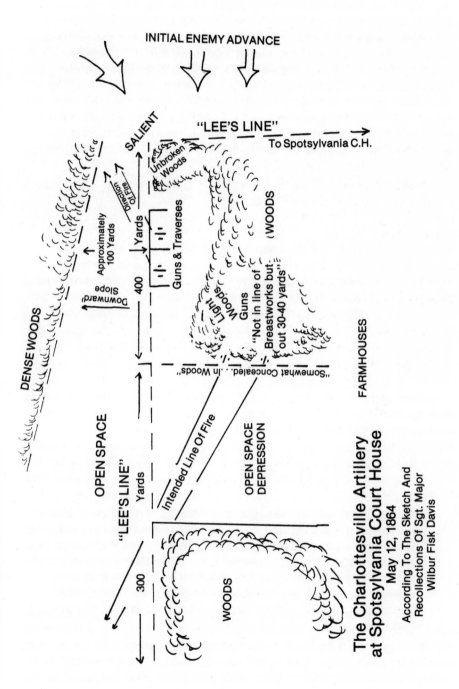

INITIAL ENEMY ADVANCE

"LEE'S LINE"

To Spotsylvania C.H.

SALIENT

Unbroken Woods

Direction Of Fire

Approximately 100 Yards

Yards

400

Downward Slope

Guns & Traverses

(WOODS

Light Woods

Guns "Not in line of Breastworks but out 30-40 yards"

DENSE WOODS

"Somewhat Concealed...In Woods"

FARMHOUSES

OPEN SPACE

Intended Line Of Fire

"LEE'S LINE"

Yards

OPEN SPACE DEPRESSION

300

WOODS

The Charlottesville Artillery at Spotsylvania Court House
May 12, 1864
According To The Sketch And Recollections Of Sgt. Major Wilbur Fisk Davis

the line of works, Carrington took time to think and began to worry particularly over the "ravine" to their right in the direction of the courthouse. Conversing with the general once more upon his return, he expressed his concerns and discussed his earlier conversation with Cutshaw. After some hesitation, Johnson agreed to move Carrington's and Tanner's batteries and stated that he would communicate the change of position and have Carrington's horses sent up. Perhaps a half-hour later, Johnson returned with word that the move would not take place because other batteries would come up to that spot some time in the morning. Now, though some still slept, the Charlottesville Artillery stood in anticipation for the day.

Near daybreak, Davis found himself unable to rest and rose to prepare for the day. Suddenly, as he was folding up his blanket, Confederate skirmishers on both the right and rear of the battery began yelling as they pulled back to the earthworks. Instantly, those of the Charlottesville men who slept were up and sprang to the guns where others had lain all night. Standing by them, the men looked out into the thick fog in their front. Though they could see nothing to open on, they sent several charges of canister into the night.

As it became apparent that the enemy were sweeping the ravine that Carrington had been so concerned about, the blue-jackets smashed into G. H. Steuart's Marylanders and began folding up the line that stood in the angle. With men falling back toward Carrington's position through the woods, Brigadier General James A. Walker, commanding the Stonewall brigade (the 5th Virginia Infantry stood on the battery's right), came up to a spot near a large oak that stood to the left of Davis's piece. Carrington recollected of Walker and the moment:

> . . .[Walker] approaching me said, hurriedly, "Carrington, can't you help my men with your battery?" . . .and raising his arm and pointing with a gesture he said they were in my rear, his men were falling back at the time up the breastworks as the enemy approached. I replied, "General it is difficult to get these guns out here in the woods and if I could see where your men are, they are between me and the enemy, and if I attempted to use canister, it would be more destructive to them than the enemy; just then a ball struck him in the arm [shattering his left elbow], evidently producing terrible shock and great pain. I remember his wheeling around, and some one coming to his aid, I had my hands full and no time to see more of him.

Davis recalled that the fallen general had called "one of my gun detachment — Walter Preston, to him, he directed him to find Col. [J. H. S.] Funk, the ranking Col. present and tell him to take command of the Brigade." While in search of the colonel, Preston suffered a fate similar to that of the general, falling with a severe wound to his arm.

In an effort somehow to aid the Stonewall Brigade, Carrington had the two pieces in the traverses point to the right front and open into the dark woods. After barking out a few rounds, Carrington felt the fire to be of little effect and they were soon ordered to cease firing.

That was the last command Davis heard for the rest of the morning. From several accounts, at this point all hell broke loose. Surrounded by fire all around, the battery could only sit idle as nothing offered a target. Confusion within the line mounted when the Confederate infantry on the left of the line began to fire into the Charlottesville company. Frantically, the men ran about in search of cover and cried out in vain to their comrades to cease fire. John Hallback, in an attempt to stop their firing, reached around a traverse and waved his hat, only to be shot dead.

A sudden wild cheer was raised, which made many men of the Charlottesville Artillery certain that the enemy had been driven. Many, like Cary Maupin and George Wood gave a cheer, "both of us waving our hats, or what was left of them." Their shouts of joy were abruptly halted when the yelling increased in intensity to the rear and the comrades of the better Shenandoah Valley days began to fall back to the guns. Carrington remembered that "the old Stonewall men using their bayonets and butts of their muskets. . . were overwhelmed by masses of the enemy." Seeing his men in danger, Captain Carrington gave the order to fall back, and, as he later wrote, "I attempted to get away myself." Only Davis's piece on the extreme right did not hear the order. A man near Davis, seeing no officers around, called out, "who is in command here?" As Davis too looked around, he found the same as the one who had called out and replied, "I am." Taking charge, the sergeant major realized that the guns were sunk too deep in the mud to be moved, so he brought the section back into action, firing into the woods in their front "as far to the right as possible." Carrington recalled:

As I was leaving, some one told me, that several of my men were at one of the guns, who had not heard my order to retire. I started back to get them off, when I got to the first gun, I looked over the breastworks into the open field. . . and there saw a number of our men, the number being so great that I thought they were charging the enemy. I could not conceive the surrender of so many of our men together, I could not take in the situation, I found a lanyard in the first of my guns, I observed several regiments of the enemy approaching to the left of our men. . . . It occurred to me that the enemy was attempting to flank us, they were in the immediate range of this gun. I got hold of the lanyard and was pulling it off, when I felt someone pulling my overcoat tail, and I found one of my men named

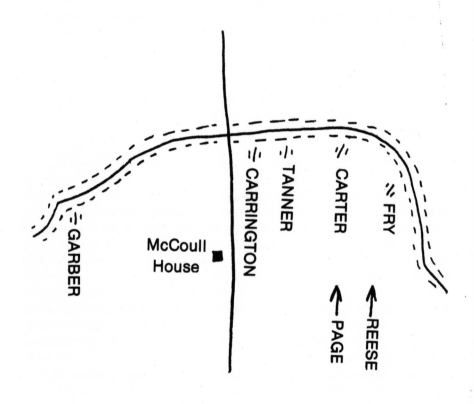

GARBER

McCoull
House

CARRINGTON

TANNER

CARTER

FRY

↑ PAGE

↑ REESE

Positions Of Artillery During
The Assault On The Bloody Angle
May 12, 1864
According to Jedediah Hotchkiss

Bishop (a game gallant fellow he was) laying at the trail of the gun, he said to me, look there, I looked a little to the right, and there stood a Federal Officer in a Colonel's uniform with a pistol cocked and directed at my head, he was very near me.... I did not know whether he was Confederate or Federal, I turned suddenly taking him as much by surprise as he had taken me, knocked his pistol off and got mine on him, when he very coolly said to me, I could have killed you, and here are my men all around you, and sure enough within twenty steps of me, there were a number of men laying down with their muskets cocked; they had come up through the woods, this is the place I was standing I suppose, when Mr. Fife. . .as he was going out he saw me standing by his gun, and said to me, "Good-bye." Of course under the circumstances I considered that discretion was the better part of valor and surrendered to this Officer.... I was turned over to a Federal soldier, whom I soon saw was of foreign birth, that soldier is now [after 1900] a Sergeant on the Police Force of Washington City, he is an Italian by the name Lombardy, he is now a great friend of mine and frequently gives a humorous account of it at my expense.

The guns of the battery to the left joined in the fight after they had wheeled the pieces around to face the right. Elevating the cannon to fire over their own works and men to the front, one of the pieces recoiled so badly as to fall back in the ditch and remain stuck. Many at these two pieces had just enough time to witness the Federal tide overrun the forward guns before they fled to the rear.

Those who were routed from the battery made it to the second or third line of defense before finally stopping. While Fitzhugh was within the second line, one of the men from the company came by and announced that some of Major Page's guns had been retaken on the right, and now needed men to serve them. Preferring to fight, Fitz went on to that position and fought until it too was overrun, escaping by fleetness of foot again.

In less than an hour, the Charlottesville Artillery virtually had ceased to exist. Some two miles to the rear, near the wagon yard, most of what was left of the company reassembled and huddled by fires to calm their nerves and catch their breath. At one such fire Fitz found Marshall and three or four others making coffee. With no cannons and over half of the men lost, the survivors (one officer, three sergeants, one corporal, and forty-five men) and horses were "temporarily" attached to Garber's Staunton Artillery.

Among the dead left in the earthworks lay 3rd Sergeant Thomas Wills, Pendleton Wash, Arch Houston, Guidon Lyman Via, Hallback,

Philip Pendleton, and William Norvell. Those wounded included William Terrell in the hip; John Old (later to die of the wound); Ned Massie; Jeremiah Wayland; Walter Preston by a gunshot in the left shoulder; James Creel, severely in the left leg; and James Sneed. Captured were Captain Carrington, 2nd Lieutenants Swoope and Massie, Sergeant Major Davis, 4th Sergeant Spooner, 1st Corporal John Lewis, 5th Corporal James Atkins, 6th Corporal Obediah Calvert (again), George Belew (died of sickness), W. F. Berry, J. H. Bibb (died of wound received at prison camp), A. G. Bishop, L. Brown (died of sickness), C. A. Chancy (died of sickness), J. L. Craven, A. H. Dillard, B. F. Dodd (again), J. H. Duncan (again), W. R. Durrett, W. F. Gillespie, H. T. Harrison, A. L. Holladay, C. P. Hornsey, H Jenkins, J. W. Miller, C. R. Perkins, L. R. Railey, A. B. Roler, G. S. Roller (received gunshot wound to back and arm), J. S. M. Sheppherd, G. W. Terrell, W. M. Thacker, Preston, S. Wood, and T. Wyant (died).

In a couple of days, some of the survivors went back to the site of their May 12 fight and found most of their comrades buried, with the exception of Wash and another. The enemy upon sweeping the works had destroyed the guns and carriages and left the shattered wrecks among the carnage.

The Aftermath

The men of the Charlottesville Artillery who survived and were not captured trudged along with the Staunton Artillery until the end. Archie Marshall was wounded at Cold Harbor by a sharpshooter, and six more were captured at Cedar Creek in October. In March of 1865 the men were posted in Fort Clifton on the Appomattox River. They numbered thirty-three present and forty-four called in, one-hundred and twenty-three on the rolls including sick and captured. With his battalion cut to such a small number in all of his batteries, Cutshaw requested — in vain — that his command be made a cavalry organization.

One month later at Appomattox, the following veterans finally surrendered, still with the Staunton Artillery: Sergeants John Hunter, Jr., and Samuel J. Coffman; Corporals Robert C. Bowman and Robert H. Fife; and Privates Dabney Clark Carver, Francis C. Fitzhugh, David L. Garton, Harry T. Harrison, George E. Humphrey, John H. Houston, Isiah P. Iseman, George T. Lowrie, George D. Mauck, William C. Maupin, Schuyler T. Rhodes, Charles Sneed, Nathaniel A. Terrell.

Those who had been captured had seen another side of the war not often written about. After being taken out of the works on May 12, 1864, the long train of men was taken through the woods at which they had been firing. The diligent writer Davis described all that took place thereafter.

> Passing. . . a four horse ambulance in which we were told was Gen. Grant — until we were completely out of range. We camped or rather bivouacked in the rain and mud, and crowded together that night — marched thro. Fredericksburg the next day and on to Belle Plains on the Potomac. . . There we were kept in a hollow square of guards, with cannon trained on us. The following Wednesday, I with other enlisted men of our battery, was put aboard a freight propeller, sea-going, at 12 m. We were till 10 p.m. Friday evening reaching Fort Delaware spending one day aground on some point of Cape Charles at the mouth of the Chesapeake Bay. They were perhaps 500-700 of us on this freight steamer crowded on the lower deck with not room enough for us to lie down. I don't remember how we slept. I maintained my position by one of the large open gangways — and so had plenty of fresh air — albeit somewhat tainted with stench that could not be avoided — the only sewer or closet be-

ing these same gangways. At least they were as far as I saw. I didn't move far away from my first stand, for fear I should lose my place and my "coigne of vantage" for seeing — during daylight and breathing fresh air all the time. The only rations served on the voyage were hardtack and cups of very brown sugar — taken and eaten by hand. I was on the starboard quarter and gazed (thro the gangway on the other side of course) mournfully at the Stratford and Nomini Cliffs as I passed. . . . A few of the captains, were taken up the ladder to the upper deck, perhaps 12 feet above us, and so had good quarters and food, I presume. . . . We got to Fort Delaware, after a very calm voyage of about 60 hours, we felt the effect of confinement in the close quarters of the ship — but not nearly so much as our comrades who had been in closer quarters still, back in the rear or forward, away from the open ports. One I remember, Lucian Brown of White Hall, Albemarle — who had been way back in the stern. He looked pale and weak, when he got in the barracks.

There were probably 7000 of us, enlisted men — in the "pens" . . . on the island under the guns of the Fort — about 400 yd off. The commissioned officers (including our three, Capt. Carrington, Lieuts. Swoope and Massie) were in a separate enclosure — between us and the Fort. We could not see them all — tho the two pens each surrounded with a close plank fence 15 or more feet high — were not too far for a stone to be thrown, with a note tied to it — when it was too dark to be noticed by the numerous sentinels. . . . We were housed in rough plank barracks, all the same pattern, built in and around the four or five acres of land enclosed. Each division was about 75 ft. long (I reckon) by 18 to 20 ft. wide. Bunks were built like berths in a ship, in three tiers, only the depth was about 6 ft. or 7, and we lay with our heads to the walls, and our feet at the plank parapet of a few inches in height — a little lower than the head. Cross pieces nailed on the supporting posts, made steps or ladders to the upper berths.

Soon after the prisoners' arrival at Fort Delaware, Captain Carrington's mother, along with his brother, Union officer Edward C. Carrington, paid a visit to the Charlottesville men. The mother was only able to come through the lines with the influence of her Federal son. Meeting in the commandant's quarters (General A. F. Schoepf), the wonderfully influential woman had lunch with Ed, the Captain, and Davis, inquiring the whole time what clothing and money the men might need. Prior to her visit, she had made arrangements with the captives' parents so that she could provide them whatever money they needed while there, and upon returning to

Charlottesville settle the debts. In all, the distribution came to about $8 or $10 per man. Money being of little value, however, suttlers tickets were provided instead. Sometime after Mrs. Carrington had returned home, she forwarded a large trunk of clothing. Davis explained what took place.

> On reaching the front of the office of the Commandant of prisoners — a 100 yds or more from the prison gate we were halted by a sergeant in charge there. I explained to him what we were doing [having already signed a receipt for it in the presence of the commandant at his office] — what was in the trunk, and that I had the order of Gen. S. to whom I had given the receipt to take the clothing to the men for whom they were intended. Nothing would do — he was partly drunk anyhow, but I must stop the trunk right there, and go to the barracks, get my men and bring them out there. I said — it is easy enough for me to get into the barracks, but I can't come out again without special orders, and that besides, it would take some time to find and get together all my men in such a crowd. "You go in and get your men together at the gate and I will be there to let you out." . . .I went in and the two men, got the men together as quickly as I could. . .

The gathering took some time for the sergeant major and the men as he collected them. After all was done, the sergeant that was to be at the gate was, as suspected, not there. After the sergeant was found, the clothes and trunk were gone. The sergeant said that he had already distributed the clothing to other men and Davis's men looked "not more ragged than those he gave to." A complaint might be forwarded to the commandant, if Davis desired, said the sergeant. The clothes and trunk were never seen again, apparently being "distributed" by the sergeant in his own favor.

Though Davis was exchanged later, many remained to die of sickness, or as in Bibb's case of a gunshot wound received at Fort Delaware. Carrington and Massie suffered yet more hardships as two of the six hundred officers who were subjected to friendly fire while in captivity at Hilton Head, S.C.; they survived the episode. They and others still were fortunate enough to survive and return home to rebuild their lives. Friendship bonds were not soon forgotten, however, as many looked back fondly on the days with their old comrades. Many joined together in the postwar years in the J. B. Strange Camp of United Confederate Veterans.

Supply Data Extracted From the Officers' Service Records
(Note: this is an incomplete accounting due to incomplete records)
19 April 1862, Richmond — 120 blankets, 140 overcoats
28 April 1862, Richmond — 12 bell tents, 3 officers (wall) tents, 15 camp

kettles, 24 skillets

28 May 1862, Winchester — 1,844 lbs. corn for 87 horses for 1 day.

29 May 1862, Winchester — 1,044 lbs. corn for 87 horses for 1 day.

6 June 1862, Harrisonburg — 3,584 lbs. corn for horses.

17 June 1862, Staunton — 8 gear straps, 2 halter straps, 2 ? straps, 2 artillery ? chains, 2 hooks, 1 new head halter, 1 sponge staff, 1 iron wire.

27 June 1862, Richmond — 1,400 lbs. corn for horses.

29 June 1862, Richmond — 1,728 lbs. corn for 72 horses for 1 day.

30 July 1862 — 3 officers tents.

22 September 1862 — 800 lbs. hay for reimbursement for trip from Gordonsville to Winchester, dated 4 October.

27 September 1862, Winchester — 1 barrel flour at $8 and 69 lbs. bacon at $24.15. For reimbursement for travel from Gordonsville to Winchester.

3 October 1862, Winchester — 1,000 lbs. hay at $10, and 400 lbs. at 3.00. (separate figures).

15 October 1862 — 19,200 lbs. corn and 22,400 lbs. hay for 100 horses for 15 days.

7 March 1863 — 5 extra wheels, 4 ammo chests, 3 poles, 18 washers, 5 lbs. packing material.

1 July 1863, different camps — 64 horses for a month. Cannot make out actual goods requisitioned.

22 July 1863, Bunker Hill — 7 artillery horses.

23 July 1863, near Winchester — 31 pair shoes, 18 pair drawers, 11 shirts, 7 pair pants.

6 August 1863, Liberty Mills — 2 artillery horses.

21 August 1863, near Gordonsville — 2 caps, 15 pants, 3 drawers, 11 shirts, 17 pair shoes, 12 jackets.

31 August 1863, at different camps — 9,300 lbs. corn, 13,299 lbs. oats, 9,899 lbs. hay for 58 horses for 31 days.

September 1863 — 14,400 lbs. barley, 6,285 lbs. hay, and 6,420 lbs. fodder.

10 September 1863, near Gordonsville — Special requisition for 5 pair of pants.

1 October 1863 — 5 quires letter paper, 1 foolscape, 75 envelopes.

1 October 1863, different camps — 18,259 lbs. corn, 2,402½ lbs. oats, 2,884 lbs. hay, 2,883 lbs. fodder for 62 horses for 30 days.

5 October 1863, near Somerville Ford — 91 jackets, 117 pantaloons, 84 shorts, 74 drawers, 28 socks, 7 blankets.

27 October 1863, Brandy Station — 7 ?, 5 jackets, 11 pair pants, 18 pair shoes, 30 pair socks, 10 pairs drawers.

29 October 1863, Brandy Station — 8 artillery horses.

1 November 1863, different camps — 18,000 lbs. corn, 2,700 lbs. hay, 3,600 lbs. fodder for 60 horses for 30 days.

1 December 1863, different camps — 18,600 lbs. corn, 2,790 lbs. hay, 3,720 lbs. fodder.

3 December 1863, near Brandy — 28 overcoats, 4 blankets, 17 pair shoes, 20 pair pants, 6 jackets, 3 pair drawers, 6 shirts.

7 December 1863 — 3 artillery horses, 2 rope halters.

10 December 1863, in the field — 41 pair shoes, 20 blankets, 9 shirts, 2 jackets, 1 pair pants.

24 December 1863, Frederick's Hall — 18 pair pants, 2 fly tents, 1 bell and fly complete, 1 flag.

January 1864 — fuel requisition for:

Allowance:

1 Captain — 1 cord wood 89 feet, 7 inches — on leave for 13 days
3 Sub? — 5 cords, 59 feet, 9 inches — one on leave 8 days
90 men — 15 cords
** — 3 cords for guard fire at stable.

2 January 1864 — 300 lbs. corn, 196 lbs. hay for 1 horse for 14 days.

8 January 1864 — 25 pairs of drawers.

11 February 1864 — 5?

12 February 1864 — 26 lbs. of leather, 1 ball of shoe thread.

17 February 1864 — 2½ quires of letter paper, 2½ quires foolscap paper, 20 pens, 100 envelopes, 2 pen holder, 2 lead pencils, 2 ?

19 February 1864 — 13 jackets, 5 pantaloons, 8 pair shoes, 10 shirts, 11 pair drawers.

22 February 1864 — 5 jackets, 8 pantaloons, 10 pair drawers.

23 February 1864 — 5 jackets, 6 shirts, 3 pair shoes.

23 February 1864 — 31 pair shoes, 9 pantaloons, 15 jackets, 6 shirts, 2 pair drawers.

27 February 1864, near Frederick's Hall — 1 pair shoes.

24 March 1864 — turned over 3 unserviceable horses.

31 March 1864 — 3 pair shoes.

8 April 1864 — Special requisition for 11 horses.

Abbreviations

AWOL — Absent without leave
Bn. — Born
Bttn. — Battalion
C.H. — Courthouse
Cav. — Cavalry
Chimbo. — Chimborazo Hospital
CM — Court-martial
Co. — Company or County
Cpl. — Corporal
D. — Died
Dau. — Daughter
Enl. — Enlisted
Ft. — Fort
GCM — General Court-Martial
GH — General Hospital
GO — General Order
GP — Grandparents
GSW — Gunshot wound
Inf. — Infantry
KIA — Killed In Action
Lt. — Lieutenant or Light
M. — Married
MWIA — Mortally Wounded In Action
NFR — No Further Record
OCH — Orange Court House
Ord. — Ordnance
Pt. — Point
Pvt. — Private
QM — Quartermaster
RC — Richmond College
Res. — Residence
SCH — Spotsylvania Court House
Sgt. — Sergeant
SO — Special Order
Surg. Cert. — Surgeon's Certificate
UVA — University of Virginia
VMI — Virginia Military Institute
WC — Washington College
WIA — Wounded In Action

James L. Dinwiddie, Charlottesville Artillery

Pvt. John G. Herndon, Charlottesville Artillery

Leroy Wesley Cox at the age of 21.

Wilbur Fisk Davis, Charlottesville Artillery

APPENDIX
Tabulations From The Roster
Commissioned And Noncommissioned Officers
Of The Charlottesville Artillery

Carrington, James McD., Captain *
Dinwiddie, James L., 1st Lt.*
Timberlake, John H., Jr. 1st Lt.
Cochran, Alexander B., 1st Lt. *
Swoope, Francis McF., 1st Lt. *
Bibb, French S., 2nd Lt. *
Massie, D. Rodes, 2nd Lt. *
Hunter, John, Jr., 2nd Lt. *
King, George M., Surgeon *
Harris, Henry H., Sgt. Major *
Davis, Wilbur F., Sgt. Major *
Harman, Charles H., QM Sgt.
McCoy, William K., 2nd Sgt. *
Coffman, Samuel J., 2nd Sgt. *
Wills, Thomas C., 3rd Sgt. (2nd)
Spooner, John H., 4th Sgt. (2nd)
Carrington, George, 7th Sgt., (1st) *
Holladay, Waller, 7th Sgt. (2nd) *
Fife, Robert H., Sgt. *
Harding, William C., 1st Cpl.
Cocke, Thomas L. P., 2nd Cpl. (1st) *
Wayland, Jeremiah F., 2nd Cpl. (2nd) *
Boyden, Daniel H., 3rd Cpl. (3rd) *
Wills, William S., 4th Cpl. (1st)
Lewis, John W., 4th Cpl.
Atkins, James H., 5th Cpl., (2nd)
Calvert, Obediah, 6th Cpl. (2nd)
Harris, Jeremiah M., 7th Cpl. (1st) *
Estill, Charles P., 8th Cpl. (1st)
Maupin, Benjamin F., 9th Cpl. (1st)
Martin, Patrick, 10th Cpl. (1st)
Brooks, John D., 11th Cpl. (1st)
Byers, Elwood, 12th Cpl. (1st)
Estill, Harry, Cpl.
Houston, Mathew H., Cpl.
McCarthy, Michael H., Cpl.

Houston, Archibald, W., Cpl.
Shreve, Samuel, Cpl.
Terrell, Nathaniel A., Buglar
Cochran, George M., Guidon (1st)
Via, Lyman, Guidon (2nd)
Madison, Dabney M., Blacksmith
Wheeler, George W., Blacksmith

*Attended U.Va.

Statistical Summary of Strengths and Losses

253	On Roster
36	Postwar References
5	Never Reported
3	Negro Servants
209	Actually Enrolled In Battery

Killed In Action	10	5%
Wounded In Action	26	12%
MIA W/NFR	1	.4%
Captured At Least Once	55	26%
Captured Twice	5	2%
Died Of Disease	6	3%
Died Of Disease While POW	9	4%
Died Of Wounds	6	3%
Died Of Wounds As POW	1	.4%
Deserted	16	8%
Total War Dead	32	15%
Sick At Least Once	117	56%
AWOL At Least Once	30	14%
Member Illegally (of another)	3	1%
Retired, Resigned, Discharged	20	10%
Provided Substitute	6	3%
Transferred	9	4%
Permanently Detached/Detailed	9	4%
Exchanged And Served Again	15	7%
Paroled And Took Oath	5	2%
Appomattox Parolees	6	3%
NFR	6	3%

Summary of Battery Strength (End Of Month)
As Extracted From The Information Provided In The Roster
Including Temporary Absences Due To Sickness And Wounds

3/62 - 114	1/63 - 96	1/64 - 57	1/65 - 36
4/62 - 142	2/63 - 87	2/64 - 81	2/65 - 35
5/62 - 136	3/63 - 97	3/64 - 97	3/65 - 36
6/62 - 113	4/63 - 99	4/64 - 103	4/65 - 37 (15 at App)
7/62 - 100	5/63 - 90	5/64 - 50	
8/62 - 86	6/63 - 77	6/64 - 52	
9/62 - 99	7/63 - 77	7/64 - 53	
10/62 - 109	8/63 - 79	8/64 - 52	
11/62 - 106	9/63 - 88	9/64 - 52	
12/62 - 101	10/63 - 86	10/64 - 44	
	11/63 - 81	11/64 - 52	
	12/63 - 57	12/64 - 56	

Occupations at Enlistment

*Approximately 27 are confirmed out of 44 supposed to have been in attendance at UVa. prior to the war and enlisting in Confederate Service. Many who were students either had recently graduated and were becoming established, first enlisted in another unit, were between sessions, or were simply waiting to see how the war would go before reentering the University.

Farmer - 5
Lawyer - 3
Blacksmith, Druggist, Shoemaker, and Stonecutter - one each

Ages At Enlistment
(Seventy-Nine Available)

12?? - 1 (R. A. Goodwyn)	Percentage in teens - 27%
15 - 1	Percentage 20 - 29 - 36%
16 - 3	Percentage 30 - 39 - 5%
17 - 3	Percentage 40 + - 5%
18 - 10	
19 - 4	
20 - 4	28 - 3
21 - 4	29 - 1
22 - 5	31 - 3
23 - 3	33 - 1
24 - 4	48 - 1
25 - 3	52 - 1
26 - 4	54 - 1
27 - 2	58 - 1

Residences at Enlistment
or
Countles of Birth of the
Former Is Unavailable

Albemarle Co.	41 +	Augusta, Ga.	1
Amherst Co.	2	Rome, Ga.	1
Augusta Co.	6	Louisiana	1
Campbell Co.	1	Maryland	1
Charles City	1	N.C.	1
Fairfax Co.	1	Tennessee	1
Fauquier Co.	3	Wheeling	2
Fluvanna Co.	2		
Louisa Co.	4		
Nelson Co.	1		
Orange Co.	3		
Rockbridge Co.	2		
Rockingham Co.	3		

A Note Regarding the Rosters

The rosters are taken from the military records of the companies, and available birth, marriage, death, and postwar dates and activities; abbreviations have been used occasionally. As far as the actual military records are concerned, all information has been copied with the exception of pay information. Sometimes it will be noted within the rosters that a veteran may have no more record than "enl. 3/15/62, present through 2/28/65." This usually will indicate that either there was no more information provided between those dates or simply that nothing of particular note occurred (e.g. sickness, hospitalization, wounds, etc.). Sometimes in the rosters lack of information is reduced by the fact that clothing was issued by the company, thus showing that an artillerist had returned.

The dates given in parentheses indicate that the actual date of an event was not given, but show when the event was next recorded.

The Charlottesville Artillery Roster

ABELL, CALEB: Bn. in Orange Co., Va., son of Caleb. Enl. 3/15/62. Later provided a substitute. Married Jane Black, dau. of William. Also a note of marrying Maria O. Garland, 3/3/56.

ANTHONY, JOSEPH: Enl. 3/15/62. Occupation: stonecutter. 7/6/62, in Richmond hospital, sick. Present (9/3/62). Admitted to Chimbo. #1 6/7/63. Deserted from the hospital 11/8/63? Had returned to duty as of 8/20/63. Present sick 12/31/63. Admitted to Chimbo. #3 with debilitas, 1/16/64. To Chimbo. #2, 4/2/64. To Chimbo. #3, 5/2/64. Took oath of amnesty in Richmond, 4/17/65, age 58.

ATKINS, JAMES H.: Pvt., 5th Cpl. Enl. 3/15/62. Absent sick in Charlottesville on surgeon's certificate, 6/20/62. Present (9/3/62). 5th corporal (4/30/63). Absent sick with chronic rheumatism at Charlottesville G.H., 6/13/63-8/14/63. Absent with paid, 2/29/64. Captured 5/12/64, S.C.H. Sent to Ft. Delaware from Belle Plain, Va., 5/21/64. Released 6/15/65, res. Albemarle Co., fair complexion, light hair, grey eyes, 5'10". M. Mary A. Webb 1/21/66.

BABER, JAMES W.: Enl. 4/24/62. AWOL 5/5/62. Deserter (9/3/62), age 26, 6'2", dark complexion, dark hair, grey eyes. Took oath in Staunton, 5/15/65.

BAKER, EDWARD W.: Postwar ref. R. E. Lee Camp Soldier's Home, Richmond. Entered 4/7/28, age 82. Died 1/6/29. Buried in Hollywood Cemetery.

BAKER, EDWIN H.: Occupation: farmer. Enl. 3/5/64. Received clothing issue, 3/5/64. Admitted to Chimbo. #2 with irritation fever, 7/25/64. To duty 8/25/64. Detached to recruit horses by order of General Early, 1/10/65. Paroled 5/5/65 Ashland, Va.

BARKSDALE, JAMES ISAAC: Bn. 1844, son of W. G. and Myra M. Wood Barksdale. Enl. first in Co. K, 19th Va. Inf. Enl. 2/1/63. Admitted to Charlottesville G.H. with chronic dysentery, 6/5/63. To duty 8/6/63. Present through 2/28/65. D. 7/27/98, Pittsylvania Co.

BARKSDALE, WILLIAM J.: Bn. 7/20/40, see above parentage. Enl. 3/15/62. Absent sick with gononrreah at Charlottesville G.H., 5/4/62. To Colony, 5/10/62. Absent sick in Albemarle Co. on Surgeon's Certificate, 5/15/62. To duty 5/25/62. Absent sick at Greenwood Hospital, 9/10/62. To duty (10/31/62). To hospital with februs remittus, 8/15/64-9/7/64. Detached to recruit horses per order of General Early, 1/10/65. Present 3/3/65. M. 12/20/66 to Nannie J. Hamilton (Bn. 1844, dau. of John and Barbara Hamsburger Hamilton of Augusta County.) He was a leading merchant in Batesville, Albemarle County. Had six children. Entered R. E. Lee Camp Soldier's Home, 3/25/20, age 86. D. 4/6/21.

BAYLOR, ALEXANDER GALT.: Enl. 3/15/62. Missing 6/27/62. Detailed as hospital nurse per S.O. #183/7, 8/7/62.

BELEW, GEORGE T.: Enl. 2/28/64 in Louisa Co. Captured 5/12/64, S.C.H. Received at Ft. Delaware 5/20/64. Died of chronic diarrhea, 3/18/65. Buried on Jersey Shore.

BERRY, WILLIAM F.: Enl. 3/15/62. Captured 5/12/64, S.C.H. Received at Ft. Delaware, 5/20/64. Released 6/15/65; res. Rockingham Co., dark complexion, dark hair, blue eyes, 5'10".

BIBB, FRENCH "FRANK" STROTHER: Pvt., 2nd Lt. Bn. 8/7/43, Charlottesville, Va. Son of John Henry and Harriet Pendleton Bibb. Paternal G. P. George and Mary Bibb. Maternal G. P. French and Mary Ann Strother. 10/60 student at Richmond College, under the "especial care of his brother-in-law, Prof. Wm. P. Louthan, M.A. UVa. '61, "student of languages and mathematics." VMI '64 MS, (matric. 4/61; attended 6 wks.) Enl. 3/15/62. Elected 2nd Lt. (chief of caisson), 4/17/62. Mortally wounded from volley fire in the groin at Chancellorsville, 5/3/63. Died in Richmond, 5/28/63. Carrington recounted of him; "a young hero. . .I recall his flaxen hair, blue eyes, florid complexion, his gentleness and his bravery." From the UVa. Memorial is written "on his coffin was laid the following lines written by a lady friend for the burial hour;

Strew flowers on his coffin'd breast,
His noble heart is now at rest;
The young, the beautiful, the brave,
We will not mourn his early grave.
Faithfully his duty done,
On earth a noble name he won;
But, nobler far than earthly fame,
He bore his saviour's holy name.
His early days to God were given,
His record in the books of heaven.
Then let him rest, till that glad sound
Which calls the nations from the ground
Full on his raptured ear is pour'd,
"Come forth, ye blessed of the Lord."

BIBB, GEORGE W.: Postwar reference.

BIBB, JOHN HENRY, JR.: Brother of F. S. Bibb. See above for parentage. Enl. 2/1/64. Captured 5/12/64, S.C.H. to Ft. Delaware. Died 12/21/64 of a gunshot wound. Buried on Jersey shore.

BIRSY, WILLIAM: Postwar reference.

BISHOP, ADOLPHUS GLENROY: Bn. 3/28/42, Augusta Co., son of Joseph Monroe and Martha Ann Finley Bishop (she was from Nelson Co.) Enl. 3/15/62. Absent sick in Charlottesville on surgeons certificate, 6/20/62. Present (9/3/62). Wounded at White Post in 10/62. Captured 5/12/64, S.C.H. to Ft. Delaware. Released 6/19/65; res. Albemarle Co., dark complexion, black hair, blue eyes, 6'0". M. 1) Annie Craven Watson, 2) Margaret Ann Scantling, daughter of William A. and Mary Elizabeth Clarks (Bn. Moorman's River 1860) he was a boot and shoemaker in Moorman's River after the war. D. 8/11/08.

BONDURANT, WALTER ERNEST: Bn. 1841, Natchez, Mississippi. Student at UVa. '60, '61, '62. No enl. date available. In Charlottesville G.H. with chronic dysentery, 8/13/62. Discharged from service 9/21/62, S.O. #217/15, 9/16/62. Later M.D. and Asst. Surgeon, C.S.A. D. 6/13/74, Natchez, Ms.

BOWEN, WILLIAM J.: Enl. 3/15/62. Captured at Gettysburg or Waterloo, 7/4 or 7/5/63. Sent to Ft. Delaware. Paroled 10/30/64. Exchanged 10/31/64. Admitted to Charlottesville G.H. with gonorrhea, 12/5/64-2/13/65. Reported from parole 2/10/65.

BOYDEN, DANIEL HANSON: Pvt., 3rd Cpl. Bn. 1843, Cobham, Albemarle Co., Va. Student at UVa. '60. Enl. 3/15/62. Promoted to 3rd Cpl. 6/19/63. Received clothing issue 3/24/64. Present through 2/28/65. Postwar Episcopal minister. D. Hopedale, Albemarle Co., Va. 12/22/71.

61

BRAGG, ROBERT S.: Enl. 4/1/62. AWOL 8/20/62. Present (10/31/62). Admitted to Charlottesville G.H. with pneumonia, 3/13/63. Sent to Colony 3/17. Present 8/25/63. AWOL 7/64. Admitted to Charlottesville G.H. with chronic rheumatism 12/8/64. Released from hospital 1/1/65. Still AWOL as of 2/28/65.

BROOKS, JOHN D.: 11th Cpl., Pvt. Enl. 4/1/62. Absent sick on leave in Augusta Co. 8/13/62. Present (10/31/62). Detailed per S.O. #44/6, 2/13/63 (without pay) through 2/28/65.

BROWN, DANIEL: Enl 4/1/62. AWOL 6/21/62. "Deserted from Charlottesville 6/20". AWOL 9/21/63, "deserted 2nd time in face of enemy at Somerville Ford 9/26/63 while in arrest". Captured at Somerville Ford 9/27/63. Sent to Old Capitol Prison, Washington, D.C. Released under oath 12/27/63. Sent north. Claimed res. as Washington, D.C., light complexion, grey hair, grey eyes, 5'9".

BROWN, JAMES: *Postwar reference.*

BROWN, LUCIAN B.: Joined from exchange from camp of instruction 10/5/63. Absent sick 10/5/63-1/3/64. Captured 5/12/64, S.C.H. Died of disease at Ft. Delaware 7/21/64, inflamation of bowels or lungs. Buried on the Jersey shore. Effects received 12/7/64, certificate #2453.

BROWN, THORNTON: Negro servant to Wilbur Fisk Davis. Present with the unit through to the battle of 5/12/64, when he returned to Davis' family.

BURGOYNE, GEORGE: Postwar reference.

BURGOYNE, MARSHALL K.: Enl. 4/15/62. "An Irishman" per Davis. Arrested as deserter from 8th Louisana Volunteers 10/4/62. See also 6th Louisiana.

BYERS, ELWOOD: 12th Cpl., Pvt. Enl. 4/14/62. Detailed temporarily as hospital steward at Gordonsville (9/3/62). Promoted to hospital steward per S.O. #230/7, 10/2/62. See personal papers of Henry J. Stansberry, Co. A, 7th Louisiana Infantry, 9/63. NFR. Member J. B. Strange Camp.

CALVERT, OBEDIAH: Pvt., 6th Cpl. Enll. 4/4/62. AWOL 11/26-12/3/62. Stoppage of pay $3.20. Sent to hospital 4/15/63. Admitted to Charlottesville G.H. with an abcess 4/18-5/27/63. Present 6/63. Promoted to 6th Corporal 7/8/63. Captured at Somerville Ford 11/11/63. Sent to Old Capitol Prison, then to Pt. Lookout 2/28/64. Exchanged 3/7/64. Captured again 5/12/64, S.C.H. Sent to Ft. Delaware. Released 6/19/65; res. Albemarle Co., sal complexion, dark hair, dark eyes, 5'10".

CARRINGTON, GEORGE: 7th Sgt. Bn. 1835, Halifax Co.? Student at UVa. '52, '53, '55? Enl. 3/20/62. Discharged 3/30/63, furnished substitute - John Riley. Postwar farmer in Halifax Co.?

CARRINGTON, JAMES McDOWELL: Captain. Bn. 1839 in Botetourt Co. Son of General Edward Coddington (d. 1857 from effects of wound received at the Battle of Sacketts Harbor, N.Y., War of 1812) and Eliza Henry Preston (8/11/96), Saltville, Va. 1/11/77, Charlottesville, Va.) Paternal G.P. Judge Paul Carrington, Jr. Materal G.P. General Francis Smith Preston (8/2/1765), Smithfield 5/26/35, Columbia, S.C.) and Sally Buchanan Campbell (4/21/1778-7/23/46), dau. of General William Campbell (commanded at the Battle of King's Mountain) and Bettie Henry (sister of Patrick). Student at Washington College '54-'55. At UVa. '56, 7, 9, 60, 65. VMI '64 MS, (matric. 5/16/61, age 22. Attended for 6 wks.) Member of University Company to John Brown's hanging at Harpers Ferry. Later as aide of his uncle, General John B. Floyd, to campaign in western Virginia. Raised the Charlottesville Artillery and elected captain 3/15/62. Acting chief of artillery 1/1/63-(3/3/63). Leave of absence 12/31/63-1/15/64. Captured 5/12/64, S.C.H. attained rank of Major, but date of rank uncertain. To Ft. Delaware. Hilton Head, S.C. 8/20/64. Ft. Pulaski, Ga. 10/20/64. Hilton Head, S.C. 1/1/65. Ft. Delaware 3/12/65. Released 6/9/65; res. Albemarle Co., light complexion, dark hair, grey eyes, 6'1". Postwar member of the bar of the District of Columbia. Member and commander of camp no. 171, U.C.V., District of Columbia. Member of the New York Ave. Presbyterian Church. D. 5/2/11 (age 72) of an "attack of nervous prostration" at Providence Hospital, Washington, D.C. Buried at the Presbyterian Church. Never married. Through the marriages of his mother's sisters, he was related to such notables as Governor James McDowell (for whom he had been named), General Wade Hampton, General/Governor John B. Floyd, Dr. Robert J. Breckinridge, Senator William C. Preston, General John S. Preston of S.C., and Colonel Thomas S. Preston of Virginia. Virginia.

_____, "JIM": Negro servant to James M. Carrington. Noted as with the company all the time up until Captain Carrington was captured. After which he returned home to Charlottesville with the captain's personal items.

CARVER, DABNEY CLARK: Enl. 3/20/62. Present through to parole at Appomattox C.H.

CASON, EDWARD P.: Enl. 3/22/62. Teamster 5/31/63-7/31/63. As of 8/31/63, stop 4 months pay, in arrest awaiting court martial. Present undergoing sentence (7/8/64). Detailed to recruit horses 1/10/65. Paroled at Charlottesville 5/15/65; res. Albemarle Co. Entered R. E. Lee Camp Soldier's Home 10/2/03, age 82. Left on his demand, 10/23/03.

CHANCY, CARY ALEXANDER: Bn. 1838, Charles City C.H., Va. Student at UVa. '59, 60. Occupation: Lawyer. Enl. 11/29/62. Admitted to Chimbo. with hydrocele, 1/30/64. Returned to duty 3/28/64. Captured 5/12/64, S.C.H. To Ft. Delaware, where he died of colic 11/10/64. Buried on the Jersey shore.

CHAPMAN, _____: Servant of Lt. F. S. Bibb. Present with the lieutenant after his wounding, but no other reference to him beyond this. Could have been one of the "half dozen servants" that were mentioned by W. F. Davis that had started with the unit.

CHEENY, JOSEPH: Enl. 5/7/62, received $50 bounty. Deserted 5/21/62 near Madison C.H. NFR.

CLARKE, T. J. B.: Enl. 3/15/62. Absent on sick leave in Albemarle Co., 8/8/62. Admitted to Charlottesville G.H. 8/8/62. Still absent 10/31/62. Discharged 8/17/63, debility. Res. Albemarle Co., 5'7", dark complexion, hazel eyes, black hair, farmer.

CLEMENTS, J. W.: Postwar reference.

COCHRAN, ALEXANDER BOYS "SANDY": 2nd Lt., 1st Lt. Bn. 5/10/36, Elk Meadows, Augusta Co., Va. Son of George Moffet and Maria T. Boys Cochran. Paternal G. P. James and Magadien Moffett Cochran. Maternal G. P. Dr. William and Jane St. Clair Boys. Matric. VMI 1855 from Staunton. Left after 10 days. Attended WC from '54-55. Attended UVa. '56, 57, 59; graduated with distinction from UVa. Law School. Enl. 3/15/62, and elected 2nd Lt. Absent sick in Staunton on Surgeon's certificate 6/14/62. Present (9/3/62). Absent sick 3/24/64. Present 5/63. Promoted to 1st Lt., 6/63. In hospital in Winchester 7/20/63-9/13/63. In arrest by order of Capt. Carrington 12/30/63. Accused AWOL. "Under impression he had been retired" by General A. L. Long. Released by order of Lt. Col. Jones 1/10/64. 1/25/64, S.O. #1/25 General Long restored him to the company and vacated or pronounced void all promotions under former orders. Sent to hospital 2/7/64. Dropped from rolls 5/64, per S.O. #103. Retired under Act of Congress to invalid corps 2/18/65. Suspended from exercise of his office per S.O. #68/11, 3/30/64, General R. E. Lee. Postwar lawyer, Commonwealth's Attorney, member Va. House of Delegates, Va. Senate. Stricken with a stroke while addressing Va. Legislature and died in Staunton 7/2/77.

COCHRAN, GEORGE MOFFETT: Guidon. Bn. 1843, see brother's (above) parentage. Enl. 4/23/62. Detailed as clerk for courts martial with Longstreet's Corps, 10/6/62. Admitted to Charlottesville G.H. with rubeola, 10/31-12/8/62. Present (3/3/63). Wounded at Chancellorsville 5/3/63, and sent to hospital. Admitted to Charlottesville G.H. 5/12. At Staunton G.H. 7/16/63. Clothing issued 7/27/63. Reported from hospital 9/28/63. Appointed Guidon 11/1/63. Attached to supply train 12/1/63-10/31/64. Attached as nurse to Charlottesville G.H. 10/22-10/25/64. Detailed as courier to General Long 3/31/64. NFR. Member J. B. Strange Camp. D. 1883.

COCKE, THOMAS LEWIS PRESTON: Pvt., 2nd Cpl. Bn. 1838, Cartersville, Amherst Co., Va. Student at UVa. '58. Enl. 3/15/62. 2nd Cpl. (7/16/62) on sick leave per S.O. #169/3, 8/1/62. "Confusio" at Charlottesville G.H. 11/27/62. Furloughed 12/13/62. Lumbago at Charlottesville G.H. 1/27-1/28/63. Discharged by order of Major General Elzey 2/19/63, due to spine injury. Age 25, 6', fair complexion, dark eyes, black hair, farmer. Posterwar farmer in Cumberland Co.

COFFMAN, SAMUEL J.: Pvt., 2nd Sgt. Bn. 4/15/36, Harrisonburg, Rockingham Co., Va. Student at UVa. '53, 54, 57, 58, 64, 67. Enl. with University volunteers. Enl. Charlottesville Arty. 3/15/62. 2nd Sgt. (7/16/62). Detailed 15 days by order of Gen. Lee 8/21/63-9/5/63. Detailed to recruit horses 1/10/65. Paroled at Appomattox. Admitted to Charlottesville G.H. 4/19/65. Professor of modern language at Stewart College/Southwestern Presbyterian University, Clarksville, Tennessee (to 1891). Principal of several all male schools in Va. and W.Va. until retired in 1899. Member of Forbes Bivouac, Clarksville, Tn. Elder of Presbyterian Church in 1877, Clarksville. Member of J. B. Strange Camp. M. Lucy Page Coffman (5/3/40-4/8/31) dau. of Mary Nelson and Benjamin B. Anderson. D. 9/25/19, Ivy Depot, Albemarle Co. Buried St. Paul's Churchyard, Ivy.

COLER, DANIEL: Enl. 8/13/62, sub. for Patrick Martin. Detailed to recruit horses 1/10/65. NFR.

COX, A. D.: enl. 3/15/62, transferred from 46th Va. per S.O. #89/4, 4/18/62. Still retained in 46th by conscriptive act.

COX, LEROY WESLEY: Bn. 11/22/45 "8 miles southwest of Charlottesville." Son of Dr. William and Mary Elizabeth Lacy Cox. Enl. with Co. D, 46th Va. Inf. "Border Guard." Enl. 3/15/62 with Charlottesville Arty. Admitted to Charlottesville G.H. with debility, 9/4/62. Present 9/25/62. Absent in arrest 5/18/63. Admitted to Charlottesville G.H. 7/23/63-8/7/63. Reported from hospital 8/17/63. Stop 3 months pay by sentence of court martial to make restitution for stolen goods. In arrest undergoing sentence (10/31/63-2/29/64). Detailed by order of General Long 4/27/64. Arrested and sent to Co. D, 46th Va. Inf. by order A&IG Office 9/1/64. Married Annie Eliza Foster (dau. of Nelson and Anne Eliza Oaks) at one time owned a gun shop on Main Street, and later operated a livery business and manufactured carriages and buggies. Also managed the National Soap and Chemical Company. Member J. B. Strange Camp. Member First Methodist Church of Charlottesville. D. 1/17/38, Albemarle Co. Buried Maplewood Cemetery.

CRAVEN, DABNEY: Postwar reference.

CRAVEN, JESSE L.: Enl. 9/1/63. Absent (12/31/63). Present (2/29/64). Captured 5/12/64, S.C.H. to Ft. Delaware. Released 5/31/65; res. Albemarle Co., ruddy complexion, light brown hair, hazel eyes, 5'10".

CRAVEN, PETER HENRY: Bn. 1840, Charlottesville. Student at UVa. '58-9. Served in Co. B, 19th Va. Inf. Enl. 10/26/64, New Market. Present through 2/28/65. Killed by accident in Albemarle Co. in 1873.

CRAWFORD, JAMES LEWIS: Bn. 4/20/47, Nelson Co. Son of Amanda M. Lewis Crawford. Enl. 3/15/62. Deserted from Richmond 7/16/62. Admitted to Charlottesville G.H. 8/27-8/29/62. Discharged per S.O. #264, AGO. 62, paragraph 11, 11/11/62; "enlisted without consent."

CRAWFORD, WADE: Enl. 10/10/62, Bunker Hill. Admitted to Charlottesville G.H. 11/26/62. Not heard from since (12/31/63). Dropped from rolls, deserter.

CREEDON, CHARLES: Enl. 4/16/62. Deserted 6/2/62 at Woodstock and captured. To Ft. Delaware. Exchanged from Aiken's Landing 8/5/62. Allegiance 8/10/62.

CREEL, JAMES C.: Enl. 3/15/62. Absent sick in Albemarle Co. on surgeon's certificate 4/1/62. Present (9/3/62). Absent (12/31/63). Present (2/29/64). 5/12/64 severely wounded in left leg, S.C.H. Admitted to Delevan Hospital 5/18/64. "Compound commuted fracture, erysipilas." Resected tibia, but complications arose and gangrene set in. D. 6/15/64 at Charlottesville G.H. Effects received 7/26/64, certificate #1264.

CRENSHAW, J. W. N.: Enl. 3/15/62. Absent on sick leave (9/3/62). Died near Charlottesville, 9/7/62. Widow - Mary E. Crenshaw filed claim 3/19/63.

CUNNINGHAM, JAMES H.: Enl. 4/25/64, Liberty Mills. Captured 10/19/64? Detailed to recruit horses, 1/10/65. NFR.

CURRIER, PORTERFIELD: Enl. 1/17/65, Fisherville. Paroled at Appomattox.

DAVIS, WILBUR FISK: Pvt., Cpl., Sgt. Major. Bn. 5/29/39 in New Bern, N.C., son of Joseph H. and Anne Tuberville Beale (m. 5/10/38). Moved with family from place to place until resided in Murfreesboro, N.C. between 1854-1857. Student at UVa. '57-8. Enl. 3/20/62. Absent sick in Richmond with leave 7/10/62. Admitted to Charlottesville G.H. with typhoid fever, 8/12-10/5/62. Present (10/31/62). Cpl. (4/30/63). Sgt. Major 6/1/63. Absent 12/31/63. Present (2/29/64). Captured 5/12/64, S.C.H. "at home on parole" 10/31/64. Reported from parole 12/19/64. Retired to invalid corps 2/13/65. Assigned to Major Campbell, topographical engineer dept. Opened a school in the Bowlsville (now Cismont) area after the war. M. Ella V. Sampson 8/30/66, at her father's home, Clifton, by his father. Moved to Lynchburg after the spring of 1869, opened another school. Settled at Hickory Hill in Westmoreland Co. between 1872-4. Superintendent of schools in Westmoreland Co. in 1878. Ella D. 8/82. He joined Va. Methodist Conference and was assigned to Martinsville 11/85. D. 2/18/12.

63

DAY, JOHN BARKSDALE: Bn. 1836, Charlottesville. Student at UVa. '57-8. Enl. 4/1/62. Absent sick in Albemarle Co. 8/8/62. Admitted to Charlottesville G.H. with debility 8/25-9/30/62. Present (10/31/62). Transferred by exchange to 2nd Va. Cav. 1/20/63. Postwar farmer in Charlottesville.

DEVERIX, ALONZO J.: Enl. 3/30/62. Admitted to Charlottesville G.H. with varioloid 3/29/63-4/17/63; morbilitis 5/3/63-5/19/63. Paroled at New Market 5/6/65; age 18, 5'7", light hair, light complexion, blue eyes.

DILLARD, ARCHALEUS HUGHES "ARCH": Son of A. H. Dillard, Sr. Enl. 3/15/62. Absent sick on Surgeon's certificate 8/22/62. Present (10/31/62). Daily duty 7/26/63 in QM Dept. Teamster 9/1/63-4/30/64. Captured 5/12/64, S.C.H. to Ft. Delaware. Released 6/19/65; res. Albemarle Co., sal complexion, light hair, grey eyes, 6'1".

DINWIDDIE, JAMES L.: 1st Lt. Bn. 6/29/37, Campbell Co., Va. student at Hampden-Sydney College. UVa. '58, 9, 60, 61. M.A. 1861. Enl. University Vols. to Lt. and Assistant Adjutant in Wise Legion. After Univ. Vols. disbanded, became a member of Wise Legion and was stationed at Roanoke Island. Escaping the surrender there, he made his way back to Charlottesville and enl. 3/15/62. To 1st Lt. Clothing issued 10/6/62. Absent with leave (10/31/62). Ordered to Col. Gorgas per S.O. #47, 2/16/63. Made Assistant Ordnance Sgt. in Richmond. Later, Major of Infantry. Postwar: married Bettie Carrington (dau. of Dr. William Carrington, of Halifax Co., Va. She d. 1899). Principal of Sayre Institute, Lexington, Ky. Professor of pure mathematics for 10 years at Southwestern Presbyterian University, Clarksville, Tn. Same position at the University of Tennessee beginning in 1880. Due to budget problems, lost chair in July 1883, only to be reinstated in August. In June 1885, purchased Central Female Institute, Gordonsville, Va. There until 1890, when he went to Peace Institute in Raleigh, N.C. At P.I. for 17 years. Due to failing health, retired 5/07. Elder in Presbyterian Church. Member of Masons and Odd Fellows. Died while visiting his son in San Francisco, Ca. Buried 7/10/07, Oakwood Cemetery, Raleigh. Survived by 7 children, and 3 brothers.

DOBBINS, RICHARD: Postwar reference.

DODD, BENJAMIN FRANKLIN: Enl. 3/15/62. Admitted to Winchester hospital 5/27. Captured 6/2/62. To steamer Coatzacoalcos. Exchanged at Aiken's Landing 8/5/62 or paroled at Winchester 6/2/62? Delivered by Lt. Palmer, 7th N.Y.M. Present (9/3/62). Wounded slightly in the face 12/19/62. Absent 12/31. Admitted to Charlottesville C.H. with chronic diarrhea 5/14-6/2/63. Present (2/29/64). Clothing issued 3/26/64. Captured 5/12/64, S.C.H. to Ft. Delaware. Released 6/19/65; res. Albemarle Co., fair complexion, light hair, grey eyes, 5'6". Admitted to R. E. Lee Camp Soldier's Home 7/21/89, age 44. Died 11/23/91. Buried in Hollywood Cemetery.

DOLLINS, R. H.: Enl. 3/15/62. Absent sick in Albemarle Co. on Surgeon's Certificate 6/6/62. Present (9/3/62). AWOL 11/20/62-2/16/63. Detailed QM Dept. 4/64. Admitted to G.H. #9 10/15/64. Admitted to Chimbo. #1 with rheumatic fever 10/16-11/17/64. Clothing issued 11/15/64. NFR.

DOUGLAS, GEORGE WASHINGTON: Enl. 3/15/62. Present through 2/28/65.

DOUGLAS, JAMES: Formerly of 7th Va. Cav. Enl. 4/29/64, Liberty Mills. Admitted to Richmond G.H. #9 6/5/64. D. 7/2/64 at Chimbo. #2.

DOUGLAS, N. J.: Enl. 3/15/62. Absent sick in Albemarle on Surgeon's certificate 5/20/62. Present (9/3/62). Admitted to Gordonsville Hospital 9/21/62. Brought to company under guard 9/8/63. Sent to Gordonsville Hospital with chronic nephritis 11/16-12/15/63. Reported from hospital in arrest 12/22/63. Sent to hospital in Richmond 1/3-4/64. At Chimbo. #2 with diarrhea 1/5/64. At Chimbo. with bronchitis 2/4/64. Admitted to Liberty Hospital with rheumatism 2/12/64. Furloughed to Albemarle Co. for 30 days, 2/3/64. Admitted to Charlottesville G.H. with debility 4/12-4/26/64. Returned to duty. Captured 10/19/64, Cedar Creek. Sent to Pt. Lookout 10/24/64. Admitted to Camp Hospital with scorbutis 2/12/65. D. 5/1/65.

DOWELL, JOHN: Enl. 3/31/63. On daily duty with medical dept. 12/10/63. Teamster 1/1/-4/30/64. Captured 10/19/64, Cedar Creek. To Pt. Lookout. Exchanged 3/28/65.

DRAPER, ROBERT O.: Enl. 3/15/62. D. at UVa. Barracks 4/10/62. Buried in Charlottesville.

DREW, EDMUND: Negro "noncombatant barber" mentioned in Leroy Cox's memoir. Participated in action of 6/8/62. No longer with the unit by the Gettysburg Campaign.

DUKE, RICHARD WILLIAM: Bn. 9/21/45, Enl. 9/20/63, Somerville Ford. Clothing issued 3/5/64. Detailed with Captain W. J. Armstrong, A.C.S. Artillery, 11/64. Paroled 5/23/65 at Charlottesville. Member J. B. Strange Camp. D. 2/12/09. Buried Riverview Cemetery, Charlottesville.

DUNCAN, G. S.: Postwar reference.

DUNCAN, JOHN H.: Enl. 3/25/62. Admitted to Winchester Hospital 5/28. Captured and followed same circumstances as B. F. Dodd. Paroled, age 31, 6'1". Absent sick in Charlottesville 8/8/62. Detailed per S.O. #28/7, 1/28/63. To duty with battery 10/9/63. Absent 12/31/63. Present (2/29/64). Captured 5/12/64, S.C.H. to Ft. Delaware. Released 6/8/65; res. Amherst Co., dark complexion, black hair, blue eyes, 6'1".

DURRETT, RICHARD WILLIAM: Enl. 3/15/62. Sent to Charlottesville G.H. 8/11/63. Admitted to Charlottesville G.H. with acute diarrhea 8/17/63. Released to duty 9/22/63. Absent 12/31/63. Present 2/29/64. Captured 5/12/64, S.C.H. To Ft. Delaware. Released 6/20/65; res. Hardaman Co., Tennessee, ruddy complexion, light hair, brown eyes, 5'6". D. 2/12/09.

ELLITON, FLEMING: Enl. 3/15/62. KIA at Chancellorsville 5/3/63.

ESTILL, CHARLES PATRICK: 8th Cpl., Pvt. Bn. 1834, Lexington, Va. Student at UVa. '55, 57, 59. Enl. 4/20/62, elected 8th Cpl. Absent sick in Waynesboro on surgeon's certificate 6/13/62. NFR. Postwar teacher. Brother of Harry.

ESTILL, HARRY: Pvt., Cpl. Said to have attended UVa., no record. Enl. 5/10/61 with the 3rd Richmond Howitzers. Transfer to the Charlottesville Arty. (9/3/62). Furlough 1/15/63-2/15/63, Cpl. ordered to Colquit's Brigade as 1st Lt. in Ordinance Dept. 2/7/63. Recommended by Lt. Col. P. T. Manning. On Colquiet's staff 10/64. Authorized leave 10/11/64, 30 days. Brother of Charles.

FARISH, SAMUEL: Enl. 3/15/62. Admitted to Richmond G.H. 1/14/63. Admitted to Charlottesville G.H. with pneumonia 1/19/63-3/10/63. Present (4/30/63). Absent when paid 2/29/64. Present 11/5/64. Admitted to Charlottesville G.H. with contusio of fingers, not a wound, 11/11/64-12/29/64. Detailed with Captain Montgomery, and worked as acting QM for the battalion since 1/65.

FERNEYHOUGH, MILTON: Bn. 1830. Enl. 4/7/62. Daily duty with QM, 11/25/63. Present (7/8/64). Absent when paid 2/29/64. Present (11/5/64). Missing 10/19/64, "supposed to have gone home." Reported to unit 11/5/64. Present through 2/28/65. D. 1904.

FIFE, ROBERT HERNDON: 5th Cpl., Sgt., 1st Cpl. Bn. 8/43, Charlottesville, son of Rev. James (of Edinburg, Scotland, 1793-1876) and Margaret Whitely Herndon (1811-1884). Student at UVa. 1861 and 1864. Enl. 3/15/62, elected Cpl. Absent sick in Charlottesville spring '62. Present (9/3/62). Promoted to Sgt. 6/1/64. Detailed as commissary sgt. for the battalion 10/29/64. Reduced to Cpl. per S.O. #25, 1/25/65. Paroled at Appomattox. Member J. B. Strange Camp. Farmer in Charlottesville. M. Martha Ann Strickler. D. 8/16/19, age 77 in Charlottesville. Obituary in Fredericksburg Star 8/18/19, P. 1 and 3.

FITZHUGH, FRANCIS CONWAY: Bn. 8/12/38, Barboursville, Orange Co., Va. Working at Jones' Bookstore at UVa. at the outbreak of the war. Enl. with the 13th Va. Inf. Enl. with the Charlottesville Arty. 3/15/62. In Richmond Hospital 7/6/62. Present (9/3/62). Wounded in left thigh at Chancellorsville 5/3/63, sent to G.H. at Howard's Grove 5/9/63. Transferred to Charlottesville G.H. 5/16. Furloughed 5/25. Admitted to Charlottesville G.H. 7/14-17/63 with debility. Returned to duty 7/30/63. Present sick (10/31/63). Received clothing issue 3/5/64. Admitted to Chimbo. #4 with typhoid fever 7/29/64. To Charlottesville G.H. 8/8/64. Admitted 8/13. Returned to duty 9/19/64. Paroled at Appomattox. Married 1) Margaret G. Conway of Greene Co. Had 2 sons, 2 daughters. 2) Roberta L. Conway (cousin of 1st wife). Had 1 son, and 1 daughter. Member J. B. Strange Camp. Member Presbyterian Church. D. 5/12/10 in Charlottesville, age 72. Physical description: 5'10", florid complexion, light hair, gray eyes.

FLYNT, SAM: Enl. 3/15/62. Absent sick 8/27/62. Present (10/31/62). "On daily duty with QM since enlisted." Teamster.

FORD, FLEMING H.: Enl. 4/21/62. Deserted at Charlottesville 4/23/62.

FRETWELL, JOHN OSTERVILLE: Enl. 3/15/62. Absent sick in Charlottesville 6/12/62. Admitted to hospital in Winchester 6/15/62-11/23/62. Transferred to Charlottesville G.H. with chronic debility 11/24/62-2/11/63. Present (3/3/63). Absent with dyspepsia 7/2/63-11/25/63. Detailed to QM Dept. 2/1/64-11/30/64? Clerk. Member J. B. Strange Camp.

FRETWELL, W. J.: Postwar reference.

GARDNER, HORACE G.: Enl. 3/29/62. Absent sick in Richmond on leave 8/8/62. Present (3/3/63). Admitted to Chimbo. #1 with syphilis 3/24-3/30/63. Sent to hospital 4/7/63. Admitted to Charlottesville G.H. with hernia 4/9-4/29/63. Discharged due to double hernia 8/7/63. Res. Albemarle Co., age 27, 5'8", light complexion, light hair, grey eyes.

GARDNER, IRA BROWN: Enl. 4/2/62. Present through 2/28/65. Paroled at Staunton 5/12/65; age 34, 5'6", light complexion, light hair, grey eyes. Entered R. E. Lee Camp Soldiers Home ?/30/91, age 59. Dropped due to AWOL. Reentered 6/12/02, age 72. Lunatic, sent to asylum 9/23/02.

GARDNER, W. R.: Enl. 3/29/62. Transferred from 46th Va. Inf. Per S.O. #89/84, 4/18/62. Still retained by 46th through the Conscriptive Act.

GARRISON, JAMES B.: Enl. 4/23/62. Absent on sick leave in Charlottesville, 8/24/62. Present (10/31/62). Admitted to Lynchburg G.H. #2 with pneumonia. D. 12/13/63.

GARRISON, JOHN QUINCY: From Co. K, 19th Inf. Enl. 3/15/62. At Charlottesville G.H. with typhoid 8/19-10/8/62. Admitted to Winchester Hospital 10/10/62. To Charlottesville G.H. 11/6-11/20/62. Present (3/3/63). In Gordonsville hospital 8/18/63. Reported to unit 10/9/63. Clothing received 3/26/64. Missing 10/19/64. Absent when paid 11/5/64. Detailed to gather horses 1/10/65. Member J. B. Strange Camp.

GARTON, L. D.: Enl. 8/22/63, Liberty Mills. Admitted to hospital 11/11/63-1/24/64. At Wayside Hospital 1/22/65-2/6/65. Paroled at Appomattox.

GAY, GEORGE WASHINGTON: Enl. 2/29/64, Louisa Co. Issued clothes 3/21/64. In Charlottesville G.H. with typhoid 9/1-9/28/64. Paroled at Charlottesville by 11th Pennsylvania Cavalry, 5/19/65.

GAY, JAMES H.: Enl. 3/15. Absent sick in Scottsville Hospital 5/16. Present (3/3/63. Absent when paid 2/29/64. Present 11/5/64. In hospital 10/22/64. Still as of 2/28/65.

GENTRY, WILLIAM F.: Enl. 3/15/62. Furnished substitute.

GIBSON, TANDY M.: Enl. 4/4/62. From Gordonsville Hospital, sent to Richmond G.H. #12 9/17-9/26/62; furloughed. Admitted to Charlottesville G.H. with fistula in ano 1/26-2/23/63. Present (3/3/63). Admitted to Winchester Hospital 7/21/63; transferred to Richmond 7/26-? at Chimbo. #3, 8/5/63-8/27/63. In Richmond with chronic rheumatism 8/28/63-7/18/64. MIA 10/19/64; captured at Strasburg. Sent to Harper's Ferry and then to Pt. Lookout where d. 12/16 or 12/17/64.

GILLESPIE, WILLIAM F.: Enl. ? 4/21/62. Wounded slightly in shoulder 12/19/62. Absent 12/31/63. Present (2/29/64). Captured 5/12/64. Released 6/20/65; fair complexion, dark hair, blue eyes, 5'7".

GLASS, JESSE MARTIN: Bn. 12/18/40, Fluvanna Co. Enl. 3/15/62. Teamster 1/1/64-3/31/64. Absent when paid 2/29/64. Present 11/5/64. MIA 10/19/64. NFR. D. 9/4/03, age 62. Buried Presbyterian Cemetery, Lynchburg.

GOODE, CALEB: Enl. 4/2/62. Absent on surgeon's certificate 8/7/62. Not heard from since and dropped from rolls as deserter.

GOODWIN, JULIUS S.: Bn. 8/12/33, Albemarle Co., son of Austin and Lucinda Mayo Goodwin. Enl. 5/8/62. Sent to Richmond Hospital 7/6/62. At Charlottesville G.H. 7/14/62, acute rheumatism. Deserted 9/17/62. Back at G.H. 10/22-11/5/62, debility. Present (3/3/63). Furloughed for 15 days to 2/24/64. Reported to Charlottesville G.H. upon its expiration. Present (11/5/64). Horse detail 1/10/65. Paroled at Charlottesville 5/17/65 by the 11th Pennsylvania Cav. M. 10/23/79 to Rebecca H. Bohannon (bn. Mathews Co. 7/28/34), dau. of William and Rosamond Billups Bohannon.) Later a farmer at Keswick, Albemarle Co.

GOODWYN, ROBERT ARCHER: Bn. 1850? in Wytheville. Assigned to company by order of General Lee, 10/22/64. Present through 2/28/65. Attended UVa. 1871, then later at Theological Seminary of Virginia. Episcopal Minister in Mecklenburg Co.

GRUBER, BENJAMIN FRANKLIN: Enl. 4/21/62; age 18, occupation: farmer. AWOL 7/10/62; not formally transferred from 1st regiment Maryland Cavalry. Present (9/3/62). Wounded 5/3/63 (bruise from shell), sent to Wayside. Transferred to Chimbo. 5/9. To Danville 5/11/63. To duty 6/30/63. At Chimbo. #1, 7/20/63. Deserted 7/26/63. NFR.

HALLBACK, JOHN W.: Enl. 3/20/62. Absent when paid 12/31/63. Clothes received 1/28/64. Present (2/29/64). Captured 5/12/64; died same day or KIA? Effects received 2/28/65, certificate #2993.

HARDING, WILLIAM C.: Pvt., 1st Cpl. Enl. 4/17/61, Kemper's Alexandria Artillery. Transferred to Charlottesville Artillery summer of 1862. Admitted to Charlottesville G.H. with acute diarrhea 8/1-8/19/62. Wounded severely in shoulder 12/13/62. In Richmond G.H. #12, 1/5/63; furloughed 60 days, 1/30/63. Admitted to Charlottesville G.H. 2/1/63 with pneumonia. D. 4/15/63. Claim certificate #4561, for $34.50. $8.00 left on person.

HARLOW, JOHN WILLIAM: See 7th Va. Inf. Enl. 5/17/62. AWOL 7/1-8/25/62. Deducted one month and 23 days pay. Leave of absence 8/3/64. Not heard from since. D. 6/17/15, age 72.

HARMAN, CHARLES H.: QM, Sgt. Enl. 3/15/62. Absent sick in Charlottesville 6/29. Still as of 8/30. At Charlottesville G.H. with debilitas 8/30-9/8/62. Present (10/31/62). Absent on detail 2/25/63. Present (4/30/63). Absent when paid 12/31/63. Present (2/29/64). Detached with QM Dept. 5/12/64-? of him Carrington wrote; "Could not be surpassed in such a position for energy, industry and shrewdness. If anything in the nature of Quartermaster stores was to be had, Charlie Harman would get his share for the Charlottesville Artillery."

HARRIS, HENRY HERBERT: 1st Sgt., Sgt. Major. Bn. 1837, at family homestead "Marvan" in Louisa Co., son of Henry and Sallie Hart Harris. Attended UVa. 1857, 58, 59. Received M.A. Served earlier with the 59th Va. Inf. Enl. 3/15. 1st Sgt. (7/16/62). Sgt. Major (4/30/63). 1st Lt. of Engineers 6/1/63. Postwar D.D., teacher, professor at the University of Richmond and Southern Baptist Theological Seminary, Louisville, Ky. Baptist minister.

HARRIS, JEREMIAH "JERE" MALCOLM: Cpl., Acting Ordinance Sgt. Bn. 3/9/40, same place and parentage as above brother. Attended UVa. 1857-1860. B.A. 7/4/60. Received his M.A. on 7/4/61. Enl. 3/15/62. Cpl. (3/3/63). Furloughed 2/22/63. In Charlottesville G.H. with irritatio spinalis 3/5-4/3/63. Detailed acting Ord. Sgt. per S.O. #23 to Colonel Crutchfield 3/31/63. Returned to company and Pvt. (10/31/64). Horse detail 1/10/65. Paroled 5/22/64, Louisa Co. To professorship at Furman University, Greenville, S.C. 2/69; Dept. of Chemistry and Physics. M. Frances "Fannie" Edna Whitmeyer (daughter of Nathan, Sr.); eight children. After teaching 10-11 years, resigned chair and turned to manufacturing oil and other products from cottonseed and established the first cottonseed oil mill in Greenville. Also established first ice factory there. In 1887, due to poor health, he retired and returned to Virginia, where he purchased two farms, one "Germanna" on the banks of the Rapidan River, in Orange Co.; the other "Western View" was a few miles up the river on the Culpeper side. Chairman of the Board of Supervisors of Culpeper Co. Became one of the first advocates of better roads and highways in the state. Deacon at Lael Baptist Church. M. 2)?. D. 10/14/19.

HARRISON, HARRY TUCKER: Enl. 8/16/62 Gordonsville. Absent when paid, 12/31/63. Present (2/29/64). Captured 5/12/64. Exchanged 10/30/64. Admitted to Charlottesville G.H. with typhoid 12/2/64. Reported from parole 2/10/65. Paroled at Appomattox.

HERNDON, JOHN GIBSON: Bn. 8/20/43, at "Washington Farm" near Warrenton, Va. Son of Reverend Thaddeus and Mary Frances Gibson Herndon. Attended Piedmont and Clifton Academies. Left home on 3/13/62 on his father's horse "Redbird" to join the Confederate Army. Enl. 3/20/62. Absent sick 8/8/62. In Charlottesville hospital convalescent from typhoid 9/5-10/30/62. Transferred to Co. A, 7th Va. Cavalry per S.O. #49/3, (dated 2/18/63) 2/22/63. Severely wounded at Tom's Brook 11/64. M. Pamela Alice Logan, 1866. Settled soon after his parent's home "Pleasant Vale" near Delaplane, Va. About 1880 moved to Lincoln, Va., to a farm called "Springdale". Early 1900's moved to East Falls Church, Va., and served for many years as mayor, an exofficio (unpaid) position. D. 3/17/28. Survived by wife, three sons and three daughters. He was a cousin of William K. McCoy.

HILL, HENRY: Postwar reference.

HILL, JOHN F.: enl. 3/15/62. Chimbo. with pneumonia 5/27/64. Farmville G.H. with dysentery, 6/3-6/14/64. Chimbo. #5 with chronic diarrhea 8/3-8/25/64. MIA 10/19/64. Reported 11/64. NFR.

HOLLADAY, ALBERT LEWIS, JR.: Bn. 2/17/44 in Persia, son of Albert Sr. and Anne (missionaries). Enl. 3/15/62. In hospital 6/8/63-7/18/63. Absent when paid 12/31/63. Present 2/29/64. Captured 5/12/64. Released 5/31/64; residence: Albemarle Co., fair complexion, brown hair, blue eyes, 5'8". Attended UVa. 1866-68. M. Nannie W. Eastham of Albemarle Co. 1876. Had one son. Teacher/farmer at Eastham. Taught in Mississippi and Albemarle Co. Member J. B. Strange Camp. D. at home in Albemarle Co., 2/1/18.

HOLLADAY, JAMES MINOR, JR.: Bn. 6/23/41, city of Ooroomiah, Persia, son of James Sr., and Anne Yancey Holladay (missionaries). Served with 19th Va. Infantry. Granted transfer to Charlottesville Artillery per S.O. #105, 5/7/62. Captured enroute, exchanged, sick and d. 8/30/62, before reported. Buried at Prospect Hill Cemetery, Fredericksburg, Va.

HOLLADAY, WALLER: Pvt., 7th Sgt. Bn. 1840. Attended UVa. 1857, 58, 60, 71. Bachelor of Science in Civil and Mining Engineering. Enl. 3/15/62. Sgt. (7/16/62). 1st Lieutenant in Ord. Dept. 2/12/63. Postwar teacher Norwood school. Nelson Co., Va. principal Select school, 1285 Broadway, New York, N.Y. D. 10/1/07, age 67 in Fredericksburg. Buried in Charlottesville.

HORNSEY, C. P.: Enl. 3/8/64, Louisa Co. Captured 5/12/64. Released on oath 3/20/65; residence: Washington Co., Md., fair complexion, dark hair, hazel eyes, 5'6".

HOUSTON, ARCHIBALD "ARCH" WOODS: Pvt., Cpl. Bn. 11/10/42, Wheeling, Va. (W.Va.). Enl. 1/3/61, at Deep Creek by Captain Mosely with the 3rd Company Richmond Howitzers. Transferred to Charlottesville Artillery per S.O. from Secretary of War (9/3/62). In hospital 5/27/63-7/30/63. Absent when paid 12/31/63. Present (2/29/64). KIA 5/12/64. Effects received 2/28/65, certificate #2994. Brother of J. W. and M. H.

HOUSTON, JOHN W.: Bn. 1844. Enl. with 3rd Richmond Howitzers 5/20/61 in Richmond by Major Randolph. Transferred as above mentioned brother. Violation of 99th Article of War. Under arrest awaiting court-martial 2/24/63. Sentenced stoppage of 4 months pay, but remitted per S.O. #4136/14, 5/22/63. Absent when paid 12/31/63. Present (2/29/64). Received an appointment as cadet from Virginia 6/15/64, accepted 7/8/64; the question here being to where was this appointment, not U.S.N.A. or U.S.M.A. Age 19, from Wheeling, 16th Congressional District. NFR. M. Mary Durham. Brother of A.W. and M.H.

HOUSTON, MATHEW HALE: Pvt., Cpl., Ord. Officer. Bn. Ca. 1840. Son of Mathew and Catherine Wilson (of Philadelphia) Houston. Attended WC. Enl. 5/5/61 with 3rd Richmond Howitzers in Richmond. Transferred as above mentioned brothers. AWOL 2/13/63 (Cpl.) Appointed Ord. Officer per S.O. #58, 2/27/63. Later D.D. and postwar Rev. and missionary to China. M. Evelyne Withrow of Waynesboro. D. 1877. Brother of A. W. and J. W.

HUMPHREY, EDMUND: Enl. 3/30/62. At Winchester hospital 5/27/62. Absent at hospital 12/10/62. Returned 5/23/63. At Charlottesville G.H. with pneumonia 10/24/63-11/13/63. At undesignated hospital through 2/1/64. Absent when paid 2/29/64. AWOL 10/1/64. At Staunton D.D. 10/12/64 of injuries inflicted by a kick from a mule; another certificate states gangrene of gsw. Effects received 11/17/64, certificate #2264.

HUMPHREY, GEORGE E.: Enl. 3/21/64, Louisa Co. Received clothing issue 3/25/64. Admitted to Wayside hospital 8/7/64, then to Chimbo. #1, where he received a clothing issue 8/16, back to Wayside and then to Chimbo. #2 in Goochland 9/27/64, where he received another clothing issue 10/13/64. At Wayside 10/13/64, received 60 day furlough. At Chimbo. #1 12/16/64-3/7/65 when returned to duty. NFR.

HUMPHREYS, ALEXANDER: Postwar reference.

HUNTER, JOHN, JR.: Pvt., 1st Sgt., 2nd Lt., 1st Sgt. Bn. 1838, Louisa Co. Attended UVa. 1857-60. VMI '64MS. Drillmaster since 7/61, serving with 51st Va. Inf. Received by John Floyd and G. C. Wharton for 2nd Lt. 12/61. Enl. with Charlottesville Artillery 3/15/62. Sgt. (7/16/62). Horse, "Madge" KIA 6/14/63. Elected 2nd Lt. 4/30/64. Fifteen day furlough 2/22/65. Promotion to 2nd Lt. Pronounced void and returned to duty as 1st Sgt. per S.O. #25. Paroled at Appomattox. Postwar "lawyer of prominence at Louisa Court House."

ISEMAN, ISAIAH PRESTON: Enl. 3/15/62. WIA 7/1/62, sent to Richmond hospital 7/63. At Charlottesville G.H. with debilitas 10/14/62-1/25/63. At Charlottesville G.H. with gsw from Fredericksburg? 1/19/63-1/20/63. Present (3/3/63). Stop pay for curry comb - $1.00, 11/15/64. Paroled at Appomattox.

JACKSON, JOHN: Postwar reference.

JENKINS, HENRY: Enl. 12/1/63, Somerville Ford. Captured 5/12/64. Exchanged 9/18/64. At Wayside 9/21/64. At Chimbo. #3 with debility 9/22/64. Furloughed 40 days, 9/26/64 to Charlottesville. At Charlottesville G.H. with chronic diarrhea 11/10/64. Paroled at Winchester 4/24/65; age 35, 6'2", fair complexion, dark hair, hazel eyes.

JOHNS, JAMES S.: Enl. 4/7/62. At hospital in Winchester 5/28. Captured 5/30. Paroled 6/62. NFR.

JONES, THOMAS SCOTT: Postwar reference.

KENNEDY, JAMES D.: Occupation: farmer. Enl. as substitute 3/15/62. Absent sick 6/13/62 in Albemarle Co., on surgeon's certificate. Present (9/3/62). Absent in hospital 3/24/63. Discharged 4/1/63; age 49, grey hair, blue eyes, fair complexion, 5'9".

KING, GEORGE M.: Surgeon. Bn. 1837, Waynesboro. Attended UVa. 1854-55; Jefferson Medical College, Philadelphia. M.D. Enl. 4/28/62. Detailed as surgeon 4/30. Attached as Bttn. surgeon for Nelson's Bttn., by order Gen. Pendleton. D. 1869, Waynesboro.

KING, W. W.: Postwar reference.

LAWSON, GEORGE: Enl. 3/20/62. At Winchester hospital 5/27, and captured 5/30. Paroled at Winchester 6/2/62; exchanged 8/8/62; age 18, 5'4". NFR.

LEAKE, F. CARTER: Enl. 3/19/62. Present through 2/28/65. NFR. Buried in Orange Co.

LEWIS, JOHN W.: Pvt., 4th Cpl. Enl. 5/5/62. Absent on 15 day furlough 8/27/63. Returned 9/11/63, sick. Appointed Cpl. 1/1/64. Absent when paid 12/31/63. Captured 5/12/64. Released 6/20/65; residence: Albemarle Co., sal. complexion, dark hair, grey eyes, 5'6".

LEWIS, ROBERT WALKER, JR.: Bn. 1839, Albemarle Co. Attended UVa. 1858. Teacher in Albemarle Co. Enl. with 2nd Va. Cavalry. Transferred by exchange to Charlottesville Artillery 1/20/63. In Charlottesville hospital with typhoid fever 8/27-11/11/63. Present (12/31/63). Chimbo. #3 to Charlottesville G.H. 8/7/64. Returned to duty 10/17/64. Present (10/31/64). Horse detail 1/10/65.

LOWRIE, GEORGE T.: Enl. 3/15/62. Present and received clothing issue 3/18/64. Present (12/31/63). WIA 5/10/64 and sent to hospital. At Chimbo. #3 5/16-5/17/64. Then to Heugonot Springs. Paroled at Appomattox.

LOYD, DAVID: Postwar reference.

LOYD, GEORGE H.: Enl. 3/21/62. At Winchester hospital 10/10/62. Present (3/3/63), in arrest. Had been in arrest under charges of desertion (2/15/63) and conduct prej. to good order, 10/31/63. CM. G.O. 97-9, 11/4/63. Deserted while in arrest near Culpeper 11/8/63. Apparently apprehended and CM again per G.O. #105-1, 12/7/63. NFR.

MADISON, DABNEY M.: Blacksmith. Enl. 4/10/62. Blacksmith (3/3/63). Detailed to ord. dept. as a smith 8/1/63-3/1/64. Pvt. after reported back. NFR.

MADISON, JACK: Postwar reference.

MALLORY, ANDREW JACKSON: Enl. 4/28/62. In Charlottesville hospital 7/31/63-9/8/63. Absent when paid 12/31/63. Present (2/29/64). Detailed to QM Dept. 5/20/64. Paroled at Charlottesville 5/19/65; residence: Albemarle Co. Tennessee Confederate Pensioner.

MARSHALL, ARCH L.: enl. 4/1/62. Absent on sick leave 8/29/62-(10/31/62). Detailed to Gordonsville by order of Lt. Col. Jones 12/29/63. WIA and sent to hospital. GSW tibia left leg. Furloughed from Chimbo. #1 7/2/64. At Charlottesville G.H. when furloughed 8/13/64. At Lynchburg G.H. when left leg was amputated 9/15-9/27/64. NFR.

MARSHALL, CHARLES E.: Enl. 10/19/63, Culpeper C.H. In Charlottesville G.H. with morbus cutus 10/31-11/14/63. Absent when paid 12/31/63. Present (2/29/64). Captured 5/12/64. Released 6/15/65; residence: Albemarle Co., light complexion, auburn hair, grey eyes, 5'8".

MARSHALL, S. M.: Postwar reference.

MARSHALL, THOMAS E.: Occupation: farmer. Enl. 3/15/62. At Charlottesville G.H. with catarrh 4/10/62, sent home 4/14. Absent sick 5/12 in Albemarle Co. on surg. cert. 11/4/62. Again at G.H. with phthesis 11/4/62. Discharged 11/5/62; residence: Albemarle Co., age 28, 5'7", light complexion, blue eyes, brown hair.

MARSHALL, WILLIAM H.: Enl. 3/15/62, transferred from 46th Virginia Inf. by S.O. #89/4, 4/18/62, but still retained with that unit by conscription act.

MARTIN, PATRICK: 10th Cpl., Pvt. Enl. 3/30/62, cpl. Absent sick in Charlottesville with hepatic disease. Furnished substitute: David Coler, 8/13/62.

MARTIN, WILLIAM L.: Enl. 3/15/62. Absent sick 6/6 in Staunton G.H. Admitted to Charlottesville G.H. with debilitas 6/24-8/19/62. Present (9/3/62). To Richmond G.H. with irritatio spinalis 1/19/63. Admitted to Charlottesville G.H. 1/27/63. To Ward F, 2/7. To Colony, 2/14. To Ward F, 4/2/63. Reported to duty 1/17/64. Detailed to Med. Dept. 2/1/64. Teamster 2/1-4/30/64. Horse detail 1/10/65.

MASON, ROBERT F.: Enl. 3/10/62. Absent sick on Surgeon's certificate at Louisa C.H. 5/15. AWOL (3/3/63). Discharged by medical board at Charlottesville 6/63.

MASSIE, D. RODES: 6th Cpl.-2nd Lt. Bn. 1836, Waynesboro. Attended UVa. 1856, 57, 59, 60. Enl. 3/20/62, Cpl. 2nd Lt. 6/25/63. On court of inquiry S.O. #225/3, 9/8/63. Fifteen day furlough from 10/30/63. Reported from furlough 11/14/63, then to hospital. At Charlottesville hospital with icterus 12/1-12/19/63. To duty 12/20/63. Captured 5/12/64. At Ft. Delaware to Hilton Head 8/20/64. At Ft. Pulaski, Ga. 10/20/64. Delivered by orders from Colonel Mulford for exchange 12/15/64. Admitted to Charlottesville G.H. with chronic bronchitis 5/22/65. Postwar professor at Washington College and Richmond College. Brother of E. B.

MASSIE, EDWIN BLACKWELL "NED": Bn. 1842, Augusta, Ga. Attended UVa. 1860, 64, 66, 67. Enl. 3/20/62. Elected to Lt. with 52nd Va. Inf. Enl. 5/3/64, after resigning a lieutenancy in the 52nd Va. Inf. WIA 5/12/64. At Charlottesville G.H. Amputated thumb after gsw to right hand. Furloughed 6/8/64. Returned and discharged as a result of wound 11/1/64, reassigned to the invalid corps. Postwar principal grade schools in Charlottesville. Also farmer. Brother of D.R.

MAUCK, GEORGE D.: Enl. 10/25/64, New Market. Paroled at Appomattox.

MAUPIN, BENJAMIN FRANKLIN: 9th Cpl., Pvt. Enl. 3/20/62. At Charlottesville G.H. for disease of back from 5/12-5/25. Absent sick in Albemarle Co. on surgeon's certificate 6/4/62. At Charlottesville G.H. for lumbago 8/15-10/4/62. At Winchester hospital 10/27. Declared deserter (3/3/63) not having reported to hospital. Present (4/30/63), stopped 3 months pay. WIA 5/3/63, back of left thigh and skull. At Howard's Grove, Richmond 5/9. Transferred to Scottsville 6/10 with "erysipelas." Detailed per S.O. #42/20, 2/20/65 for collection of captured property. Order revoked per S.O. #53/16, 3/4/65. NFR.

MAUPIN, WILLIAM CAREY: Bn. 1845, Rome, Ga. Enl. 6/15/63. Absent sick 7/24/63. At Charlottesville G.H. with debility 8/17-9/15/63. Reported from hospital 9/16/63. Paroled at Appomattox. Attended UVa 1866-68. Farmer at Liberty, Bedford Co., Va.

MAYO, URIAH B.: Enl. 3/15/62. Detailed to the ord. dept. by order of Col. Jones 6/17/63. Reported to Wayside for duty 3/8/64. NFR.

McCARTHY, MICHAEL H.: Pvt., Cpl. Enl. 5/5/62. Cpl. (6/63). WIA at Winchester and sent to hospital 6/14/63. Reported from hospital 8/7/63. Furloughed 1/25/64. Deserter 2/1/64.

McCAULEY, WILLIAM J.: Enl. 3/2/63, near Milford. Present sick (12/31/63). Furloughed for 8 days, 1/27/64. At Charlottesville G.H. with debilitas 4/4-5/27/64. Present (7/8/64). Horse detail 1/10/65.

McCOY, WILLIAM KENNETH: Pvt., 2nd Sgt. Bn. 1/31/43, at Brookland in Fauquier Co. "Flaxen haired, oval faced boy, with large rich grey eyes, always full of life and merriment." Moved with his family to Charlottesville in 1852, where "Kenny" remained under home instruction until 1857. After the death of his father he was sent to Raleigh, N.C. under the care of an elder brother. After one year there, he attended Hampden-Sydney 1858. Preparing to enter UVa., "Kenneth" decided otherwise and enlisted with the Charlottesville Artillery on 3/15/62. Sgt. (7/62). Absent sick on surgeon's certificate at Charlottesville G.H. 8/10-10/30/62, having been run over by a caisson, temporarily crippling him. Present (3/3/63). WIA by shell exploding in his hands (see narrative) 5/3/63. At G.H. #4 in Richmond 5/8/63. D. at the residence of Mrs. John B. Martin 5/19/63, attended by Dr. James. Effects received 2/9/64, certificate #437. Buried in family plot at University cemetery. In a letter to his mother, McCoy's messmates expressed their sympathy in his loss; as quoted from the University Memorial:

"Camp near Guinea's Station, Va.,

June 3d, 1863.

Mrs. McCoy will not, we trust, consider it an intrusion upon the sacred privacy of parental grief, for us, the messmates of her lamented son, Kenneth, to unite our voices in bearing testimony to his worth, and to mingle our tears of heartfelt sympathy and sorrow over his honored but too early grave. The relations into which we were thrown, and the ties of community of interest, community of sentiment and feeling, community of action and of suffering by which we were bound to him, we believe to have been second in intimacy and affection only to those of home itself. Cut off from relatives and friends and dependent upon each other for society and sympathy, while we shared daily the same fare and occupied nightly the same shelter, our mess had grown into a family circle. What, at the outset, had been acquaintanceship, blossomed into friendship and ripened into mature affection. In him our hitherto unbroken circle has lost its first link, and we feel as though a brother had been struck down from our midst. As we look back upon the past, we can scarcely realize the fact that who he was, to so large an extent, the light and life of our band, has passed away... The more we knew him we loved him; we loved him for his kind and obliging dispositions, his warm and affectionate heart the vivacity and bouyancy of his spirits, and the frankness, generosity, unaffected simplicity and real nobility of his nature... with great respect and heartfelt sympathy, W. F. Davis, R. A. Lewis, Jr., A. B. Roler, F. M. Swoope, P. T. Wash, Albert L. Holladay, D. Hanson Boyden, A. L. Marshall."

McGRATH, MAURICE: Enl. 3/15/62, from 46th Va. Inf., by S.O. but retained in regiment under the conscription act.

McGUIRE, JOHN G.: Enl. 2/2/63, near Milford as substitute. Deserted 2/5/63.

McINTIRE, GEORGE MALCOLM: Bn. 1846, Charlottesville. Enl. 9/20/63, Somerville Ford. Captured by cavalry at Milford Ford 11/11/63. Sent to Old Capital Prison 11/14/63, and then to Pt. Lookout 2/3/64. Exchanged 5/3/64. Present (7/8/64). Horse detail 1/10/65. Attended UVa. 1866. Merchant in Chicago, Ill.

MILES, B. B.: Postwar reference.

MILLER, JAMES W.: See Co. E, 15th Va. Inf. Enl. 5/5/62. Absent sick on surgeon's certificate in Albemarle Co. 5/10. Present (3/3/63). At Charlottesville G.H. with stricture of urethra 10/1-11/1/63. Absent with paid 12/31/63. Present (2/29/64). Captured 5/12/64. Released 5/28/65; residence: Rockingham Co., fair complexion, brown hair, hazel eyes, 5'7". Entered R. E. Lee Camp Soldier's Home 4/3/99, age 63. Left at own request 5/31/12.

MINOR, JAMES HUNTER, JR.: Bn. 3/7/48, Orange C.H., Va., son of Dr. J. H. (11/15/18-4/12/62), UVa. 1838), of Music Hall, Albemarle Co., Va. and Mary Watson Morris (1821-7/92). Paternal G. P.: Samuel Overton and Lydia Laurie Lewis Minor. Maternal G. P.: William and Nacy Watson Morris, of "Sylvania", Louisa Co. Matriculated at V.M.I. from Cobham, Va. 9/11/63. Cadet Pvt. in Co. C at Battle of New Market. Did not return to the institute the following session, but enl. 1/7/65 at Fisherville with the Charlottesville Artillery. On horse detail 1/10/65. Postwar merchant. Elected recorder of deeds in Audain Co., Mo., served in this capacity and as deputy for fifteen years. M. 5/31/80, Ida (D. 1895), daughter of Jeptha Lake, of Farber, Mo. had two daughters. Later years he was in the real estate business in Mexico, Mo. M. 2)? He d. 1/4/14, Mexico, Mo. Buried in Elmwood Place.

MORGAN, MICHAEL: Enl. 1/11/63, near Milford, as substitute for R. R. Nelson. Deserted 1/14/63.

MORRIS, A. B.: Enl. 3/15/62. AWOL 11/26-12/31/62. Stop pay $3.20. At hospital with syphillis 4/9-12/25/62. Detailed as hospital guard per G.O. #137. Returned to duty 7/64. At hospital with variola 3/12-5/28/65.

MORRIS, WILLIAM F.: Enl. 4/22/62. Detailed blacksmith 5/18. Then to daily duty with QM Dept. 1/1/64-(teamster 1/1-4/30/64) captured at Waynesboro 3/2/65. Sent to Ft. Delaware where received 3/12. Released 6/20/65; residence: Albemarle Co., dark complexion, mixed hair, grey eyes, 5'7".

NELSON, ROBERT R.: Enl. 4/3/62. Absent sick 8/8. Present (10/31). Discharged 1/11/63, furnished substitute, Michael Morgan.

NORVELL, WILLIAM H.: Bn. Albemarle Co. Enl. 3/15/62. At hospital in Winchester 5/27. Captured 5/30, and sent to steamer Coatcoalos. Paroled 6/62; age 16, 5'6". Present (9/3/62). In hospital 6/5/63-Richmond G.H. #1 (7/2/63) then to Charlottesville G.H. with blistered feet 7/27-8/8/63. Clothes issued 8/7/63. Absent when paid 12/31/63. Present (2/29/64). KIA 5/12/64. Effects received 11/22/64, certificate #2312.

OLD, JOHN NELSON: Bn. 1827 Albemarle Co., son of Abijah S. and Sarah Fretwell Old. Enl. 3/15/62. Absent sick on surgeon's certificate in Albemarle Co. 6/6. Present (9/3/62). In Charlottesville G.H. 9/4/62. With debilitas at G.H. 9/12/62 — sent to Colony 9/13. To Ward F 1/9/63. Present (3/3/63). AWOL 3/23-4/10/63, stop $7.20. Absent when paid 12/31/63. Clothing issued 1/28/64. Present (2/29/64). WIA 5/12/64, d. of those wounds in Fredericksburg. Effects received 12/7/64, certificate #2529. M. Catherine R. Grooms, 1830.

PACE, HENRY H.: Enl. 3/15/62. At Charlottesville G.H. with debility 2/7/63-6/2/63. Again from 6/8-9/11/63, ordered to company. Captured at Somerville Ford 11/11/63. Sent to Lincoln U.S. Army G.H., Washington, D.C. with pneumonia 1/3/64-1/14/64. Transferred to Point Lookout 2/3/64. Exchanged 2/24/64. At Charlottesville G.H. with acute diarrhea 12/14/63-1/4/64?? at Charlottesville G.H. with inflamation of the bowels 5/24 — 60 day furlough — 8/31/64. At Richmond G.H. from Charlottesville 9/16/64. At Charlottesville G.H. with chronic diarrhea 10/24-11/21/64. Paroled 5/3/65, Columbia, Va. by Major Henry Terwilliger 1st Regt. N.Y. Mtd. Rifles, Provost Marshall.

PACE, HILARY C.: Enl. 5/8/62. Detailed as hospital nurse at Winchester 9/29/62. Absent sick 2/10/63. Detailed per S.O. #214/11, 9/9/63 to hospital through 5/13/64. Clothing issued 3/16/64. Horse detail 1/10/65. Member J. B. Strange Camp.

PAGE, HENRY CLAY: Enl. 4/22/62. WIA 6/8/62. Sent to Charlottesville G.H. 6/12. Discharged on surgeon's certificate 7/28/62.

PATTIE, DUDLEY MARSHALL: Bn. 1/19/46, Fauquier Co. Enl. 3/17/64, Frederick Hall, Louisa Co. at Charlottesville G.H. with abcess of ear 9/27-10/12/64. Horse detail 1/10/65. Paroled 4/28/65 at Winchester; age 19, 5'9", fair complexion, light hair, blue eyes. M. 1)? M. one son. 2) Bertha Harrison, daughter of W. F. Harrison of Madison Co. One son. Assistant doorkeeper of the Virginia Senate for 14 years. Member of the Linn Banks Lodge of Masons, Madison Co. Commander of Kemper-Strother-Foy Camp, UCV, Madison Co. Steward of Methodist Church. "Always celebrated his own birthday and that of General Robert E. Lee by giving on this occasion 'Lee's farewell address to his army', which he did with rare feeling and emphasis." At the 1920 Culpeper Reunion. D. 2/4/30 in Madison, Va. Buried in Cedar Hill Cemetery.

PATTON, HUGH F.: Enl. 3/15/62. Transferred 8/22/62 by promotion to Adjutancy in 7th Va. Cav. Transferred to Cook's staff 11/26/62. Absent wounded 1/3/63. Paroled at Appomattox as 1st Lt. and aid-de-camp.

PEGRAM, GEORGE E.: Enl. 8/1/63, Liberty Mills. Admitted to Charlottesville G.H. with icterus 12/11/63 — Richmond G.H. #4, 12/26-12/29/63; then back to Charlottesville G.H. where released 1/11/64. Present (2/29/64). Transferred to Co. C, 1st Engineer Regiment per S.O. #66/2, 3/8/64.

PENDLETON, PHILIP HENRY: Enrolled as conscript at Camp Lee 1/20/64, assigned to Charlottesville Artillery 1/26 at Louisa C.H. Captured/KIA 5/12/64. Effects received 2/28/65, certificate #3044.

PERRY, BENJAMIN H.: Enl. 3/15/62. D. at hospital 3/23/63. Effects in charge of H. Black, surgeon in charge. Certificate #2173, 11/23/64 and certificate #946, $20.00.

PINCKNEY, HOPSON: Enl. 3/15/62. Detailed as nurse at Jackson hospital 11/5/63-12/21/63, Pegram's Brigade. Transferred to Treasury Dept. 12/21/63.

PRESTON, WALTER CREIGH: Bn. 12/31/41, Lexington. Attended UVa. 1858-60. Enl. 3/15/62. Absent on 15 day furlough 10/25/63-11/10/63. Absent when paid 12/31/63. Present (2/29/64). WIA and captured 5/12/64. GSW by minie, fractured left humerus, upper third. Amputated at left shoulder joint - flaps. Transferred to Lincoln G.H. 6/10/64 from Douglas G.H., Washington, D.C. Sent to Old Capitol Prison 7/30/64. Sent to Elmira, N.Y. 8/12/64. Exchanged 10/29/64. Application for retirement received 1/25/65, dated 1/19. Retired to Invalid Corps 1/19/65. Postwar farmer, Rapidan Station, Culpeper Co. D. 1905.

PRITCHETT, H. W.: Postwar reference.

PRITCHETT, J. W.: Postwar reference.

RAILEY, L. RANDOLPH: Enl. 2/29/64, Louisa Co. Captured 5/12/64. Released 6/5/65; residence: Albemarle Co., ruddy complexion, black hair, hazel eyes, 5'6".

RHODES, C. DALLAS: Enl. 3/29/62. WIA 6/27/62. Sent to hospital at Manchester. Present (9/3/62). Stop pay by board survey for 1 curry comb. (11/5/64). Absnt (2/28/65).

RHODES, SCHUYLER T.: Enl. 3/15/62. Detailed for Government work per S.O. #82/14, 4/4/62. Present (10/31/62). In Charlottesville G.H. with debilitas 6/8 — to Colony 6/9 — released 7/30/63. Paroled at Appomattox.

RHODES, THOMAS D.: Enl. 4/20/62. At Chimbo. #1 with chronic diarrhea 11/18/63-12/17/63. Absent when paid 2/29/64. MIA 10/19/64. Captured at Strasburg 10/31/64. Sent to Pt. Lookout 12/28/64. Released on oath 6/17/65; residence: Louisa Co., fair complexion, black hair, blue eyes, 5'11¼".

RILEY, JOHN: Enl. 3/31/63, near Milford. Deserted 4/4/63. Arrested 4/26 and sent to Hamilton Crossroads, Fredericksburg. Substitute for Sgt. Carrington. Released by presidential proclamation 8/63. Deserted again. NFR.

RILEY, JOHN H.: Enl. 9/8/64, Charlottesville. Horse detail 1/10/65.

RISK, JOHN W.: Enl. 3/15/62. On 15 day furlough 12/30/63-1/14/64. Absent when paid 2/29/64. MIA 10/19/64. Captured 10/19/64 at Strasburg. Sent to Point Lookout, where released 6/17/65; residence: Staunton, dark complexion, brown hair, hazel eyes, 5'8¾".

RODES, JAMES: Postwar reference.

ROLER, ADDISON B.: Bn. 1835, Mt. Sidney, Augusta Co., Va. Attended UVa. 1860. Enl. 4/23/62. WIA 7/1/62. Sent to hospital in Richmond 7/64. Present (9/3/62). Absent when paid 12/31/63. Present (2/29/64). Captured 5/12/64. Sent to Ft. Delaware, from where he was released 6/5/65; residence: Augusta Co., dark complexion, brown hair, grey eyes, 6'2".

ROLLER, GEORGE S.: Enl. 1/29/64, Louisa Co. Captured 5/12/64. Sent to Old Capitol Prison Hospital with gsw of arm and back 5/20/64. Sent to Ft. Delaware 6/15/64. Paroled 9/14/64. Admitted to Chimbo. #3 with debility 9/22/64. Furloughed for 40 days to Augusta Co., 10/1/64. Reported from parole 1/1/65. Horse detail 1/10/65. NFR.

ROLLER, JOHN HOUSELL: Postwar reference.

SAMPSON, ROBERT: Bn. 1847, Albemarle Co. Enl. 1/7/65, Fisherville. NFR. Attended UVa. 1868. Lawyer at Keswick, Albemarle Co.

SCANTLING, W. N.: Postwar reference.

SHANNON, PATRICK: Enl. by transfer from 19th Va. Inf., 4/10/62, officially 5/21/62. AWOL 7/13. Deserted at Gordonsville 9/20/62.

SHEPHERD, JAMES S. M.: Enl. 3/15/62. Absent sick in Albemarle. Present (9/3/62). Absent when paid 12/31/62). Present (2/29/64). Captured 5/12/64. To Ft. Delaware. Released 6/21/65; residence: Albemarle Co., light complexion, dark hair, grey eyes, 5'5".

SHEPHERD, JOHN: Enl. 5/17/62. Found to have deserted from 5th Va. Inf. 6/19. Retained in 5th by Conscription Act.

SHIFLETT, ANFIELD: Postwar reference.

SHIFLETT, L. G.: Postwar reference.

SHREVE, A.: Postwar reference.

SHREVE, SAMUEL: Pvt., Cpl. Bn. 1833. Enl. 4/21/62. Took 15 day furlough 1/13/64. Deserter 2/1/64. Cpl. (11/5/64). D. 1898, Ballston, Arlington Co.

SINCLAIR, CEPHUS: Enl. 11/64. Horse detail 1/10/65.

SINCLAIR, CHARLES G.: Enl. 9/1/63, Liberty Mills. At Chimbo. #2 with diarrhea 7/26/64-8/16/64 when sent to Charlottesville G.H. at Charlottesville G.H. 8/17-10/12/64. Present (10/31/64). Horse detail 1/10/65. Paroled 5/17/65, Charlottesville. Member J. B. Strange Camp.

SMITH or SMYTH, IRA G.: Enl. 5/5/62. Absent sick in Charlottesville on Surgeon's certificate 6/3/62. Present (9/3/62). Richmond G.H. #6 10/30/62-?. Same 12/16/62-?. Detailed per S.O. #12/7, 1/12/63. Clothes issued 7/3/63. At Richmond Medical Directors with single reducable hernia 8/24/63. Detailed as clerk 9/1-9/12/64. Present (10/31/63). Absent when paid 12/31/63. Clothing issued 3/26/64. AWOL (7/8/64) since last of May. Temporarily assigned to Thompson's Battery, Stuart's Horse Artillery 9/21/64-1/10/65. In Chimbo. 12/4/64. In Staunton Hospital 12/14/64.

SNEED, CHARLES: Enl. 3/8/64, Louisa Co. Clothes issued 3/5/64. Detached at army headquarters (courier) 2/2/65 (at that time with 1 private horse belonging to Pvt. Cochran, now absent with leave) until paroled at Appomattox.

SNEED, JAMES: Enl. 4/1/62. At hospital 6/5/63-7/30/63. Absent when paid 2/29/64. At Chimbo. #1 5/27/64 wounded. Returned to duty 6/9/64. MIA 10/19/64. Present 11/1/64. Detached to QM Dept. at Ivy Depot, Albemarle Co. since 1/1/65 (2/28/65).

SNEED, MILES A.: Enl. 3/15/62. At hospital in Richmond 7/6/62. Present (9/3/62). At hospital 3/24/63-5/27/63-2/28/65. NFR.

SNEED, RICHARD: Bn. Henrico Co. occupation: shoemaker. Enl. 4/10/62. Absent sick in Albemarle Co. on surgeon's certificate (7/16/62). Present (9/3/62). At Charlottesville G.H. 3/27/63 with febris int. tertiary. To Colony 4/3/63. At Charlottesville G.H. 12/14/63 with general debility and old age. Discharged 12/14/63. Age 55, 5'8", florid complexion, grey eyes and hair.

SPARROW, LEONARD K.: Bn. 1839, Fairfax Co., Va. Attended UVa. 1857-59. Transferred from Fredericksburg Artillery per S.O. #32, 2/1/63. Assigned per S.O. #38/5. S.O. #44/34, 2/23/64, to rejoin company (report to chief of ordinance). Appointed to 2nd Lt. 3/26/64. Accepted 4/6/64. Confirmed 5/16/64. Postwar merchant in Baltimore, Md.

SPOONER, JOHN H.: Pvt., 4th Sgt. Enl. 3/15/62. Cpl. (5/62). At Winchester hospital 5/27/62. Absent sick in Charlottesville by order Dr. J. S. Davis. At Charlottesville G. H. with debility, 6/20-8/30/62. Present (9/3/62). 4th Sgt., (6/63). Absent at hospital 12/20/63 (Charlottesville G.H. with neuralgia 1/11-1/14/64). Captured 5/12/64, sent to Ft. Delaware. Released on oath 6/21/65; residence: Albemarle Co., dark complexion, hair, and eyes, 5'8". Member J. B. Strange Camp.

SPROUSE, HENRY: Enl. 3/15/62. Absent sick in Greenwood Depot on Surgeon's certificate (7/16/62). Present (9/3/62). Sent to hospital 9/4/62. At Charlottesville G.H. with debility 10/10-11/14/62. To Colony 10/22. AWOL 2/23/63-3/19/63, stop $10.00 pay. Present (3/3/63). Absent sick 6/26. MIA 7/7/63, captured at Chambersburg, Pa. 7/4/63. Sick at Chambersburg Hospital 7/5. To West Walnut Street Hospital, Harrisburg 7/21/63. To Provost Marshall 8/4/63. At Ft. Delaware 8/12. Notation for C. M. per G.O. #87, 8/21/63. At post hospital with dysentery 9/8. Notation as d. 9/24/63, ward #2, however another notation has as exchanged 9/30/64. Clothes issued 10/10/64, 11/22/64.

STARK, ALLEN W.: Enl. 3/15/62. At hospital in Richmond 8/8/62. AWOL 2/1/63. Present (3/3/63). Present under arrest awaiting C.M. for AWOL 8/31/63. Sentenced loss of 21 days of pay. Undergoing sentence (10/31/63). Released from arrest (2/29/64). Sent to Gordonsville by Major Turner with extra horses. Present (11/5/64). Horse detail 1/10/65.

STRANGE, TUCKER: Enl. 3/15/62. At Lovingston Hospital (9/3/62). Present (10/31/62). Absent furloughed 2/22/63. Detailed by Colonel Crutchfield 4/1/63 - ? at Charlottesville G.H. with acute dysentery 4/16-5/12/63. At Chimbo. 5/27. At Charlottesville G.H. with chronic diarrhea 6/8-7/7/63. (To Ward K, 6/25). Reported from hospital 7/17/63. Clothes issued 3/21/64. To hospital sick 5/24/64. At Chimbo. #1, wounded, and returned to duty 7/18. At Chimbo. 7/25. At Chimbo. #2 with diarrhea 7/26, furloughed 35 days, 8/18/64, to Albemarle Co. at Charlottesville G.H. with chronic diarrhea 9/23/64, furloughed same day. NFR.

SWOOPE, FRANCIS McFARLAND "FRANK": Cpl., 2nd Lt., 1st Lt. Bn. 1839, son of George Washington and Eliza M. Trent Swoope. Paternal G.P.: Jacob (member of 11th Congress and Federalist from 1809-1811) and Mary McDowell (sister of Gov. James McDowell of Va.) maternal G.P.:? and ? Lewis (sister of John and Andrew Lewis of American Rev. fame) Attended Washington College 1858-59; UVa. 1859-60; VMI '64MS, matriculating from Staunton on 5/15/61 and remaining for no more than one month. Enl. 3/15/62. Cpl. (7/16). At Staunton Hospital 9/10-? Present (3/3/63). At Richmond G.H. #18 with chronic rheumatism 3/13-3/26/63. 2nd Lt. 6/3/63. On leave for 10 days 1/22/64. Captured 5/12/64. Promoted to 1st Lt. Pronounced void per S.O. #?, 1/25/65. Sent to Ft. Delaware. Released 6/8/65; residence: Augusta Co., dark complexion, brown hair and eyes, 5'10". Never married. Studied for ministry after the war until health failed. Also prospected in W.Va.

70

TERRELL, GEORGE WASHINGTON: Enl. 3/15/62. Absent sick 9/12/62. Wounded in the thigh and left knee 5/3/63. Sent to Howard's Grove, Richmond 5/10. Transferred 5/16-8/7/63. Reported from hospital 8/10/63. Captured 5/12/64. Sent to Ft. Delaware. Released 6/7/65.

TERRELL, JOHN A.: Enl. 3/15/62. Absent sick on Surgeon's Certificate 6/6/62. Present (3/3/63). KIA at Winchester 6/14/63.

TERRELL, NATHANIEL A. "NAT": Enl. 3/15/62. Bugler 5/1/62. Captain Carrington remembered of him, "He had the reputation of being the biggest blower in the army; though he was not called upon to expose himself greatly in battle, yet he was called upon to blow under trying circumstances on many occasions it was his duty to sound all sorts of calls, and to be present early and late at every company meeting, and I think the unanimous voice of his comrades would be that no one could surpass him in the position to be filled." Paroled at Appomattox. Member J. B. Strange Camp. Alive in 1911.

TERRELL, WILLIAM H.: Enl. 3/15/62. Absent sick on Surgeon's certificate 8/21/62 (Charlottesville G.H. with typhoid fever 12/2/62-4/29/63)-4/30/63. Wounded in hip 5/12/64. At Charlottesville G.H. 5/15-8/5/64. Reported back 8/9/64. Detailed with Captain W. J. Armstrong ACS Artillery from 11/1/64-?. NFR.

THACKER, WILLIAM: Enl. 3/29/62. Absent sick on leave 8/24/62. Present (10/31/62). In hospital 3/24/63-6/3/63. At Charlottesville G.H. with debility 10/5/63. Detailed to Ord. Dept. by Brig. Gen. Long, 11/1/63. At Wayside for duty 4/1/65. NFR.

THACKER, WILLIAM M.: Enl. 3/31/62. At Winchester Hospital 5/27. Captured 5/30/62 and sent to steamer Coatzacoalcos. Paroled at Winchester 6/2/62. Present (9/3/62). With Ord. Dept. 1/64. Captured 5/12/64. Sent to Ft. Delaware and exchanged 9/30/64. At Chimbo. #1 with diarrhea 10/7/64. Furloughed for 60 days 10/10/64 to Mt. Garden Depot. Reported from parole 12/12/64. NFR.

THOMAS, SAMUEL P.: Postwar reference. Admitted to R. E. Lee Camp Soldier's Home 12/16/20, age 80. D. 12/27/20. Body sent to Caroline Co., Va.

THOMPSON, JAMES H.: Enl. 3/22/62. At Charlottesville G.H. with acute bronchitis 3/30-4/11/62. Deserted 6/23 at Louisa C.H. at Charlottesville G.H. with chronic rheumatism 7/16-7/26/62. In arrest 10/12/62. Furloughed at Richmond 11/13/62 for 40 days. Detailed to Col. Crutchfield 4/1/63, stop 3 months pay. Returned 7/8/63. Deserted 7/25/63, at home. Absent 8/10. Present 9/2/63. To hospital 9/25. Reported from hospital in arrest 11/30/63. Released, charges withdrawn. Deserted 8/1/64. Took oath in Alexandria, Va. 11/4/64; residence: Fluvanna Co., dark complexion, brown hair, blue eyes, 6'1". Transferred to Harrisburg, Pa. Claimed he was drafted 10/62. NFR.

TIMBERLAKE, JOHN HENRY, JR.: 1st Lt. Bn. 5/8/40, Charlottesville, Va., son of J.H., Sr. and E.W. Timberlake. Paternal G.P.: Horace and Anne Timberlake. Maternal G.P.: Rev. Walker (from Fluvanna Co.) and Sallie Strange Timberlake. Attended UVa. 1856-58. VMI '64, matriculating from Greenwood Depot, Albemarle Co. 6/61, attending for 4 weeks. Enl. with Co. F, 10th Va. Cav. (Wise's command). Transferred to Charlottesville Artillery 3/15/62. Detailed by order of Major Gen. Ewell for 10 days, 7/11/62. Present (9/3/62). Absent sick 12/6/62. At Charlottesville G. H. 12/8/62-4/8/63. Returned from hospital 4/15/63. Resigned due to poor health 6/20/63. Of him Captain Carrington remembered; "Lieutenant Timberlake is remembered with pride, and justly so, in Albemarle County; he was every inch a soldier, a remarkably handsome man, fastidious in his dress, an elegant horseman and always well mounted, as brave as a lion and gentle as a woman, a sincere friend and prompt in the discharge of every duty." Merchant and farmer near Crozet after the war. D. 12/10/81 near Brownsville, Va. when he was killed by his own horse trying to rescue a boy on a runaway horse. L. W. Cox wrote of him; "I always felt I had a friend and protection in him, at least one that that would see that those under him were treated with due consideration."

TIMBERLAKE, JOHN W.: Enl. 3/15/62. Absent sick on Surgeon's certificate at Charlottesville 6/21/62. At Charlottesville G.H. with pneumonia 6/30-8/26/62. Present (9/3/62). Discharged 2/2/63, substitute was John Maguire. At Charlottesville G.H. with scabies 2/9/63. NFR.

TIMBERLAKE, WILLIAM CLARKE: Bttn. QM Sgt. Residence: Louisa Co. Occupation: farmer. Enl. 3/15/62. Detailed per order #15 by Lt. Col.Jones to QM Sgt. of Bttn., 4/20/63. Dropped from that position by order of Lt. Col. Jones 12/1/63. Apparently reinstated 1/1/64-4/30/64. Age 18, blue eyes, auburn hair, fair complexion, 6'.

VIA, LYMAN: Pvt., Guidon Bearer. Enl. 3/15/62. Absent sick on leave 8/28/62. Present (10/31/62). To Charlottesville G.H. with debilitas 9/1-9/15/62. To hospital 6/63. At Charlottesville G.H. with morbilitas 6/8-7/14/63. Reported from G.H. 7/19/63. Absent when paid 12/31/63. Present (2/29/64). Captured/KIA 5/12/64. Effects received 2/28/65, certificate #3094.

WADDELL, ALEXANDER A.: Enl. 3/9/64, Louisa Co. Detailed to guard over guns at Waynesboro 1/15/65. At Charlottesville G.H. 3/2/65. Furloughed 3/11. NFR.

WADE, MAT GOOD: Enl. 3/21/62. Deserted at Gordonsville 9/20/62. Present (3/3/63). Clothes issued 2/64. Absent when paid 2/29/64. MIA 10/19/64. Captured at Strasburg same day. Sent to Pt. Lookout. At Camp Hospital 11/26. Died with fever 12/4/64 or chronic diarrhea 12/5/64. Grave 676, POW graveyard.

WALLER, FRANK C. F.: Postwar reference.

WALTON, W. CHAP.: Enl. 3/24/62. AWOL 7/1. Deduct 1 months pay. At Charlottesville G.H. 2/23/63. Sent to Colony 2/27. Released 4/19/63. Present (4/30/63). AWOL 9/4/63. Deserted at Liberty Mills.

WASH, PENDLETON T.: Son of Judge Wash of St. Louis, Mo. Attended UVa.? Enl. 3/15/62, age 19. There was an apparent drive to have him appointed as a Lt. in the engineers from 6/??/64. Never transpired. Absent when paid 12/31/63. Present (2/29/64). KIA 5/12/64. Effects received 11/22/64, certificate 2440. Former student of Lt. Dinwiddie's, "proficient at Mathematics and Modern Languages."

WAYLAND, JEREMIAH FINKS: Pvt., 2nd Cpl. Bn. 9/25/41 Albemarle Co., son of J. Wayland and Mary Ramsey. Attended UVa. 1860, 66, 67. Enl. 3/20/62. Cpl. (3/3/63). At hospital 6/5/63-(Charlottesville G.H. with chronic diarrhea 6/8-7/10 7/18/63). Absent when paid 12/31/63. Clothes issued 2/64. Present (2/29/64). Captured 5/12/64. To Ft. Delaware. Released 6/15/64, per G.O. #9. Residence: Albemarle Co., light complexion and hair, blue eyes, 6'. Postwar farmer at Covesville, Albemarle Co. M. 7/12/70 in Baltimore to M. Bledso (dau. of Dr. Albert T. and Harriett Cox Bledso; bn. in Philadelphia 5/5/46).

WEST, J. W.: Postwar reference.

WHEAT, ALONZO M.: enl. 3/15/62. Absent sick at Charlottesville on Surgeon's certificate 6/20. Present (9/3/62). Wounded at Fredericksburg by a caisson running over him 12/19/62. D. in hospital 3/12/63.

71

WHEELER, B. J.: Enl. 3/15/62. Captured 6/5/62 at Harrisonburg. Sent to steamer Coatcoalcos. Paroled 6/62; age 20, 5'11". Exchanged 8/5/62. Present (9/3/62), in arrest awaiting sentence of C.M. Stop 3 days pay for being AWOL. (10/31/62) Present undergoing sentence. Absent when paid 2/29/64. Present (7/8/64). At Chimbo. #3 8/7-8/20/64. Present (11/5/64). MIA 10/19/64; captured. Sent to Pt. Lookout. At Camp Hospital 3/10/65-5/15/65 when he d. of chronic diarrhea. Buried in POW Graveyard.

WHEELER, GEORGE WASHINGTON: Occupation: Blacksmith. Enl. 3/15/62. Detailed as blacksmith 5/20. Absent sick on surgeon's certificate at Charlottesville 8/8/62. At Charlottesville G.H. with chronic diarrhea 8/17-11/4/62. Discharged 12/24/62. At Charlottesville G.H. with chronic rheumatism 1/5/63, though discharged earlier, record was omitted. Residence: Albemarle Co., age 32, 5'9", light complexion, grey eyes, light hair.

WHITE, THOMAS B.: Postwar reference.

WHITE, THOMAS J.: Enl. 3/8/64, Louisa Co. Clothes issued. KIA 5/18/64. Effects received 11/22/64, certificate #2441. Buried in Spotsylvania Confederate Cemetery.

WIDDIFIELD, JAMES M.: Enl. 3/31/62. AWOL 8/13-8/23/62; deduct 12 days pay. In arrest awaiting C. M. (8/31/63). Present (10/31/63). Clothes issued 2/64. Absent when paid 2/29/64. Present (11/5/64). On 24 hour leave 9/22/64. Reported back 11/5/64. Present (2/28/65). NFR.

WILKERSON, J. A.: Postwar reference.

WILLS, ALEXANDER: Postwar reference.

WILLS, BENJAMIN BOWLER or BOWLES: Pvt., Artificer. Bn. 1832. Enl. 3/15/62. Absent furloughed 8/27/63 for 15 days. Reported back 9/11/63. Artificer 1/1/63. Clothes issued 2/64. Horse detail 1/10/65. Paroled at Columbia, Va. 5/4/65. Member J. B. Strange Camp. D. 12/13/15.

WILLS, THOMAS CARY: Pvt., 3rd Sgt. Enl. 3/15/62. Sgt. (7/16/62). At Charlottesville G.H. with debility 12/4-12/13/62. Detailed by order of Lt. Col. Jones to QM Dept. 12/14/63-12/30/63. Again 1/64. Clothes issued 2/64. Present (7/8/64). Detailed with Captain W. J. Armstrong 11/64.

WILLS, WILLIAM S.: 4th Cpl., Pvt. Attended UVa. 1861. Occupation: druggist? Enl. 3/15/62. Cpl. (7/6/62). Detailed by Col. Crutchfield as Pvt. 4/30/63. Attached to hospital 4/10/63. Clothes issued 2/64. To duty with Med. Dept. per S.O. #276/22, 11/21/64. Hospital steward. Paroled at Columbia, Va. 5/4/65.

WOOD, EDWARD S.: Enl. 9/7/63, Albemarle Co. In hospital 9/21/63. At Charlottesville G.H. with chronic rheumatism 9/28/63-2/11/64. At Jackson Hospital, Richmond with rheumatism. Detailed to Ord. Dept. 6/64. Present (7/8/64). Absent when paid 9/30/64. Present (11/15/64). At Chimbo. #1 12/13-12/20/64. NFR.

WOOD, JOHN REUBEN: Bn. 6/24/42 in Albemarle, son of Reuben (vet of 1812) and Martha M. Kinsolving Wood. Attended UVa. 1860. Enl. Univ. Vols. then to 48th Mississippi Inf. as Asst. Surg. M. In Richmond 5/20/63 to Abbie H. Enl. 3/15/64, Louisa Co. Clothes issued 3/21/64, 3/26/64, 3/31/64. Captured 7/4/64, below Richmond on Major Allen's farm. Confined at military prison, Bermuda Hundred, Va. Sent to Pt. Lookout 7/14/64. To Elmira, N.Y. 8/3/64. Released 7/3/65; residence: Charlottesville, fair complexion, dark hair, grey eyes, 5'6". M.D. at Goshen, Rockbridge Co.

WOOD, SILAS: enl. 3/15/62. Absent sick 11/7/63 (at Chimbo. #4 11/8 furloughed 11/23, 30 days) 12/27/63. Absent when paid 12/31/63. Present (2/29/64). Clothes issued 2/64, 3/31/64. Captured 5/12/64. To Ft. Delaware. Claimed to have d. 1/31/65, however another record shows him as released 6/21/65; residence: Albemarle Co., dark complexion, hair, eyes, 5'6".

WOODY, AUSTIN: enl. 3/15/62. At hospital 12/7/63. Chimbo. on 12/9. At Charlottesville G.H. with fever 1/1-1/28/64. Deserted 1/28. Readmitted 2/6/64. Returned to duty 4/19/64. At Chimbo. #1 with debility 5/2-5/7/64. At Chimbo. #2 with iscitis 5/26-6/15/64. Present (7/8/64). At Chimbo. #3 with debilitas 8/8/64-8/14/64. Discharged 11/7/64. Another is dated 11/12, reason: disability.

WYANT, JAMES R.: Postwar reference.

WYANT, THOMAS E.: Enl. 3/15/62. Absent when paid 12/31/63. Present (2/29/64). Clothes issued 3/25/64. Captured 5/12/64. Sent to Ft. Delaware. D. of small pox 1/31/65. Buried on Jersey Shore.

YAGER, JOHN ALBERT: Enl. 3/25/62. Provided substitute 10/10/62, Wade Crawford.

YOCHUM, JOHN: Enl. 4/13/62. Deserted at Harrisonburg 6/5/62. Captured 6/9/62. Sent to Ft. Delaware and took oath 8/10/62.

THE LEE BATTERY

A Volunteer For Virginia

1861

By the middle of May 1861, the daily comings and goings of troops to Lynchburg had become routine, with a mix of the various cultures from all of the Southern states arriving daily. One such organization was Colonel Peter Turney's 1st Tennessee Infantry. Among the regiment's volunteer staff rode Major Pierce Butler Anderson.

Anderson, age 57, held high promise of the Confederate Army. A son of Senator Joseph Anderson, the major was a former student at West Point, having matriculated in the summer of 1823 along with several other men who would make their place in history. Among the lot were Leonidas Polk, Gabriel James Rains, and Philip St. George Cooke (future Union Major General and father-in-law to J.E.B. Stuart). The young Tennesseean's years at the Academy proved successful. He finished the first year first in his class, and the second year as fourth. Though not members of his own class, Anderson did have the opportunity during the height of his education to meet and in fact drill other future notables, including Jefferson Davis, Robert E. Lee, and Joseph E. Johnston.

Though he earned praise in the West Point years, Anderson's time between sessions proved difficult because of his yearning for a love back in East Tennessee. In the summer of 1824, that love took priority over all else and he was married. Returning to New York shortly after, the young man kept his marriage secret; however, in December of the following year, Anderson submitted his resignation and temporarily disappeared from military life.

Back on his homestead at the "Bend of Chunky" in East Tennessee, Anderson continued a productive and successful life, becoming a lawyer, professor of mathematics at Franklin College, and state legislator. Military life again summoned the intelligent Tennessean through a call for troops in the war with Mexico. Anderson was quick to respond, raising Company B, 2nd Tennessee Volunteers, and leading it off to war as its captain. Months later at the Battle of Chapultepec, the company suffered a tremendous loss of men as a shell exploded in their ranks (supposedly killing sixteen in that blast). With the company in a panic, Anderson held his ground and shouted to rally his men, "Company B! Remember you are Tennesseans! Follow me!" Anderson was successful in his gallant stand; the company rallied and continued on. Upon the company's return to New

Orleans, the captain was warmly received by friends and admirers. In a token of appreciation his admirers, along with a presentation from General Winfield Scott, awarded Anderson for his valor a "very handsome and valuable sword." On one side was inscribed the phrase that rallied his men, and on the other simply "Captain Pierce B. Anderson, Chapultepec."

Once home, the local war hero concentrated his attention on land investments. An ardent supporter of two rail systems, Anderson, along with a few others, founded the town of Tullahoma on one of the railways in Coffee County.

Just ten years later, the aging speculator again found himself on the eve of a war, and again he raised a company for the service of the state. Joining with Peter Turney's 1st Tennessee, Captain Anderson found his place at the front of another Company B. Once the regiment was mustered in, and before it set off for Virginia, Anderson and Daniel W. Holman were elected majors.

Upon their arrival in Lynchburg, Virginia, Turney was informed that he could only have one major, whereupon another election was held and Anderson was left without a command. Feeling his experience of war warranted forming a new company, the old captain set the wheels in motion and held a meeting of interested men. On May 28 the meeting proved a success and a Virginia company intended for light artillery service was raised with Anderson at its head. In honor of the new commander of Virginia's forces, the company chose the name the Lee Battery. The new company with ninety-nine enrolled had what appeared to be a fine staff of officers including Anderson, 1st Lieutenants Charles W. Statham and John R. Massey (Massey also from Turney's Tennesseans), and 2nd Lieutenants Charles I. Raine and William H. Hughes.

Mustered into service on June 7, the company, still without cannon, received orders to join the forces already near Rich Mountain in western Virginia. Already there were some that earlier had signed on but did not report for the trip. Boarding cars of the Virginia Central on June 8, the Lee Battery, with Shumaker's Danville company, moved to Staunton, then by foot to Monterey, Beverly, and finally to Cheat Mountain Pass by June 16. Encamping there for eight days, the company received four six-pounders delivered by Captain William Rice's Eighth Star Artillery. The battery then moved again, reaching Camp Garnett at Rich Mountain on June 26.

As General Garnett's forces massed around Rich and Laurel Mountains, Major General George B. McClellan prepared his own forces for an attack against Garnett. The plan of Federal attack involved one column against what was supposed the stronger position at Rich Mountain, and only a smaller force against the "weaker" Confederate force at Laurel Mountain. Though McCelllan confused the relative strength of the Confederate positions, "Little Mac's" forces would still prove to be the victors.

The Lee Battery had been deployed in front of Camp Garnett on Rich Mountain shortly after its arrival. As the threat of enemy attack became more imminent, on July 10 Anderson made his lieutenants aware that changes in positions should soon be expected. The first gun moved was that of 2nd Lieutenant Raine, to a point on the extreme right, in front of Camp Garnett. Another gun under Captain J. A. DeLagnel was placed one and one-half miles in the rear of the camp. The last two places, under Lieutenants Statham and Massey, were posted on the left.

It was from Raine's position that the enemy was first detected about dusk July 10. The chopping of axes on both the left of the camp and along the creek near where Raine was stationed provided the first indication of movement, causing Captain Anderson to reinforce the piece with thirty additional "musketeers." The Captain also posted himself nearby.

At about midnight the bugle of the enemy's 19th Ohio Infantry was inadvertently sounded, causing Raine's cannoneers to peer out into the pitch-black night. In a half an hour more, drums were heard along with a bugle. Soon the Confederates noticed lights passing in the distant darkness. Feeling that the enemy were in motion, Anderson ordered his lieutenant to report their sighting to Colonel John Pegram. When Raine returned, Pegram's adjutant, A. R. H. Ranson, accompanied him and remained as they watched for the enemy into the morning. Suspicions of movement were soon after confirmed from an enemy trooper captured before light.

With Pegram growing more concerned over this concealed advance, Anderson was ordered to move a piece back to the middle of the line. Lieutenant Statham's gun and his detachment of twenty-one men quickly came into the new position at about 1 p.m. While Anderson went forward with this group, Raine was ordered to move to a better position that could rake the road and ravine coming down into camp from near Hart's house.

While waiting by their guns under overcast and drizzling conditions, in less than two hours Statham's men spotted Brigadier General William S. Rosecran's Federal troops as they advanced across the hill to the south of the pass. Turning their gun around in the opposite direction from which they had been facing (it originally faced down the pass), the crew readied their piece for action.

Lieutenant Massey, meanwhile, between 10 and 11 a.m. had been informed by Colonel J. M. Heck that Anderson wanted his piece moved to the top of Stonecoal Hill, farther on the extreme left of camp. Once posted, the Tennessee lieutenant had also discovered the enemy "cavalry on top of Rich Mountain opposite Hart's house, about one and a half miles in the rear of our breastworks. . . ." Upon witnessing the enemy,

Massey immediately requested that Colonel Heck inform Pegram. Massey reported: "About 12½ o'clock the firing of a gun at Hart's Hill, on Rich Mountain commenced. After the fire of that gun had continued for some time firing, forty or fifty of the enemy's infantry appeared on the turnpike road in front of our breastworks. I commenced firing on them as they retired."

Between 2:30 and 3 p.m. Lieutenant Statham caught sight of the 10th Indiana Infantry as it came across the opposite crest. After opening fire on the Confederate pickets, the enemy column pressed on through "dense brushwood, emerging into rather more open brushwood and trees." Once this line came to within two or three hundred yards, the Federals commenced taking shots at Statham's crew from behind rocks and trees. Unhampered, the crew responded with spherical case against the main body of enemy farther off, cutting fuses at first to one second and a quarter. As the lieutenant reported, he ". . .could distinctly see them burst in their midst. I knew we did good execution, as I could distinctly hear their officers give vehement commands to close up ranks. After firing this way some little time at the rate of near four shots per minute we forced the enemy to retire."

As the enemy closed in and Pegram's situation grew more desperate by the minute, Captain Anderson received word from Captain DeLagnel asking for another gun. In response, Anderson rode out to Raine's position and again ordered the gun moved. With Anderson riding in advance of the gun, Raine followed with the caisson and ammunition. Once the lieutenant reached the turn in the road, he met Confederates streaming back in retreat. At this place also, word came to Raine that one of the wheel horses of his piece had been killed and the other wounded. Worse yet, in an explosion, the tongue of the gun carriage had been broken off, throwing one of the drivers and sending the carriage down the side of the hill. Wheeling his caisson around in the road, the lieutenant watched as Anderson attempted to rally the fleeing Confederates.

Meanwhile, Statham's gun had fallen prey to an assault of the enemy, forcing the lieutenant to withdraw higher up the hill and reopen. The spherical shot now cut "as low as one second down to three quarters." For a time, Statham's artillerists and the supporting infantry seemed to throw back their assailants. The men "rent the air with their shouts, confidently believing that we had gained the day." Those cheers were short-lived, however, as the enemy reformed and renewed the assault. The next few minutes turned to total chaos about the lone piece as green horses bolted and soon took off down the mountain with caisson and drivers, leaving the crew stranded with nothing but the gun and the ammunition in the limber box. Hurriedly the crew scrambled to harness the remaining horses to the limber and pull the piece out of danger. They found an adequate position near a small log stable, unlimbered the gun, and sent the horses behind the stable for cover. Though the determined crew believed that their new position was better, within minutes many of its men fell with wounds. As Lieutenant Statham reported:

> Sergeant Turner, of the gun, had both legs broken and shot through the body; I. I. Mays had his left arm splintered with a musket ball; Isaiah Ryder shot through the head and died instantly; John A. Taylor had his thigh broken; E. H. Kersey, shot in the ankle; Lewis Going, wounded in the arm; William W. Stewart badly wounded in the head and breast. This left me but few men to man the gun. Captain DeLagnel, who was the commander of the post, having his horse shot under him and seeing our crippled condition, gallantly came and volunteered his valuable aid, and helped load and fire three or four times, when he was shot in the side and I think in the hand." [DeLagnel had been in the act of bringing a cartridge from the limber box to the gun, having only two others at the gun.]

With the enemy upon them, DeLagnel ordered the men to save themselves, but the surrounding blue-jackets and their fire proved too intense. As Private W. H. Broyles pricked the last cartridge and the gun fired, the crew was overrun and the remaining survivors surrendered. Those captured included James Brooks, James M. Brooks, Thomas Brooks, William Broyles, Amos Curren, Warren Curren, Benjamin H. Davidson, James B. Creasy, Joseph Lambden, William J. Lipscomb, John Madden (also severely wounded), John J. Mays, Reese W. Walker, Lewellyn Wooldridge, William Worley, and Lieutenant Statham. The lieutenant also suffered a wound to the hand. Isaiah Rider was killed.

In an effort to retake the guns, Captain Anderson tried to take volunteers from those rallied, but Pegram soon rode up and proposed to make an attack in the night instead, as dust just then was falling.

Massey's gun, still posted atop Stonecoal Hill, had a busy day of it as well, firing on the enemy movements on Sugar Hill opposite them. At the close of the day, that crew remained unscathed. Between 2 and 3 a.m. on July 12, the lieutenant was ordered to spike the gun and return to camp, there finding the companies organizing for a retreat. With the command of the company, now eighteen men, devolving upon Lieutenant Statham, Anderson and Raine moved forward into the night with Colonel Pegram and several men.

As Pegram's contingent passed along a trail of "clustering bushes, overlarge logs, and often steep and slippery" they attempted to make their way to the enemy camp. Soon however, it was discovered that they were lost. Pausing amidst a heavy rainfall, the captain in a couple of hours moved farther along and encountered "two companies of the column, from whose captains (Bruce and Jones) I learned that Colonel Pegram had returned to camp after directing Major Tyler to take the men on to Beverly." Now within eight miles of General Garnett's camp, Anderson, along with Raine and three others, determined to make it to him and obtain assistance. As the group rambled through the darkness, they finally reached the turnpike, only to find Garnett's picket positions abandoned. It was apparent that Garnett too had withdrawn. Anderson wrote:

> Surrounded by foraging parties of the enemy, who were moving about in different directions, I was compelled to remain in the mountains of Cheat for several days and nights before I could come out safely. At length I succeeded in doing so. During this time Lieutenant Raine and my three men, each armed with a musket, suffered much from fatigue, hunger, and thirst, but they were prompt and fearless in the discharge of duty.

The loss of the Lee Battery at the conclusion of this fiasco totaled all the guns, carriages, equippage, horses, ordnance, officers' clothing, baggage and accouterments. Including Statham's crew, two men were killed, twelve wounded (two commissioned officers, two non-coms, and eight privates), and eighteen captured in all.

Uniting with the remnants of Pegram's command, Lieutenant Statham led the Lynchburg company out of danger. By July 22, one day after comrades had been victorious at Manassas, the battery reunited as the scattered remnants had found their way to Monterey. After receiving three more guns, the company marched west a short distance along with the 12th Georgia Infantry. They served there as a warning element for the main body at Monterey and in front of McClellan's lead elements along Shaver's Fork of the Cheat River. Marching back to Camp Alleghany by August 8, the battery then moved back to Monterey, where it arrived on August 13; and then on to a campsite on the Greenbrier River on August 19. Here at the new campsite, a green but confident Lieutenant R. P. Chew began his career in the field. The former VMI cadet, having graduated early, now had the opportunity to perform what he had been well trained for.

At Camp Bartow and under the command of Brigadier General Henry R. Jackson, the Lee Battery stood as one of three batteries in the Army of the Northwest. Tending to the duties of camp life and daily drilling, the Lynchburg men, for the first time since their organization, found time to settle down. Sometime in late September the enthusiastic Chew was detached from the Lynchburg company and by November was launched on his way to immortal fame under "Stonewall" Jackson.

By October 2 the enemy began to threaten again, as they were found moving in the direction of the river encampment. General Jackson briefed

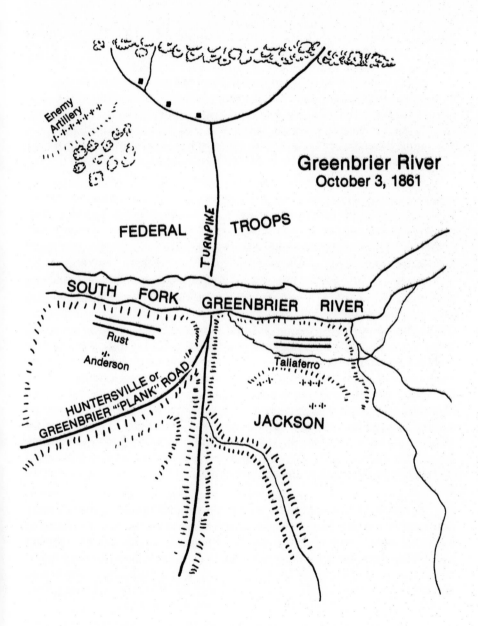

Greenbrier River
October 3, 1861

his officers and delivered instructions for the following morning in anticipation of an attack.

One section of Anderson's pieces was to move to the extreme left flank along with the 3rd Arkansas, the 31st Virginia, and Hansbrough's Battalion of Virginia Infantry. There, under command of Colonel Albert Rust of the 3rd Arkansas, Anderson was to enfilade the Huntersville Road. Another piece was ordered to the right on a hill near the Yager house, under the command of Lieutenant Massey. Massey, being considerably ill, would continue to remain with his piece, the battery command actually being assumed by Captain James Deshler, aide-de-camp to Colonel Edward Johnson. In this position Massey's crew found themselves in the company of William B. Taliaferro's men and the guns of both the Danville and Eighth Star Artillery.

As the enemy artillery opened the action near 8 a.m. on October 3, Anderson's men stood separated once more at their respective positions. Though the guns near Rust remained quiet, not having the opportunity to fire during the day, Massey's gun under Captain Deshler actively participated. Massey fired approximately ninety-three rounds and did good execution, dismounting an enemy cannon. General Jackson complimented the crew, saying that they ". . .directed a rapid fire with marked effect." By the close of the action and following a Federal withdrawal, the Lee Battery had sustained no casualties.

After being positioned upon the Greenbrier for almost two months, Anderson's men moved with Jackson's forces to Camp Alleghany and into winter quarters by November 22. Back at the familiar camp, the Lynchburg men looked on as the infantry labored in developing trenches around the areas. The company also made another transaction with the Eighth Star Artillery turning over to it some iron smoothbore six-pounders. Anderson found supplies wanting. Due to lack of any stationery of any form he was unable to make out muster rolls. Furthermore, forage was in short supply, forcing the battery to turn in all but eleven horses to the quartermaster to be sent back to Staunton to graze.

In November, a sickly Lieutenant Massey took leave from the company to return to Tennessee for proper medical attention. The lieutenant never did return, because of the severity of his ailment. This did not keep the horrors of way at bay however; in 1864 Massey was shot down "riddled with bullets" by Federals as they made their way through his home town.

Though the enemy too had gone into winter quarters on Cheat Mountain some distance from the Confederate camp, threat of an attack did not subside, as both sides continued to scout actively along the Greenbrier River. On December 12, scouts from Colonel Ed Johnson's 12th Georgia Infantry came upon an enemy party close to Camp Alleghany, and engaged in a brief skirmish. Alarmed by the proximity of enemy troops, the camp became aware that action should soon follow.

December 13 dawned to sporadic fire along the picket line at about 4 a.m. When the Confederates were driven back, the crews of both Anderson's Lee and Miller's 2nd Rockbridge batteries manned their guns and opened fire on the Greenbrier Road at about 7:15 a.m. The fight that followed first pressured the Confederate right, leaving the batteries safe from harm. Within half an hour, however, an enemy column approached the guns in their entrenchments on the left.

Captain Anderson, believing the enemy skirmishers to be returning friendly pickets, called on the line to hold their fire, and rode out of the trenchline to invite the men in. The decision to do so was fatal: he was shot out of his saddle. In response, the line let the enemy column have it, forcing them in a short time to fall back into the fallen timber and brush about fifty paces from the works. The enemy kept up a constant harassing fire against the line and the exposed artillerists as they moved about. Captain Deshler of Colonel Johnson's staff once more stood with the cannoneers. This time he went down with a severe wound, shot through both thighs. Though in pain and losing blood, the captain remained among the Lynchburg battery and refused to be sent from the field until the enemy were repulsed. During this attack on the left, the right flank sent reenforcements, and the enemy attack was soon thrown back.

Though the engagement proved a Confederate victory, and though the Lee Battery suffered only one casualty, the men mourned the loss of their gallant captain from Tennessee. The body of the slain commander was appropriately sent back to Tullahoma and buried in the city cemetery. Having sported his famous Chapultepec sword in the fight, it too was returned with the body and taken charge of by his brother, Dr. Thomas A. Anderson. He kept the fine specimen as a fond but sad memory of his brother. After Braxton Bragg's withdrawal from Tullahoma in 1863, the doctor fled with the sword among other valuable possessions to Atlanta. While waiting in a train station, he left his valise and the sword in a waiting room while he went out to visit his convalescing son, a soldier with Bragg's army. Upon his return a few minutes later, he found the valise where it had been left but the sword gone. Throughout the rest of the war and after, Doctor Anderson made every effort to locate the valuable piece, but was never successful.

The Lee Battery after the battle returned to the routine in its winter quarters and set to trimming and burning the brush in front of the camp in an effort to prepare for a renewed attack. None ever came. On December 21 an election was held with Charles I. Raine rising to the rank of captain and Hardwicke to fill Raine's lieutenancy.

Season of Victory
1862

The Lee Battery endured the season in their winter quarters relatively undisturbed. They broke the monotony with notorious stag dances, prayer meetings, and several snowball battles against various infantry companies. Life was not all fun and games, however, as the close quarters provided poor water, and extreme winter temperatures on the mountain contributed significantly to camp illnesses and death. The first of the returned paroled prisoners of Rich Mountain, William Lipscomb, rejoined the company in camp and reenlisted on February 14. The rest would not follow until the next year.

Welcoming orders to burn and abandon the camp, Raine's company marched out along with the rest of the Army of the Northwest on April 1. The destination was the rough and rugged Shenandoah Mountain, putting "Alleghany" Johnson's command closer to the recently defeated army of "Stonewall" Jackson, since withdrawn to Mt. Jackson.

In mid-April the command marched through Buffalo Gap and eventually to Staunton where, on April 26, Johnson divided his command into two brigades. The Lee Battery was assigned to the second, under the command of Colonel John B. Baldwin of the 52nd Virginia Infantry. The brigade included the 44th, 52nd, and 58th Virginia Infantry and the 2nd Rockbridge Artillery.

On May 6, "Stonewall's" troops reached Staunton and made a rendezvous with the forces already there, with the intention of striking out against Milroy's force at Shenandoah Mountain. On May 8 the combined Jackson-Johnson army arrived at McDowell and defeated the enemy, securing the safety of Staunton and the Virginia Central Railroad. Though the Lee Battery did not arrive in time to see action, the terrain had not allowed proper deployment of the artillery already there. From McDowell, the Confederates pursued the enemy to Franklin, where the Federals were forced to destroy a great quantity of their stores, arms, and camp equippage.

Jackson gave up the pursuit on May 13 and made his way across Shenandoah Mountain, still unable to draw Milroy out for an open fight. Once in the vicinity of Lebanon Sulpher Springs, the combined force rested for three days.

With General Nathaniel P. Banks's Federal army at both Winchester and Front Royal, Jackson set his sights on a new target. On May 17, the army was put in motion, marching through Harrisonburg and New Market and across the Massanutten to Luray. There the growing Confederate Valley army was boosted again by addition of the command of General Richard S. Ewell.

With this strengthened mass of men, Jackson struck and surprised the Front Royal garrison on May 23, capturing stores valued at $300,000. The Lee Battery was not a participant in the day's action.

Following up on this success, "Blue-Light" struck again on May 24 by attacking Banks again as he retreated toward Winchester. By the end of the day, the enemy army was in its full retreat. Raine's battery did not partake in the action again.

The morning of May 25 proved a different story for the Lee Battery as it, along with Caskie's Hampden Artillery, was ordered to pursue the enemy. Colonel Stapleton Crutchfield commented that they ". . .were handled with uncommon tact, energy, and effect." By the close of the afternoon, the battery returned to its camp unscathed.

Poised for a strike across the Potomac, Raine's, Caskie's and Wooding's batteries accompanied the Valley army on May 28 as it marched in the direction of Harpers Ferry. The battery was slightly engaged on Bolivar Heights during the next two days. The "seige" was abruptly lifted because of the rapidly closing enemy armies under Fremont and Shields. As the pincers closed from both the east and west, Jackson retreated up the Valley, reaching Strasburg on June 1. Atop a hill overlooking the town, the batteries of Raine, Poague, Courtney, Cutshaw, and Caskie fired a few shots in the direction of the enemy to keep them at bay.

Onward through heavy rains Jackson pressed his army through Edinburg, Woodstock, and Mt. Jackson. Near the village of Mt. Jackson, Ewell's division was ordered to fight a delaying action to delay Fremont's pursuit. Only slightly engaged, the Lee Battery kept with its division from there through Harrisonburg and finally reached a point near Port Republic on June 7.

The following morning dawned bright and beautiful, but the Sabbath was not to remain holy. Fremont's men had moved toward the Confederates at Cross Keys, and in an effort to stall the enemy, General Ewell prepared his division for a defense. Just two miles southeast of Cross Keys, the division was thrown out in a line of battle facing the northwest, from which the enemy was approaching. The Lee Battery and the Henrico, Eighth Star, Second Rockbridge, and Baltimore Artillery batteries were all wheeled into position barring an advance along the Harrisonburg-Port Republic Road.

At about 10 a.m., Fremont's lead elements arrived and opened a half-hearted attack against the defiant Confederate line. Brigadier General Ar-

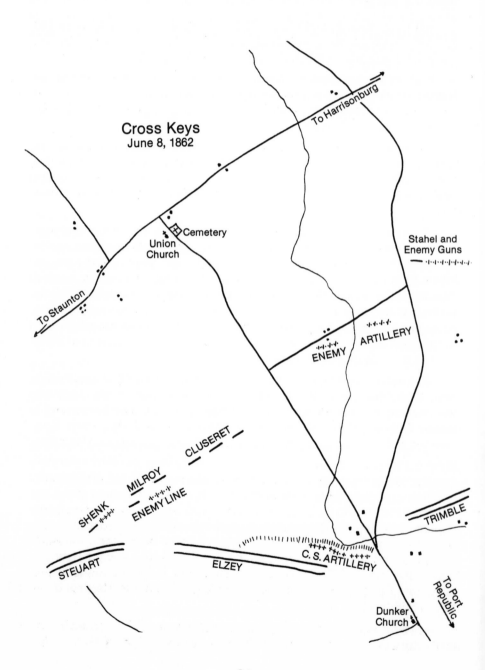

Cross Keys
June 8, 1862

To Harrisonburg

Cemetery

Union
Church

Stahel and
Enemy Guns

To Staunton

ENEMY   ARTILLERY

CLUSERET

MILROY

SHENK

ENEMY LINE

TRIMBLE

STEUART

ELZEY

C. S. ARTILLERY

To Port
Republic

Dunker
Church

nold Elzey, with his own brigade behind the batteries, came forward and personally coordinated the artillery fire on Blenker's German Division as it trudged forward. In supervising this, Elzey fell wounded in the late afternoon. As the action intensified, the enemy artillery fire found its mark among Ewell's batteries. That, combined with the effect of small arms fire and depletion of their own ammunition, forced the Lee and Star batteries to retire. Crutchfield reported: "Raine's . . . was particularly well and gallantly managed, he having his horse shot, and serving a gun himself when short of cannoneers." Though having to serve the guns himself, Raines either failed to report casualties or had none.

On the morning of June 9, the Lee Battery moved forward with some of Ewell's infantry to join Jackson in the attack on E. B. Tyler's Federals just outside of Port Republic. Reporting to Winder with two pieces (one without cannoneers), Raine was sent forward with the lone piece and into action in the rear of Taylor's Louisianans. From behind a fence beside the batteries of Poague and Carpenter the piece joined in the fight.

As Winder attacked with the Stonewall brigade and the 7th Louisiana Infantry, the group of nine guns advanced rapidly behind them. The infantry was soon driven back, however, and the guns exposed to the onslaught of the enemy. One of Poague's guns was captured. The second Confederate attack proved successful and ended the day in favor of Jackson once more. Crutchfield wrote of the artillery service, "Their fire was good, and they were generally well managed. . . ." The Lee Battery apparently only suffered one casualty, Thomas Coffee, who eventually died of jaundice on June 18.

With the Shenandoah Valley won for now, Jackson's victorious army moved into Brown's Gap, encamping near the summit. The two Federal armies withdrew down the valley and Jackson moved his men back into the lowland and encamped first at Mt. Meridian, and then on June 17 at Weyer's Cave.

In true "Blue Light" style, Jackson discreetly and rapidly slipped his army out of the Shenandoah through Jarman's Gap and into Albemarle County. From the railroad station near Mechum's River, the infantry boarded cars for Frederick's Hall and Beaver Dam Station, while the cavalry, artillery, and wagons were forced to march along the hot and dusty roads. The end of the long trek brought most of Ewell's artillery up too late to repulse their old foe, McClellan.

The new commander of the Army of Northern Virginia, Robert E. Lee directed his attention after defeating "Little Mac" toward the threat of General John Pope as he advanced in the direction of Fredericksburg. In response, the Lee Battery, along with the rest of the division artillery, was ordered to march to Gordonsville on July 13. The guns and caissons moved by rail.

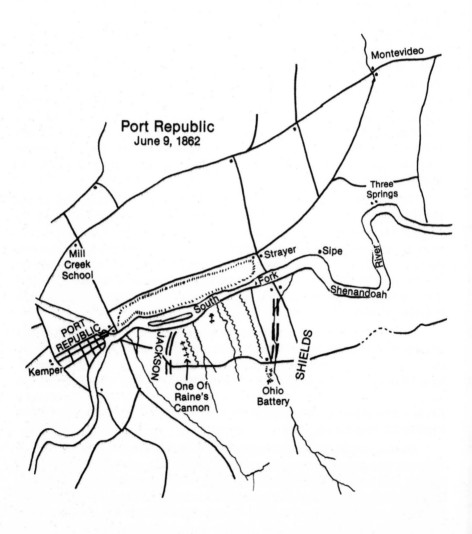

Port Republic
June 9, 1862

The Lynchburg men remained near the peaceful village for sometime. By the beginning of August Raine's men found themselves caught up in a reorganization of artillery. Under the command of Major Lindsey M. Shumaker, former comrade of the Greenbrier River episode, the Lynchburg company was placed into a battalion along with the Eighth Star, Hampden, Danville, Alleghany, Jackson, Rockbridge, and Baltimore batteries.

July and August brought a different and ugly experience to the Lee Battery as several men, mostly substitutes, began to desert. When twenty-two deserted in August, Captain Raine issued an order by direction of General Jackson for the return of thirteen of those men, offering $15 each if returned to local officials, or $30 apiece if brought back to the camp of the battery. Those on the list of wanted included George Wilson, John Suddith alias Riley, Edward Hite (Hill), William Martin, John Campbell, James Burham, James Sheehan, William G. Thomas, John Kelly, William L. Johnson (from Scottsville), Samuel Mays (from Amherst), William O'Conner (from Chester, Chesterfield Co.), and Robert Worley. Others not on the list included Patrick Costello, Jr., David J. Craddock, Thomas P. Franklin, Thomas Haw, Thomas E. Johnson, Marion Norvell, John Smith, and Thomas Sullivan. Of the entire set, only Thomas Johnson and Marion Norvell were brought in. Norvell was courtmartialed and assigned to hard labor and stoppage of pay for one month.

The Lee Battery could only sit back and listen on August 9 as the guns at Cedar Mountain engaged in yet another Confederate victory. On August 17, the Lee Battery fell in with General William B. Taliaferro's Division as it started on a line of march. In the lead of the third brigade, the battery's first-night bivouac was on the Crenshaw farm near Orange Court House. With short rations and no tents or baggage, Shumaker's Battalion marched again on August 20 behind Ewell's division, crossing the Rapidan at Somerville Ford and bivouacking at Stevensburg for the night.

Continuing the leg northward on August 21, Taliaferro advanced his troops in front of Jackson's other divisions at Brandy Station. From Brandy on to Cunningham's Ford on the Rappahannock, the artillery battalion spent the day on the road until it halted near Beverly's Ford. There the long range guns of the battalion were sent along with J.E.B. Stuart's cavalry and drove off an enemy force. The Lee Battery spent the day in reserve on August 22.

On August 23, Shumaker's Battalion continued its trek into Northern Virginia, passing through Jeffersonton and finally going into camp in a driving rain just short of Fauquier Springs. Pressing on again on August 25, the Lee Battery along with the battalion marched through Washington, Flint Hill, and Warrenton, resting for the evening near Salem. Resuming the flank maneuver on the next day, the route of the artillerists took them

87

through Thoroughfare Gap and Gainesville to within a few miles of Bristoe Station.

The division started again on August 27 as tall pillars of smoke clouded the sky, rising from the sack and burning of railcars at Manassas Junction. Passing the depot, men could not resist the temptation to fall out and partake of the bountiful harvest so generously supplied by their enemy. As night came on, the cannoneers found their path well lighted from the fires that continued to glow, finally arriving at Sudley Church and bivouacking for the night.

Though Shumaker's Battalion was actively engaged in the battles that followed, there is no record of Raine's battery participating in the fights of the next five days. On September 2, the Lee Battery joined its sister batteries as they moved northwestward through Leesburg and, on September 5, across the Potomac at White's Ford to within a short distance of Frederick. In camp that night, some of the Lee men got in an argument with men from the Rockbridge Artillery. Turning from insults to fists, the men broke the quiet of the night. Nearby the men of the Alleghany Artillery overheard the ruckus and many rushed to the aid of the Rockbridge men. Before they could get well started in the affair, officers broke up the fracas and returned the men to their proper places.

Marching to Frederick the next day, the guns went into park for five more days. On that fifth day, the battalion resumed the march on through Boonsboro, and on the next day back across the Potomac at Williamsport. With the rest of Jackson's artillery, the Lee Battery went into a position opposite Bolivar Heights on September 13 and participated in the bombardment that rocked the hills around Harper's Ferry. At the end of the day, the guns prepared for another bombardment to be preceded by an infantry advance; but before the advance could get underway, a white flag went up and the garrison surrendered.

Back across the Potomac on September 16, Jackson's corps moved through the town of Sharpsburg and into the lines developing around it. Raine's battery was ordered up near the West Wood on a slight rise behind a fenceline, facing the area just on the northern side of the Dunker Church. Harry Hays' Louisiana Brigade stood poised just to their front across the fenceline, while Jubal Early's occupied the left of the battery and faced the West Wood.

As soon as it was light enough to see on the morning of September 17, the Federal batteries opened a terrific fire. In response to the enemy's heavier guns, the light artillery batteries of Jackson's corps attempted to return fire. Poague requested that the short-range guns be moved up in order to conserve his own long-range ammunition. In consequence the Lee Battery moved up slightly. In their advanced position, Raine's two three-inch rifles and one twelve-pounder howitzer barked out rounds in their first real fight since Port Republic. Not long after, Union infantry assaulted the position and forced the one piece of Poague, under Lieutenant Brown, and Raine's battery to withdraw to a safer position on the Poffenberger farm. Brown, unable to find a suitable position, reported back to Poague. Sam Bateman was the only casualty reported by Raine that day; he was listed as missing. What happened to Bateman cannot be ascertained, but he was alive after the war.

On September 18 the Lee Battery crossed back into Virginia and camped on the Opequon. Four days later, General W. N. Pendleton inspected the battery and reported that it had two three-inch rifles, two twelve-pound howitzers (the new twelve-pounder being from the stores captured at Harper's Ferry), one forge, horses and harnesses. The company needed thirty horses.

Eight days later, the battery went into camp at Bunker Hill and remained through November, untouched by the great reorganization and consolidation ordered for the artillery on October 4.

At the end of their comfortable rest in the valley, the Lee Battery joined Jackson's corps as it marched up the valley and out at Fisher's Gap, with its destination Fredericksburg. "Stonewall's" army raced across the Virginia countryside to join Lee in countering a new Federal commander, Ambrose E. Burnside. Arriving at Port Royal on the Rappahannock several days later, the men were subject to short rations and bitter cold weather. Late on December 12, the battery moved to Hamilton's Crossing on Jackson's right.

In the chilling air before dawn on December 13, Jackson's guns completed their deployments in a line extending from the crossing north to Deep Run. Near the crossing and on Prospect Hill Colonel R. Lindsay Walker commanded fourteen cannon. North of that position and near Deep Run waited twenty-one guns under Captain Greenlee Davidson. There was one problem, however, in the placement of the pieces. Between the two heavy concentrations of guns lay an eight-hundred-yard stretch of land that could not be reached by artillery fire. In order to cover the gap, Colonel Crutchfield ordered twelve guns, under Captain John B. Brockenbrough, to move in front and slightly to the right of Davidson, just across the railroad tracks. That left nine guns with Davidson.

In Davidson's position on the left of Jackson's line, near the Bernard slave cabins, stood the batteries of Davidson, Raine, Caskie and Braxton. The batteries had orders to fire only at the enemy infantry. Anxious and cold cannoneers stood by their pieces. As the Federal guns unleashed a hail of iron upon their positions, the Confederate artillerists remained true to their orders and did not counter. It was not until about 9 a.m. that the first of the enemy infantry, (Pennsylvanians) began closing on Brocken-

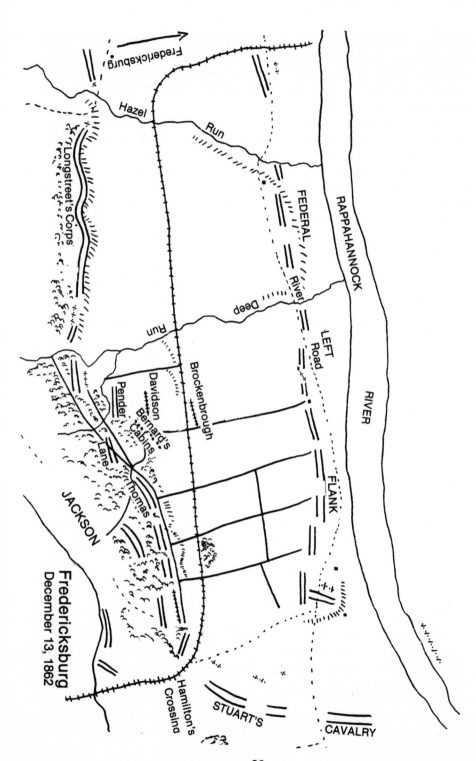

Fredericksburg
December 13, 1862

brough's crews. Driving them off with canister, the forward guns drew even more unwanted attention as the Federal batteries found good targets in their exposed position. In vain these men looked to Davidson's guns for assistance against the advancing Federal guns, but the response was only "a very slow fire."

Davidson's guns, in fact, were hampered by their own problems in the form of a rapidly advancing line of infantry. Blasting them with double-shotted canister, the Lee Battery and the others found success, mowing the blue line down. After two more shots of that same form, the enemy withdrew from their front. The Lynchburg company, under command of Lieutenant Statham, did not participate in the fight long. Finding the ammunition defective and not bursting, they were forced to pull off the line. Apparently, however, the battery returned with better ammunition later, and stood in battle for nine hours, firing eighty-seven rounds of shot and shell. With only one man wounded (Private Thomas L. Brooks), the battery remained on the front for the next two days, not firing another shot.

On December 15 the battery marched to Moss Neck and into camp, remaining until December 29, when they were ordered to Bowling Green and into winter quarters.

With The Maryland Battalion
1863

Making the best of a cold winter, the Lee Battery built a fine group of cabins and welcomed a pause in the hostilities. In the days that proved suitable, the battery along with others took the opportunity to drill. Life in the camp was not unlike the winter before: snowball fights, prayer meetings, etc. On January 16, the peace of the temporary village was interrupted when the men were ordered out to General Robert E. Rodes near Grace Church, arriving on the 18th. From there, Raine reported to General Taliaferro at Moss Neck again and remained in camp in that vicinity until January 28, when the battery returned admist a heavy snowfall to Bowling Green.

Numerous individuals began returning to the company that winter who had been captured at Rich Mountain. Among those who reenlisted on February 14 were James M. Brooks, Thomas Brooks, William H. Broyles, Warren Curren, and Edward H. Kersey.

Others of the Lee Battery spent their winter in the brigade brig and became some of the many men who were to be taken before courts martial. A total of eight from the company either met the board of officers or were fortunate enough to be released for some unstated reasons. Of the lot, Daniel DePriest, Timothy Hughes, and Sterling Wright were sent to Castle Thunder.

In the great organization of artillery in February, the battery was placed in Lieutenant Colonel Richard Snowden Andrews's Battalion along with Caskie's Hampden, Brown's Chesapeake, and Dement's Maryland Artillery.

An inspection held four days following the organization showed Raine's battery with the following: three three-inch rifles in good order; ammunition well kept; harnesses good; forty-eight horses in tolerable order; two wagons in good condition; three officers and eighty-five men present; one officer and five men detached; eleven absent with leave; and eleven absent sick.

On April 16 the battalion was modified when the Hampden Artillery was transferred to the 38th Battalion Virginia Light Artillery, and Carpenter's Alleghany Artillery transferred in. Other battalion matters included the selection of the executive officer. Raine, being senior captain in the battalion, would have been a natural selection, and the officers of the other batteries displayed their support in the form of a petition.

"Stonewall" felt differently, however, and decided that the proper selection would be Joseph White Latimer.

Latimer, a Prince William County native, had matriculated at VMI in July 1859, and in two years of training at the Institute gained high praise from Jackson as a pupil. Assigned as one of twelve drillmasters to Richmond in April 1861, eighteen-year-old Latimer was assigned to drill the Hampden Artillery. He later was commissioned as 2nd Lieutenant in Alfred R. Courtney's Henrico Artillery. In this capacity the young man distinguished himself as an excellent artillerist; Ewell later called Latimer his "little Napoleon." Now in the spring of 1863, Jackson found it just to reward the valor of Latimer, promoting him and made him second to Snowden Andrews. The decision angered Raine and caused some degree of competitiveness between the two men. Captain Raine could not live the decision down easily.

As Federal troops crossed the Rappahannock near Deep Run, the new battalion moved toward Hamilton's Crossing. On May 1, two of Raine's rifled pieces and a Whitworth of Graham's Battery were placed in some works in the open field between Deep Run and the marshy area on the right, some 200 yards in rear of the railroad. Under the command of the "Boy Major," all remained quiet that day.

The following morning was not so peaceful. Noticing a large number of enemy on the other side of the river, Lieutenant Colonel Andrews ordered Raine to open on the right, while the other batteries opened on other positions to feel the enemy out. After twenty-five rounds, Raine received no response and Latimer ordered the guns to cease fire. At 2 p.m. Andrews received orders to march with Early's division on the Telegraph Road. Leaving their positions with fires going, and cheering so as to deceive the enemy, the battalion reached the road and replenished ammunition stores and corn enough for three days for the horses. At 9 p.m. the battalion was ordered to countermarch to the old position.

On the morning of May 3, reports came back that the enemy was in motion in their front. With the pieces of Dement's Battery, Raine went forward to the same position he had occupied two days before. This group of eight rifled cannon, under the command of the ever-present Latimer, opened up and lay a concentrated fire upon the head of a ravine where an enemy battery of six guns was posted just left of the Bernard house. The Federals returned the fire in short order, and were soon joined by two more guns. The two guns proved too great a distance for the Maryland cannoneers to reach and Carpenter's pieces were moved up to join the fight. The counter-battery fire cost the Lee Battery William A. Owens killed, W. H. Eades wounded in the head slightly, John Norvell wounded in the hand slightly, and Tilghman A. Marsh wounded in the hand and arm slightly. At about 1 p.m. the area went quiet and Andrews moved his battalion "to the heights back on the Corduroy Road." Remaining there for several hours, the batteries were again moved before dusk to a position behind Lee's Hill, where they remained all the following day until 6 p.m., when they came up to support charges by Gordon, Hays, and Hoke.

With the battle won and the Federals back across the river, the Lee Battery remained with the battalion near Fredericksburg until they all moved again on May 8 a short distance toward Massaponax Heights.

By June 5, the Lee Battery was en route to the Shenandoah Valley, passing through Culpeper on the 9th, then on through Sperryville, Little Washington, through Chester Gap, to Front Royal and finally reaching Cedarville by June 12. Arriving within sight of Winchester at noon on June 13, Andrews' Battalion stood ready for orders, but only Carpenter's men were engaged that afternoon.

It would not be until the following evening at about dusk that the battalion would next go into line for a march. Along with General Ed Johnson's division, a section of Raine's battery, Dement's Marylanders, and the Alleghany men, all under the direction of Andrews, proceeded until they reached Stephenson's Depot, approximately two and a half miles from Winchester. There they waited, either to intercept the enemy retreat or to repulse an attack. Just as they reached the position, the Confederates could hear the Federals nearby in retreat toward Martinsburg.

Forming a line parallel with the pike and behind a stone well, General G. H. Steuart's men were posted on the right while the Louisianans drew up on the left, and the artillery was "favorably" posted. The wait was a brief one, as Milroy's Yankees soon slammed right into Johnson's force. With Raine's guns faced to the left on the line, the battery was exposed to considerable fighting as Milroy unsuccessfully attempted to flank the Louisiana brigade. Johnson reported, "a rifle section belonging to Raine's battery... fired on the flank move at right angles with his former line of fire with good effect." Surprisingly, the Lynchburg company sustained a loss of only three horses disabled. Colonel Andrews fell with a severe wound, leaving Major Latimer in command.

On June 16, the "Maryland" battalion moved out of Stephenson's Depot and marched toward Sheperdstown. Crossing Boteler's Ford on June 18, the batteries passed over the Sharpsburg battlefield of the previous September, then moved via Hagerstown and Chambersburg, Pennsylvania. The column came to within three miles of Carlisle on June 29. Ordered to countermarch, the battalion continued with Johnson's division and camped on the last day of the month near Greenville. With a distinct sound of battle in the distance, the battalion raced with its division down the Chambersburg Road until it reached the crossroad town of Gettysburg by dusk. Just northeast of the town, the battalion halted and went into camp between the York and Baltimore roads.

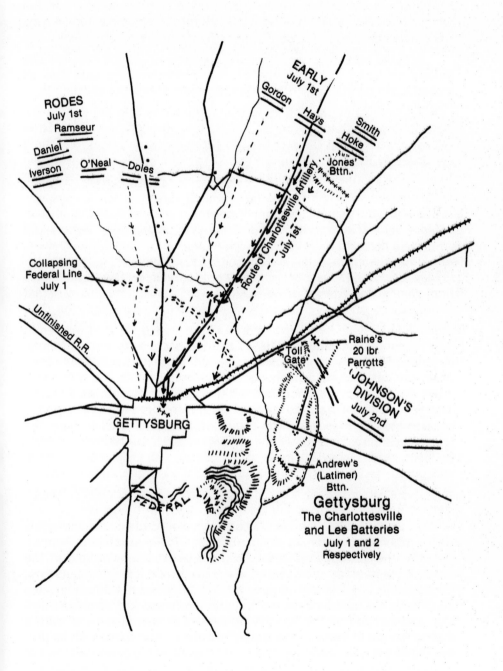

RODES
July 1st
Ramseur
Daniel
Iverson O'Neal Doles

EARLY
July 1st
Gordon
Hays
Smith
Hoke
Jones'
Bttn.

Route of Charlottesville Artillery
July 1st

Collapsing
Federal Line
July 1

Unfinished R.R.

Toll
Gate

Raine's
20 lbr
Parrotts

JOHNSON'S
DIVISION
July 2nd

GETTYSBURG

FEDERAL LINE

Andrew's
(Latimer)
Bttn.

Gettysburg
The Charlottesville
and Lee Batteries
July 1 and 2
Respectively

Young Major Latimer, in command of the battalion since Andrews' wounding at Winchester, took the night to examine the terrain in his front for best fields of fire. The most eligible site was on Benner's Hill. Unfortunately, this ground was clear and terribly vulnerable to return fire. Furthermore, the exposed site was so narrow that the battalion's pieces "had to be crowded. . ." rather than spaced as normally desired.

With Latimer's decision made, the battalion remained poised for the proper moment on the following day. At 4 p.m., the order was delivered and the guns driven to the top and unlimbered. From right to left the batteries stood Brown's, Carpenter's, Dement's, and a section of Raine's. The other section of Raine's, 20-pounders, were in position with Captain Graham's battery somewhat to the rear of Benner's Hill near a Toll Gate. As soon as the Confederate batteries opened, the enemy guns under Colonel Charles S. Wainwright replied with well-directed fire from a superior number of pieces. Wainwright commented that the fire from the Southern guns was equally well directed and "was the most accurate I have ever seen on the part of their guns." The fire intensified and after two hours, Latimer sent word to General Johnson of his deteriorating situation. Johnson approved the withdrawal of all but four pieces to remain in anticipation of a Confederate advance.

The batteries rumbled off the eminence as Latimer stood firm with his remaining artillerists. Riding back and forth among the guns the "Boy Major" cheered on his men with every shot. To end the glory of his finest hour, a shell burst nearby and sent fragments through the rider and his mount. Latimer was struck in his right arm, shattering it, and was thrown to the ground. Calling upon Raine to withdraw the rest of the guns, Ewell's artillerist held up the mangled stump of an arm and continued to prod his men to avenge his loss as he was carried from the field. Those would be the last orders young Latimer would give in battle, as he expired one month later near Harrisonburg.

Raine's battery suffered less than the others, losing on Benner's Hill one severely wounded, several others slightly, but not enough to keep them from duty, and three horses killed. Lieutenant Statham, at the twenty-pounders, suffered three men severely wounded and the axle-tree of the number one gun damaged by a solid shot. The horses for Statham's crews were held safely in the rear. Those most severely wounded were Patrick Costello, Jr., with a gunshot wound to the shoulder and head (he later was captured and died August 8); William Kinlock with a gunshot wound to his right arm near the wrist, shattering bones, and his face badly burnt (captured and arm amputated, but paroled and returned home in the fall); and William E. Walker wounded in both legs (captured and exchanged in the fall).

The battalion remained out of action the next day, even though being sent forward late in the afternoon. On July 5, Raine led the battalion behind Johnson's division along the long road home, regretfully leaving three of his most severely wounded behind. Crossing the Potomac at Falling Waters on July 14, the battalion went into bivouac at Darkesville for two days before countermarching with the division to Martinsburg. Ordered to destroy a section of the Baltimore and Ohio, the artillerists looked on as the infantrymen completed the task.

The month of August was spent restfully by the men of the Lee Battery in a peaceful bivouac below Liberty Mills, having to contend with nothing more than a passing thunderstorm. In early September the campsite was moved into Orange County. Captain Raine took leave and left Lieutenant Statham in charge on August 21.

On October 9 the battalion broke its camp near Morton's Ford and marched via Orange Court House, crossing the river at Munson's Ford, and went into camp that night on the county line between Madison and Culpeper. The following morning, Andrews's guns joined with Johnson's division and moved with it until it reached Auburn, near Catlett's Station, on the morning of October 14. The long-range guns were ordered up. Lieutenants Hardwicke and Early with one section were placed on the left of the road. Six other guns of the battalion came up also. So did Lieutenant Statham's two twenty-pounders. They fired against batteries commanding a hill on the left of Auburn. The duel lasted approximately an hour before the Federals were forced from the field. The only casualty sustained by the Lynchburg battery was Alexander East, who suffered a painful "but not serious" wound.

Remaining in the rear of the division, the battalion followed Johnson's men through Bristoe Station, Brandy Station (there detaching from the division), and across the Rapidan at Rapidan Station by way of Slaughter Mountain. By November 9, the battalion was back at its old campsites at Morton's Ford.

In October several of the men attempted a mutiny for some unknown reason. Only two were arrested and charged in late October or early November — Richard Shepherd and Lewellyn Wooldridge.

On November 27, the Lee Battery roused early and hitched their horses to move again with the battalion, under orders to join Johnson's division near Hume's Shop. Once the connection was made, the battalion pressed on toward Locust Grove by way of Bartlett's Mill. Through the thick forest the batteries marched behind the Stonewall Brigade. At about noon, after passing the intersection of the Raccoon and Jacob's Ford roads, the enemy struck the ambulance trains in rear of Johnson's column. As the country was mostly wooded, the battalion pulled to a field to the right of the road until an appropriate position could be found. Though

Carpenter's battery went into action, the others did not, and the battalion moved across Mine Run to a position near Zoar Church, where the men began construction of earthworks.

The Federal forces to Johnson's front did not threaten during the next two days, but just after sunrise on November 30, a Federal battery opened on the Lee Battery position. Returning the fire, Raine's company was soon joined by the Alleghany and Chesapeake Batteries. Within an hour it was all over, but the Lynchburg battery had suffered tremendously. During the duel, the captain from Appomattox took a ball in his hip and fell from his horse into William Stanley's arms; by night he was dead. Raine was just short of being made major and executive officer of the battalion. Samuel Alvis and Fleming Coleman also were killed. Samuel Dunn was fortunate to escape the fight with only a scalp wound. Johnson crossed Mine Run in an effort to capitalize on the victory, but the Federals had fled beyond reach.

With Lieutenant Statham in command, the Lee Battery followed the battalion back to Morton's Ford, and then on to winter quarters at Frederick's Hall.

A Deteriorating Chain of Events
1864

Lieutenant Statham held together his company to the best of his ability in the winter of 1863-64 and was successful to such a degree that none of his men were reported as AWOL or deserters. The peace the Lee Battery enjoyed was interrupted when a force of cavalry under Colonel Ulric Dahlgren approached within sight of Frederick's Hall on the morning of February 28. With the word out of the enemy approach, the Confederate batteries made preparations for a possible attack. Dahlgren veered away from the nervous and awaiting artillerists and a general pursuit of the Yankee cavalry was launched. The Lee Battery left no record of the affair.

On January 31 Lieutenant Colonel Carter M. Braxton, formerly of the Fredericksburg Artillery, took the reins of the battalion with Lynchburg resident Marcellus N. Moorman as his executive officer. Transitions also took place within the Lee Battery while in winter quarters. William W. Hardwicke was elected captain. Feeling denied proper credit for holding the battery in his charge for the past three months, Statham filed his resignation on March 1. In fact, Statham's fate may have related to his being put on court-martial in late January under the charge of conduct unbecoming an officer.

The first of April brought with it orders to abandon the battery's winter home and march to Gordonsville, where the horses of the batteries enjoyed much-needed grazing. A shift in battalion organization took place at the quaint village when the Maryland batteries were taken out and replaced by Raleigh L. Cooper's Stafford Artillery. The armament list of the battalion at the time also indicated that the Lee Battery's two twenty-pounders had been replaced by two ten-pounders.

On May 4 Braxton received orders to move his all-Virginia battalion to Locust Grove, where the Second Corps Artillery would soon be concentrated. Two days later, the battalion left its position at Locust Grove and marched to the extreme right of the Second Corps deep in the Wilderness. Occupying the interval between Rodes's right and A. P. Hill's left, the batteries lined up between the Orange Turnpike and the Orange Plank Road. These guns in the following action, according to General William N. Pendleton, "did well such work as offered, aiding in successfully driving back the enemy whenever and wherever he attempted to advance." There was no record of casualties for the Lynchburg company.

Moving out from the Wilderness, Braxton's battalion moved toward Spotsylvania Court House and settled into the apex of the Muleshoe Salient. The position was a poor one, offering little use for the artillery due to thick woods. On the morning of May 10, Braxton's battalion was relieved by William Nelson's battalion and moved to a reserve battalion in the rear near the courthouse.

On the morning of May 12, severe fighting around the former position in the salient could be heard by those in the rear. Braxton's battalion, among others, held the second line of defense in an effort to stop the enemy onslaught. The casualty rate for the Lee Battery was high and included Reuben Bellomy with a gunshot wound to the right shoulder; Thomas Brooks with a gunshot wound; James Corley with a gunshot wound to the left groin/hip area; Tilghman Marsh wounded for the second time; and William Stanley wounded in the right thigh. Lieutenant Early narrowly escaped a wound when his horse was shot from under him.

Of what transpired between the salient fight at Spotsylvania and May 18 cannot be ascertained. On the latter day, however, Braxton accompanied General Ewell with six guns of "select caliber" and moved to flank the enemy. Finding the roads "impracticable" for artillery movement, the guns were returned to their positions.

On May 21 the battalion was again put in motion as it followed the Second Corps to Hanover Junction, where it arrived on the following day. Hardwicke's battery along with the guns of the Stafford Artillery was placed on the Confederate right near the Doswell House to guard the fords on the North Anna River. The night of May 23 the battalion pulled up stakes and drew westward with General John B. Gordon's division to a position on the Virginia Central Railroad as a support to Mahone's division near the Anderson House.

The Army of Northern Virginia continued its bounds and recoils southward for the following days in an effort to meet each of Ulysses S. Grant's attempts to find a weak spot in the Confederate line. The Second Corps Artillery in turn followed along the road to Richmond through Pole Green Church and finally settled in at the William Gaines Farm on June 9.

Though occupied with the formidable army under Grant, Lee sent out Jubal Early with the Second Corps on June 13 to rid the Shenandoah Valley of a menacing army under David Hunter. Unable to reach Lynchburg in time to aid in the repulse of the Federal force, Braxton's battalion turned northward and reached the infantry at Salem on June 22. Pressing on to Staunton from there, the Second Corps savored a rest from marching for several days.

After a trek down the valley, the Confederate troops reached Winchester on July 2 and began to throw the Union capital into a panic when

100

they crossed the Potomac a few days later. Virtually unopposed, Early's men marched until they finally met a strong Federal force on the east bank of the Monocacy River near the Baltimore and Ohio Railroad junction. Moving in support of Gordon's assaults, the Lee Battery became engaged against the Federal flank and served with "great effect."

Victorious at Monocacy, Early pressed his men on along the Georgetown Pike until coming up in front of Washington, D.C. Though the temptation stood before them, after two days the Confederates pulled out under cover of night back toward Leesburg on July 12, and across the Potomac at Edward's Ferry on July 14.

Back into the Shenandoah Valley two days later, Early gave his men a deserved rest at Strasburg for five days before becoming victorious again when routing the enemy at Kernstown on July 20. As the Second Corps embraced their summer of victory, General Phil Sheridan advanced to put an end to it.

Early withdrew before the oncoming threat to the heights at Fisher's Hill and was successful at warding off the demonstrations of his enemy, eventually pursuing the Federals down the valley and settling in at Bunker Hill on August 19. Hardwicke's artillerists advanced with the battalion in the following days as Early put on his own demonstrations at Shepherdstown before finally falling back to Bunker Hill.

Encamping at Stephenson's Depot until September 17, Braxton's battalion was then sent along with Rodes's and Gordon's divisions in an effort to harass enemy working parties on the Baltimore and Ohio Railroad. Reaching Martinsburg on September 18, the entire force made its way back to Stephenson's Depot by the next morning. Shortly after arriving on that day at about 9 a.m., the Alleghany Artillery unlimbered and commenced firing from its position near the Berryville Road. Shortly after, the remaining guns of the battalion arrived and were placed in support of Rodes's division.

Along with some of the other guns of the battalion, the Lee Battery set up just north of the Hackwood Farm Lane in support of Gordon's division. As the Confederate infantry broke and began to run, the weight of the fight rested upon Braxton's seven pieces. Under the direction of Braxton and the Second Corps Chief of Artillery, Thomas H. Carter, the guns were double-shotted with canister and mowed down the columns that advanced toward them. Successfully driving the Federals from their assault, the cannoneers could take pride in their accomplishment.

As the day progressed, the battalion shifted its position frequently until at 3 p.m., when it came under another heavy assault. This time the opponent was a bold, hard-charging force of cavalry. Almost wrecklessly, the cavalrymen charged head-on toward the cannoneers with their

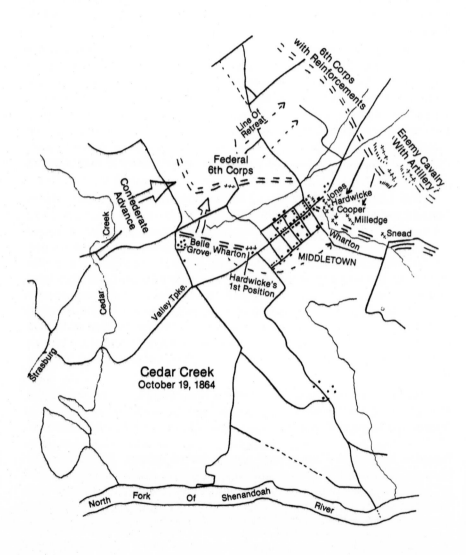

Cedar Creek
October 19, 1864

double-shotted pieces. Blasting holes in the ranks of the horsemen, the artillerists stood in awe to see that this herd of horses and men continued onward, almost undaunted. Firing round after round, the men at the guns finally found themselves overwhelmed as the blue-coats hurdled guns and flew past them in an unending tide. In turn, the Confederate turned the pieces around and loaded again. At the same time, the Union commander called his horsemen to about-face and recharged the guns. Again the Virginians blasted their Yankee foe with canister, and the gallant but torn cavalry ranks rode on and passed the guns back to their original lines.

The day still not ended. The daring cannoneers found themselves in more trouble as Early's lines collapsed late in the afternoon, leaving the guns as the forefront of the defense. Hitched to drag ropes from the limbers to the trails of the pieces, the cannons were carefully removed to follow the failing infantrymen. Defiantly, however, Early's artillerists held the lines they formed long enough that the infantry could be reformed and brought up to align on the pieces. Gallant resistance proved futile, however, and at 5 p.m. the last line broke, leaving Early to withdraw his corps to Newtown.

The Lee Battery took an appaling number of casualties: Henry Sprouts was killed; 2nd Lieutenant William Hughes took a wound and had his horse shot from under him; Craig Callahill received a gunshot wound to the right hand; Alexander C. Day took a round ball in his abdomen, perforating his intestines, and was captured; Louis Going received a similar wound but the ball also reached his pancreas and he died two days later in enemy hands; James McCormick was wounded, but the degree was not indicated; William Worley took a gunshot wound in the hip and through the ilium to the bladder, of which he died on September 28; James A. Sheffield was wounded severely and captured; a minie hit Andrew J. Wood in the knee, but was "uninjured" when captured; and William Kinlock was captured.

Retiring to the works on Fisher's Hill, Early's forces set about strengthening their positions while the Confederate artillery engaged in occasional duels with enemy guns below. At about 4 p.m. on September 22, Sheridan came at Early again and commenced to roll up the Confederate left flank. Following a strong frontal attack, Braxton's cannoneers attempted to save themselves this time, but lost most of their ordnance and wagons. In this engagement Hardwicke's company had four men and two guns captured. The following day the captain recorded one more captured and William Eades wounded by a gunshot to the right forearm.

Early's once-victorious corps now retreated post-haste up the valley through New Market and on to Brown's Gap on September 25. The Lee

Battery, with two cannon remaining, engaged enemy cavalry on the 27th near Weyer's Cave and forced their withdrawal after two hours of fighting. By the end of the month the battalion only totaled twelve officers, two-hundred-and-ten enlisted men, two ten-pounders, and four iron Napoleons.

On October 1 the Second Corps moved out across the Valley to Mt. Sidney, before marching back to New Market five days later. Almost tempting more disaster, Early moved his forces back to Fisher's Hill on October 12.

Setting his sights on a surprise attack on the enemy, Early began to position his forces on the night of October 18. The following morning went spectacularly well. Gordon's and Kershaw's divisions slammed into the unsuspecting Yankees, while a full complement of eighteen to twenty Confederate cannon pounded the elevated position of General George Getty's division. At around noon, Colonel Thomas H. Carter placed his cannon on the northern edge of Middleton in support of the infantry. As the afternoon progressed matters deteriorated as the Confederate left began to fall apart. The right, where Braxton was positioned, stood firm against assailing cavalry. Early saw an impending disaster and ordered the right to fall back.

Bringing off the artillery was not as easy as anticipated. With their path closed by a blocked bridge at Spangler's Mill below Strasburg, the retreating column was brought to a halt. Immediately the Federal cavalry began to take advantage of the opportunity and descended upon an assortment of wagons and limbered batteries. Though the Lee Battery had fired as they fell back, the enemy cavalry charged and captured their remaining two guns and caissons. The battery also lost nine captured, William Wright killed, and James Watkins wounded.

Once more at the haven of New Market, Early rested his shattered army for several days. Though Old Jube would move down the Valley once more on November 10 to confront the Federals at Winchester, the Lee Battery remained unengaged. When Hardwicke's battery obtained two more Napoleons is uncertain; however, the worn and tired company of survivors remained with the Second Corps as it made its way back to New Market and then on December 16th to Staunton and five miles east to Fishersville, into winter quarters.

The inspection reports for the battalion at the end of the year showed the men and batteries in pitiful condition due to poor clothing, and hardly enough men to man the six guns that remained.

Merciful Peace
1865

The new year brought nothing for the Lynchburg men or the men of the battalion to celebrate. The Valley was ruined, there country was on the decline, and their battalion had been reduced to two guns. To worsen matters, the enemy posed a never-ending threat to the remnants of the Second Corps.

The Lee Battery left scant information about their role hereafter. Whether they participated in the defense of Waynesboro on March 2 cannot be determined; however, the company did accompany Colonel Carter to Petersburg and into Drewry's Bluff in mid-March. Through the strong efforts of Braxton, the old battalion attempted a refit, but met with considerable problems. The batteries of Crispin Dickenson and David Walker turned over their guns, equippage, and horses to Braxton sometime late in the month, whereupon the battalion moved to Burgess's Mill. It cannot be ascertained if the Lynchburg battery participated again in the battle that took place on April 1 at Five Forks, though it appears possible. Lieutenant Early, having detached to the Alleghany Battery, served at the engagement and was killed.

It appears also that the Lee Battery was involved in the engagement at Petersburg on the day of Grant's huge offensive of April 2 and lost nine captured.

Seven days later, near the grave of Captain Raine, thirteen of the Lynchburg cannoneers surrendered along with the Army of Northern Virginia, including Captain Hardwicke, Lieutenant William Hughes, Levi Armsworthy, James Brooks, Thomas Brooks, Callahill Craig, William Eades, Beverly Eames, John Gilliam, John L. Green, Frank Milstead, Richard Shepherd, William Sprouts, Henry T. Walker, and William Walker. In an effort to save the remnants of their beloved guidon, Captain Hardwicke wrapped the flag (of "superior quality bunting" and with not less than "twenty-seven bullet holes" in it) around his body and "buttoned his coat closely over it." Upon returning to Lynchburg, the captain presented the flag to Miss M. L. Latham, "daughter of. . .Dr. Henry Latham (and later wife of Mr. O. T. Mingea). . .as a valuable momento of the stormy period in which it figured."

The Murder of Lieutenant Massey

In June 1864, Fayetteville, Tennessee was under occupation by Federal soldiers under the command of General Payne. In an effort to shake out some of the local marauding bushwhackers, orders were issued to apprehend and execute three suspects: William Pickett, F. Burrough and a man named Massey.

In the search that followed, the Federals first went to the home of Thomas Massey, the older brother of the lieutenant. In the process of arresting the younger Massey, John was alerted by the screams and cries of Thomas' wife and children and he quickly appeared on the scene. After inquiring as to why the soldiers were seizing his brother, John replied, "My name is Massey, and if you want a man by the name of Massey, arrest me." In turn, the soldiers inquired if he were a bushwhacker, to which Massey stated, "No, . . .but I would shoot you from the bushes or anywhere else, if I could." The former lieutenant was then arrested and taken off to join the others in captivity.

The death march which followed, proceeded north up Water Street and past the home of the Webb residence. As the condemned Massey marched by he called out to Mrs. Webb to ask for a drink of water. Mrs. Webb turned to her son Frank and told him to go to the cistern and get the water. By the time he had returned, the column had continued by, but the youth took up a hurried pace to catch up. When he reached Lieutenant Massey, the procession was halted and the men allowed to drink.

After the boy was thanked by Massey for his kindness, the three were placed in line facing the town, "north and near the Female Academy, and a squad of soldiers were placed ten or fifteen feet from them, and facing them." When the men were asked if they wished to pray, only one protested to do so. Following the prayer, Captain Cason, commanding the Federals, asked if anyone wished to make a final statement. Massey was quick to respond when he said, "I fought you as a Confederate soldier, but I am not a bushwhacker neither have I harbored bushwhackers." He then bared his breast and said, "Don't shoot me in the face." Mr. John M. Bright in a 1910 article from the *Fayetteville Observer* stated that next, one of the execution party exclaimed, "Capt. Cason, I can't shoot as brave a man as that." After the man was removed from the squad, another took his place and the order to fire was given.

Though the bodies were not to be removed for several hours, Federal soldiers did not refrain from robbing a gold watch from Massey's body and, upon returning to his home, his violin, piano, and gold buttons from a military coat.

As a closing statement of Massey's courage, Bright wrote, "Massey was a man of pride. When it came to the crucial test, John Massey displayed the magnanimity and bravery of Marshall Ney or Sam Davis. He was murdered an innocent victim, to glut the vengance of a heartless tyrant."

Sometime after the appearance of the article, a rough rock marker was placed at the sight of the execution, two blocks north of the square. It was later removed to the lawn of the Lincoln County Courthouse where it still stands today. The inscription upon it reads simply, "John Massey, William Pickett, F. Burrough. Martyred June 15, 1864. Erected June 15, 1914. U.D.C."

Available Supply Data From the Lee Battery

Requisitioned by Captain Raine:
>27 May - 31 May 1864
>For 50 horses - 1600 lbs. corn.

>1 June - 30 June 1864
>For 50 horses - 18,000 lbs. corn and 21,000 lbs. hay

By Lieutenant Statham:
>9/23/62 - 3" Rifle Shell - 150 rounds
>Friction Primers - 200

By Captain Hardwicke:
>10/1/63 - 1 battle flag.

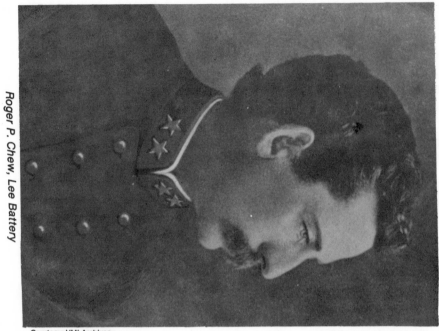

Courtesy: VMI Archives

Courtesy: Eleanor S. Brockenbrough Library, Museum of the Confederacy, Richmond

Pierce Butler Anderson (right, back row). Father is front left.

APPENDIX

Tabulations from the Roster
Commissioned And Noncommissioned Officers
Of The Lee Battery

Anderson, Pierce B., Captain
Raines, Charles I., Captain
Hardwicke, William W., Captain
Massey, John R., 1st Lt.
Statham, Charles W., 1st Lt.
Early, William, 1st Lt.
Hughes, William H., 2nd Lt.
Gaddess, John B., 2nd Lt.
Chew, Roger P., Lt. (Temporary)
Hughes, James., 2nd Lt. (Postwar Ref)
East, William C., Sgt. Major
Turpin, William R., 1st Sgt.
Franklin, Thomas P., 1st Sgt.
Milstead, Frank D., Jr., 1st Sgt.
Broyles, William H., 1st Sgt.
Fletcher, Lucien, 2nd Sgt.
Turner, Wythe R., 2nd Sgt.
Fisher, Alban T., 2nd Sgt.
Moodie, Robert P., 2nd Sgt.

East, Alexander L., 3rd Sgt.
Eades, William H., 3rd Sgt.
Johnson, William L., 4th Sgt.
Adams, Lynch, Sgt.
Wood, Thomas J., Sgt.
Branson, John T., 1st Cpl.
Sheppard, Joseph B., 4th Cpl.
Mosby, Henry B., 4th Cpl.
Goolsby, Joshua, 7th Cpl.
Broyles, Samuel A., 8th Cpl.
North, John Q. A., Cpl.
Goolsby, Alexander, Cpl.
Green, John L., Cpl.
Grubbs, Richard M., Cpl.
Watkins, James L., Cpl.
Mitchell, William H., Buglar
Raine, Charles J., Guidon
Rule, Peter H., Blacksmith
Ransome, James M., Artificier

Statistical Summary of Strengths and Losses

220 On Roster
35 Postwar References
185 Actually Enrolled in Battery

Killed In Action	10	5%
Wounded in Action	30	16%
WIA W/NFR	3	2%
Captured At Least Once	48	26%
Captured Twice	4	2%
Died Of Diseases	9	5%
Died Of Diseases While POW	2	1%
Died Of Wounds	2	1%
Died Of Wounds As POW	4	2%
Deserted	12	6%
AWOL With NFR	8	4%

Under Arrest At Least Once	13	7%
Apprehended Deserters	1	1%
Total War Dead	27	15%
Sick At Least Once	61	33%
AWOL At Least Once	27	15%
Member Illegally (of another)	1	1%
Retired, Resigned, Discharged	12	6%
Permanently Detached/Detailed	6	3%
Sent to CS Military Prison	3	2%
Furloughed and NFR	2	1%
Exchanged And Served Again	20	11%
Did Not Return After Exchange	7	4%
NFR After POW	5	3%
Appomattox Parolees	14	8%
Received Paroles Elsewhere	59	32%
NFR	20	11%

Summary of Battery Strength (End Of Month)
As Extracted From The Information Provided In The Roster, Including Temporary Absences Due To Sickness And Wounds

5/61-99	1/62-34	1/63-73	1/64-94	1/65-62
6/61-102	2/62-62	2/63-88	2/64-102	2/65-62
7/61-80	3/62-77	3/63-86	3/64-101	3/65-62
8/61-67	4/62-78	4/63-88	4/64-100	4/65-53
9/61-63	5/62-78	5/63-86	5/64-93	(14 at App)
10/61-64	6/62-76	6/63-85	6/64-92	
11/61-63	7/62-93	7/63-82	7/64-89	
12/61-54	8/62-87	8/63-90	8/64-88	
	9/62-82	9/63-91	9/64-71	
	10/62-81	10/63-90	10/64-63	
	11/62-80	11/63-91	11/64-61	
	12/62-76	12/63-93	12/64-62	

Occupations at Enlistment

Tobacconist	6
Laborer	6
Shoemaker	3
Student	2
Carpenter	2

Clerk, Farmer, Merchant, Merchant Clerk, Painter, Printer, Salesman - one each

Occupations at Enlistment

Tobacconist	6
Laborer	6
Shoemaker	3
Student	2
Carpenter	2

Clerk, Farmer, Merchant, Merchant Clerk, Painter, Printer, Salesman - one each

Ages At Enlistment
(Ninety-Two Available)

15 - 1 (W. H. Stanley, Jr.)	32 - 2
16 - 1	33 - 1
18 - 7	34 - 1
19 - 5	35 - 3
20 - 4	36 - 2
21 - 4	37 - 1
22 - 8	38 - 2
23 - 5	39 - 3
24 - 4	41 - 2
25 - 4	42 - 1
26 - 2	45 - 1
27 - 4	50 - 2
28 - 6	55 - 1
29 - 1	57 - 1 (Anderson)
30 - 7	60 - 1 (James Roche)
31 - 4	

Percentage in teens - 15%
Percentage 20-29 - 46%
Percentage 30-39 - 28%
Percentage 40 + - 11%

Residence at Enlistment
or
Counties of Birth If the Former
Is Unavailable

Appomattox Co.	3	Jefferson Co.	1
Albemarle Co.	2	Prince Edward Co.	1
Amherst Co.	9	Rockbridge Co.	1
Buckingham Co.	1	Washington, D.C.	1
Campbell Co.	25 +	Baltimore	1
Charles Co.	1	Ireland	5
Fluvanna Co.	1	England	1
Hanover Co.	1		

The Cannons

Types	Caliber	Lgnth of Tube	Wt. of Tube	Wt. of projectile
6 lbr.	3.67	60"	884	6.10
12 lbr.	4.62	66"	1227	12.30
10 lbr. Nap	3.00	74"	899	9.5
3" Ord. Rif.	3.00	69"	820	9.5
20 lbr.	3.67	84"	1750	20.0

The Lee Battery

ADAMS, LYNCH: Pvt., 3rd Cpl., Sgt. Enl. 5/28/61, age 41. Cpl. from 6/7-7/11/61, then Pvt. 12/21/61, 3rd Cpl. Present through 12/31/63, (sick 10/31). Received clothing 1/12/64 and 3/14/64. On hospital muster at G.H. #2, Lynchburg, attached at nurse 8/5/64. Returned to duty 10/64. Sgt. in 1864. NFR. Paroled 4/13/65. D. 1878.

ADKINS, JOHN: Pvt. Enl. 7/29/62, Lynchburg. Admitted to Chimbo. #2 with injury to ankle. Transferred to Chimbo. #1, 12/16/62. Transferred to Farmville G.H., ward #14, 12/21/62. Returned to duty 1/3/63. Transferred to Co. A, 11th Va. Inf. Per S.O. #78/4, 3/19/63.

ALMAN, REUBEN R.: Pvt. Enl. 7/22/64, Lexington. Captured at Petersburg 4/2/65. Sent to Ft. Delaware where he was received 4/4/65. Released 6/19/65, signed by "X"; resident of Rockbridge Co., fair complexion, dark hair and eyes, 5'9½".

ALVIS, SAMUEL H.: Pvt. Bn. Campbell Co. Enl. 5/28/61, age 22. Present through 10/63. KIA during Battle of Payne's Farm and operations on Mine Run, 11/27 or 11/28/63. Claim made for by father, John, 8/23/64.

ANDERSON, PIERCE BUTLER: Captain. Bn. 1804 in Jefferson Co., Tn., the fourth son of Judge (and later senator from Tennessee) Joseph Anderson and Only Patience Outlaw (daughter of Col. Alexander and Penelope Smith Outlaw. Patience was bn. 3/1/1777, N.C. Married 10/4/1791. D. 9/19/64, Forsythe, Ga.) Pierce married Anna Madison Luke in 1824, near Lewisburg, Ky. Entered U.S.M.A. 7/1/23, age 17, 10 months. Stood #1 in class in first year, #4 in second year. Resigned before third year 12/31/25. Supposibly acted as drillmaster for Robert E. Lee and Joseph E. Johnston. He was said to have been "of elegant appearance and manner." Lived several years after the academy in the "Bend of Chucky" in East Tennessee. He was a lawyer and member of the Tennessee Legislature from Athens. Later professor of mathematics at Franklin College. Served in the Mexican War 1847-48 as Captain of Co. B, 2nd Tennessee Infantry. Distinguished service at Chapultepec. Prior to 1850, with the coming of the Nashville and Chattanooga R.R. through Coffee Co., Anderson was one of the surveyors and owners of the Town of Tullahoma (founded in 1851). Acted as an agent to establish the McMinnville and Manchester R.R. Formed Co. B, 1st Regt. (Col. Peter Turney's) Tennessee. In Tullahoma in April 1861, elected Captain. When the regiment was officially mustered into Confederate service, Anderson was made Major. However, when the regt. reached Virginia, Turney was informed he could only have one major instead of the two he had brought with him. Daniel W. Holman was elected to be the major, whereupon Anderson left the regt. and formed an artillery company (The Lee Battery) in Lynchburg, Va. Mustered in 5/28/61, Anderson as Captain. Present 8/61. KIA 12/13/61 at Camp Alleghany. Claim made by his second son Alexander L. Andreson 9/12/62, certificate #364. Found due $480.00 per requisition #1586. Survived by five children, two (Joseph and William) of which served in the Confederate Army; William was killed at Chancellorsville, 5/2/63. Another son, George W., served later in the U.S. House of Representatives.

ARMSWORTHY, LEVI: Pvt. Enl. 7/25/62, Lynchburg. Detailed per S.O. #199/3, 8/26/62. Detailed to QM office by order of the Secretary of War 10/12/62. Detail extended per S.O. #200/10, 8/24/63. Returned to duty 10/1/63. Received clothing allowance 4th qtr./63, 2/6/64, 3/14/64. Detailed extra duty as driver for the bttn., 12/31/64. Paroled at Appomattox.

BAILEY, EDMUND J.: Pvt. Enl. 7/7/61, Lynchburg; age 36. Present through 2/28/63 (sick in camp). Sent to Staunton G.H. with dropsy 3/10/63. "Improving very slowly" 4/7/63. Entry cancelled. Died by 10/31/63.

BANTON, GEORGE WASHINGTON: Pvt. Enl. 4/11/63. Clothing receipt for 12/22/63 and 2/20/64. Captured at Fisher's Hill 9/22/64. Sent to Pt. Lookout 9/30/64, in Camp Hospital. Received from Harper's Ferry 10/3/64. Exchanged 2/10/65. Admitted to Chimbo. #2 with pneumonia 2/15/65. Furloughed for 60 days, 2/22/65.

BANTON, WILLIAM H.: Pvt. Enl. 8/15/63, Lynchburg. Clothing receipt for 1st qtr./64, 2/20/64. Died at Mt. Jackson Hospital with typhoid fever, 9/9/64. Effects turned over to the QM Dept. Certificate #6961 ($6.91) received 12/20/64, certificate #2584.

BATEMAN, SAMUEL "SAM": Pvt. Ben. 4/15/41. Enl. 6/7/61, Lynchburg. Sick in camp with measles 8/31/61. In hospital with same through 2/28/62. MIA Sharpsburg 9/17/62 (dated 2/28/63). D. 11/10/14, buried in Presbyterian Cemetery, Lynchburg, Range N, Lot 36.

BELLOMY, REUBEN WHITTLE: Pvt. Bn. 11/16/14. M. 1) Frances Carver 6/27/43 in Albemarle Co. M. 2) Sarah Jane Stephens 5/2/61. Enl. 12/17/63. Clothing receipt for 2/20/62, 9/15/64. Wounded by gsw to right shoulder 5/12/64. Admitted to Chimbo. #3, 5/15/64; Chimbo. #9 5/16; Charlottesville G.H. 5/17/64. Returned to duty 9/16/64. Captured 4/2/65 at Petersburg. Sent to Ft. Delaware where he was received 4/4/65. Released 6/19/65; residence: Albemarle Co., ruddy complexion, brown hair, grey eyes, 5'9". Amnesty certificate dated 6/10/65. D. 4/12/89.

BORDEN, ANDREW S.: Postwar reference.

BOWMAN, JOHN JAMES: Postwar reference. Bn. 6/1/39, Winchester, Pennsylvania. D. Lynchburg, 5/20/07. Buried in the Presbyterian Cemetery, Range K, Lot 4.

BOWMAN, JOHN M.: Pvt. Occupation: tobacconist. Enl. 6/7/61, Lynchburg; age 22 clothing receipt for 12/24/63, 4th qtr./64. Present until captured 10/19/64. Arrived from Harper's Ferry to Pt. Lookout 10/25. Released on oath 5/12/65; residence: Lynchburg.

BRANSON, HEZEKIAH: Pvt. Bn. Campbell Co. Enl. 2/9/63. Clothing receipt for 11/21/63, 4th qtr./63, 2/6/64. D. at Warrenton or Gordonsville Hospital of smallpox, 3/23/64. Effects received 4/6/64, certificate #827, and 4/7/64 cert. #630.

BRANSON, JACKSON: Postwar reference.

BRANSON, JOHN T.: Pvt., 1st Cpl., Pvt. Enl. 6/6/61, Lynchburg; age 28. 2nd Cpl. 12/31/61. 1st Cpl. 2/28/63. Clothing receipt for 4th qtr./63, and 2/6/64. Pvt. 12/31/64. Captured 4/2/65, Petersburg. Sent to Ft. Delaware where received on 4/4/65. Released 6/19/65; residence: Campbell Co., dark complexion, brown hair, blue eyes, 5'10". Received 1900 pension, Amherst Co.

BROOKS, GEORGE WASHINGTON: Pvt. Bn. Lynchburg. Enl. 6/7/61, Lynchburg, age 43. Present through 8/61. D. at Lynchburg Hospital 12/7/61. Deceased claim dated 2/17/62, certificate #407, due $96.65 to widow, Henrietta Brooks.

BROOKS, JAMES: Pvt. Bn. Campbell Co. Occupation: laborer. Enl. 5/28/61, age 25 or 33. Captured 7/11/61. Paroled and then later discharged by order of General Winder, 8/29/61. 5'7", dark complexion, brown hair, blue eyes. Reenl. 6/1/63. Present 10/63 and 12/64. Clothes issued 12/12/63, 2/22/64. Paroled at Appomattox and again at Lynchburg 4/14/65. Amherst Co. Pensioner 1900.

BROOKS, JAMES M.: Pvt. Bn. Campbell Co. Occupation: Laborer. Enl. 5/28/61, age 27. Captured 7/11/61. Paroled and later discharged by General Winder 9/3/61. 6', light complexion, dark hair, grey eyes. Reenl. 2/14/63. Present sick (10/31). Present 12/64. Clothes issued 12/24/63, 1/30/64. Paroled at Lynchburg 4/14/65.

BROOKS, LINDSEY THOMAS: Pvt. Enl. 3/3/62, Lynchburg. At Chimbo. #25 10/20/62. Wounded at Fredericksburg? at Chimbo. #20, 1/9/63. At home 2/28/63. Present 10/31/63. Clothes issued 4th qtr. 1863, 11/21/63, 2/12/64. Admitted to Chimbo. #9, 5/15/64. NFR.

BROOKS, THOMAS S.: Pvt. Bn. Campbell Co. Occupation: tobacconist. Enl. 5/28/61, age 38; noted as AWOL 6/7/61. Captured 7/11/61. Paroled and later discharged by General Winder 8/22/61. 5'10", dark complexion, black hair and eyes. Reenl. 2/14/63. At Chimbo. #20, 1/10/63. Present 2/63, 10/63. Clothes issued 4th qtr./63, 2/6/64, 3/14/64. At Chimbo. #3 with gsw, 5/15/64. To Charlottesville G.H. 5/22/64. Clothes issued 11/21/64. Present 12/64. At Chimbo. #20 with "bubo sump" 3/13/65. Paroled at Appomattox and later again at Lynchburg, 4/13/65.

BROOKS, WILLIAM: Pvt. Enl. 3/7/62. Present 2/63. D. 7/19/63 at Darksville, Va.

BROYLES, SAMUEL A.: Pvt., 8th Cpl. Enl. 5/28/61, age 25. Sick in Lynchburg with rheumatism, 8/61. Present 12/31/61. Sick at Lynchburg hospital 2/28/62. Present 2/28/63, 10/63 (cpl.). Clothes issued 4th qtr./63, 11/21/63, 2/20/64. Present 12/64. Paroled at Lynchburg as Cpl.

BROYLES, WILLIAM H.: Pvt., 5th Cpl., 1st Sgt.? Occupation: Tobacconist. Enl. 5/28/61, age 30. Captured 7/11/61. Paroled and discharged by order of General Winder, 9/3/61. Native of Appomattox Co., 5'9½", light complexion and hair, blue eyes. Reenl. 2/14/63. Present 10/63, 12/64. Clothes issued 4th qtr./63, 2/19 and 24/64. Paroled at Lynchburg 4/65. D. 12/3/09, age 78. Buried at Presbyterian Cemetery, Lynchburg, Range M, Lot 27.

BURHAM, JAMES: Pvt. Enl. 8/4/62. Deserted at Lynchburg 8/17/62. Substitute for James C. Wilson.

CALDWELL, ARCHER: Postwar reference.

CALDWELL, EDWARD: Pvt. Enl. 8/18/63. Clothes issued 4th qtr./63. Present 10/63, 12/64. Paroled 5/27/65 at Campbell C.H.

CAMPBELL, JOHN: Pvt. Enl. 8/12/62, Lynchburg. Deserted at Lynchburg. Substitute for Tazewell M. McCork.

CHEW, ROGER PRESTON: Temporarily attached acting Lt. Bn. 4/9/43, Loudoun Co., son of Roger and Sarah West Airidge Chew of Jefferson Co., Va. (W.Va.). Paternal G. P.: John and Margaret Chew. Maternal G.P.: John Aldridge and Harriet West. Attended VMI, matriculating on 7/30/59 from Kabletown, Jefferson Co., Va. Class declared graduated 12/12/61, standing 8th of 35. Drillmaster in Richmond 4/61. Temporarily assigned to Lee Battery at Monterey 7/15/61 - 9/61. Commanded battery of horse artillery under General Turner Ashby, considered "Ashby's pet." Later Lt. Colonel commanding horse artillery of the A.N.V. Paroled 5/3/65 at Greensboro, N.C. M. Louisa Fontaine Washington (1844-1927) 8/15/71. Three children. Postwar farmer; and into real estate and insurance business. D. 3/16/21. Charlestown, W.Va.

CHILDRESS, ANDREW JACKSON: Pvt. Enl. 8/15/63, Lynchburg. Present 10/63. Present under arrest 12/31/64. Clothing issued 4th qtr./63, 11/21/63, 2/22/64. Paroled at Lynchburg 4/13/65.

COFFEE, THOMAS: Pvt. Enl. 5/28/61, age 30. Present through 2/62. Admitted to Charlottesville G.H. 6/17/62 with gsw. D. 6/18/62 of jaundice and erysipelas.

COLEMAN, FLEMING: Pvt. Enl. 8/15/63, Lynchburg. KIA, on list of casualties of the Battle at Payne's Farm and Mine Run operations 11/27 and 28/63.

COLEMAN, GEORGE T.: Pvt. Enl. 8/15/63, Lynchburg. At hospital 10/31/63. Present 12/31/64. Clothing issued 12/12/63, 4th qtr./63, 2/22/64. Paroled at Lynchburg 4/13/65.

COLEMAN, SINGLETON: Postwar reference.

CORLEY, JAMES D.: Pvt. Enl. 2/9/64, Louisa Co. Wounded by gsw left groin/hip 5/12/64. Sent to Chimbo. #5, admitted 5/16/64. D. 7/17/64. Left no effects. Register of effects of deceased soldiers #6635.

COSTELLO, PATRICK SR.: Pvt. Enl. 8/62, Lynchburg. Deserted near Rappahannock 8/26/62. Substitute for David C. Shanks.

COSTELLO, PATRICK JR.: Pvt. Enl. 5/28/61, age 23. Present through 2/63. Wounded by gsw to shoulder and head at Gettysburg. Captured and taken to DeCamp G.H., David's Island, N.Y. 7/23/63. D. 8/16/63. Effects received 9/17/63, certificate #2189.

COX, JAMES M.: Pvt. Enl. 9/1/63, Lynchburg. Present 10/31/63. Issued clothes 4th qtr./63. Detailed as Battalion Courier (12/31/64). NFR.

COX, JOHN M.: Postwar reference. Amherst Co. Pensioner 1902.

CRADDOCK, DAVID J.: Pvt. Enl. 7/28/62, Lynchburg. AWOL 8/17/62. Substitute for Samuel B. Hunt.

CRAIG, CALLAHILL: Pvt. Enl. 3/18/62, Lynchburg. Present 2/63 and 10/63. Wounded by gsw to right hand 9/19/64, Winchester. Admitted to Lynchburg G.H. Admitted to Charlottesville G.H. 9/23. Transferred back to Lynchburg 9/28. Absent 12/64. Clothes issued 1/12/64, 2/22/64, and 3/14/64. Paroled at Appomattox.

CREASEY, JAMES B.: Pvt. Bn. in Amherst Co. Occupation: Shoemaker. Enl. 5/28/61, age 31. Captured 7/11/61. Paroled and later discharged by order of General Winder, 9/3/61, or 8/29/61, or 2/62. Age 20, 5'10", light complexion, auburn hair, black eyes.

CURREN, AMOS: Occupation: tobacconist. Enl. 5/28/61, age 18. Captured 7/11/61. Paroled and later discharged 10/3/61. Native of Albemarle Co., 5', light complexion and hair, blue eyes. Reenl. 8/1/63. Clothes issued 11/21/63, 4th qtr./63, 12/24/63, 2/6/64. Captured 10/19/64, Cedar Creek. Sent to Harper's Ferry and then to Pt. Lookout 10/23/64. Exchanged 3/28/65.

CURREN, WARREN: Pvt. Native of Fluvanna Co. Occupation: laborer. Enl. 5/28/61, age 28. Captured 7/11/61. Paroled and later discharged 9/3/61. 6', light complexion, dark hair, blue eyes. Reenl. 2/14/63. On extra duty as teamster (10/31/63). Clothes issued 11/21/63, 4th qtr./63, 12/24/63, 2/22/64. Captured 10/19/64, Cedar Creek. Sent to Harpers Ferry and then on to Pt. Lookout where arrived 10/25. NFR.

DANIEL, JAMES H.: Pvt. Enl. 2/25/64, Frederick's Hall, Louisa Co. Captured 10/19/64, Cedar Creek. From Harpers Ferry to Pt. Lookout where arrived 10/25/64. Exchanged 2/10/65. Sent to Chimbo. #9 2/14/65. Granted 60 day furlough from 2/22/65. Paroled at Culpeper C.H. 5/27/65.

DARCY, MICHAEL: Pvt. Enl. 5/28/61, age 28. Present until furloughed 2/20/62 for 15 days. NFR.

DAVIDSON, BENJAMIN H.: Pvt. Bn. Campbell Co. Occupation: carpenter. Enl. 5/28/61. Captured 7/11/61. Paroled and later discharged 9/3/61. 5'10", dark complexion, grey eyes, black hair. NFR.

115

DAY, ALEXANDER C.: Pvt. Enl. 5/28/61. Age 21. Present 8/31/61. AWOL 12/16/61. Apprehended in Lynchburg and in hospital (2/28/62). Present 2/28/63. Wounded by gsw (round ball) to abdomen (perforating intestines) and captured 9/19/64. Treated in U.S. Field Hospital, Winchester; simple dressing and anodymus. Critical as feces passed through both perforations and for 5 weeks from the day of the wound. Transferred and received at Ft. McHenry, Md. from West Buildings of the U.S.G.H., Baltimore, 1/5/64. Transferred to Pt. Lookout for exchange 2/20/65. To Camp Winder Hospital, Richmond, 2/25/65. Paroled at Lynchburg 4/13/65.

DEPRIEST, DANIEL G.: Pvt. Enl. 5/28/61, age 35. 2nd Cpl. 7/11/61. 4th Sgt. 12/21/61. 3rd Sgt. 2/1/62. Sent to Castle Thunder 6/7/63, dated 10/31/63. NFR.

DEPRIEST, WILLIAM: Postwar reference.

DONIVAN, WILLIAM: Postwar reference.

DUNN, SAMUEL H.: Pvt. Resident of Buckingham Co. Occupation: farmer. Enl. 5/28/61, age 25. Sick at Staunton G.H. (8/31/61). AWOL since 12/17/61. Present 2/28/62. Wounded at Battle of Payne's Farm and operations at Mine Run, 11/27-28/63. Shell wound of scalp; admitted to Chimbo. #4, 12/3/63; Chimbo. #9, 12/4/63, furloughed for 30 days, 12/18/63. Clothes issued 4th qtr./63, 2/20/64. Returned to duty 1/64. Captured 9/23/64, Fisher's Hill. Sent to Harper's Ferry and then to Pt. Lookout 10/1/64. Released by oath 5/13/65, G.O. #85. Entered Lee Camp Soldier's Home 12/4/08, age 72. D. 11/8/16. Buried in Hollywood Cemetery, Richmond.

DUNNIGAN, WILLIAM: Pvt. Enl. 5/28/61, age 34. AWOL 12/12/61 apprehended and placed in Lynchburg G.H. (2/28/62). Detailed as guard at G.H. (10/31/63-12/31/64) by order of Genera. Lee. Absent in quarters and furloughed for 60 days 12/8/63. Patient 2/11/64, haemoplegia. NFR.

EADES, GEORGE W.: Pvt., Bttn. Butcher. Enl. 5/28/61, age 24. Present until AWOL 12/16/61. Present 2/28/63. Detailed as Bttn. Butcher (10/31/63). Clothes issued 12/24/63. AWOL 11/25/64. Deserter. NFR.

EADES, JOE: Postwar reference.

EADES, SAMUEL: Postwar reference.

EADES, THOMAS H.: Pvt. Enl. 5/28/61, age 24. Present throughout until paroled at Lynchburg 4/13/65. Clothing issued 11/21/63.

EADES, WILLIAM H.: Pvt., 3rd Sgt. Enl. 5/28/61, age 23. Present until wounded slightly in the head at Hamilton's Crossing 5/3/63. Under arrest as 4th Sgt. (10/31/63). CM for neglect of duty under G.O. #105-1, 12/7/63. Per S.O. #23/12 subject will report to duty. Clothes issued 4th qtr./63. GSW to right forearm 9/23/64, sent to Charlottesville G.H. Furloughed for 40 days 9/28/64. Present as Sgt. 12/31/64. Paroled at Appomattox with private horse.

EAMES, BEVERLY: Pvt. Enl. 5/28/61, age 33. Sick at Lynchburg G.H. (12/31/61) and still (2/28/62). Present 2/28/63. Clothes issued 11/21/63, 12/24/63. Captured at Fisher's Hill 9/22/64. Apparently paroled and in receipt of more clothing 11/7/64. Paroled at Appomattox.

EARLY, WILLIAM: 2nd Lt., 1st Lt. Bn. 3/13/43. Enl. 8/1/62, 2nd Lt. Horse which he had just come into possession of on 5/10 or 5/11/64 was wounded at Spotsylvania C.H. 5/12/64; died of wounds, received $900 for loss. 1st Lt. 6/8/64. KIA 4/1/65 at Five Forks. Buried at range 11, lot 1, Presbyterian Cemetery, Lynchburg.

EAST, ALEXANDER L.: Pvt., 1st Cpl., 3rd Sgt., Pvt. Enl. 5/28/61, age 31. 1st Cpl. 6/7/61. 3rd Sgt. 7/11/61. 1st Sgt. from 10/31/61-12/20/61, then to Pvt. Wounded 10/63, at Catlett's Station. Admitted to Richmond G.H. #9, 10/19/63. Returned to duty before 12/63. Clothing issued 12/12/63, 1/30/64. Present 12/31/64. Paroled at Lynchburg 4/13/65.

EAST, WILLIAM C.: Pvt., 1st Cpl., 5th Sgt., 2nd Sgt., Sgt. Major. Enl. 5/28/61, age 35. 1st Cpl. 7/11/61. 5th Sgt. 12/21/61. Clothes issued 2/20/64. Captured as Sgt. Major 10/19/64, Cedar Creek. Sent to Harper's Ferry then onto Pt. Lookout 10/23/64. Released 6/11/65; residence: Lynchburg, light complexion, greyish hair, hazel eyes, 5'11".

FALWELL, JOHN M.: Postwar reference. Bn. 1826. D. 11/10/65. Buried range 15, lot 11, Presbyterian Church, Lynchburg.

FARMER, ALONZO W.: Pvt. Enl. 5/28/61, age 21. Under arrest for desertion (2/28/63). CM Per G.O. #57, 4/18/63. Present 10/31/63. Clothes issued 4th qtr./63, 12/24/63, 1/30/64. MIA 7/30/64 near Williamsport, Md. Supposed captured. NFR.

FARMER, BERRY T.: Pvt. Enl. 3/64, Louisa Co. on extra duty as driver in Bttn. Ordinance Dept. (12/31/64). Paroled at Lynchburg 4/14/65.

FARMER, DAVID T.: Pvt. Enl. 6/7/61, Lynchburg. Sick in camp with cold (8/31/61). Teamster for Bttn. (10/31/63). Clothes issued 4th qtr./63, 2/12/64, 2/22/64. Paroled at Lynchburg 4/14/65.

FISHER, ALBAN T.: Pvt., 3rd Cpl., 1st Sgt., Pvt. Enl. 5/28/61, age 28. 3rd Cpl. 7/11/61. 1st Sgt. 12/21/61. Absent on furlough from 2/20/62-3/7/62. Present as Pvt. 2/28/63. Clothing issued 4th qtr./63. Detailed with Lt. Gregory as corps ordinance Sgt. of Artillery -end. paroled at Lynchburg 4/14/65.

FITZGERALD, JOHN H.: Pvt. Enl. 5/28/61. AWOL 6/7/61. NFR.

FLETCHER, LUCIEN: Pvt., 3rd Sgt., 2nd Sgt., Pvt. Enl. 5/28/61, age 37. 3rd Sgt. 6/6/61. 2nd Sgt. 7/11/61. PVt. 12/21/61. Present at Richmond undergoing GCM (12/31/64). Per S.O. #65/1, sentence of GCM was remitted. Clothes issued 4th qtr./63, 2/20/64, 2/22/64. Captured 4/2/65 at Petersburg. Sent to Ft. Delaware from City Point 4/4/65. Released 6/20/65 residence: Amherst Co., dark hair, grey eyes, 5'7".

FLIPPIN, ALBERT: Pvt. Enl. 12/11/63, Lancaster Co.? Clothes issued 2/12/64. Admitted to Charlottesville G.H. with chronic diarrhea. D. 9/6/64. Effects sundries, received 10/1/64, certificate #2033. Register of effects #6499 - $19.50.

FOLTZ, BENJAMIN: Pvt. Enl. 5/28/61, age 19. Present through 2/28/62. NFR.

FRANKLIN, THOMAS POWELL: Pvt., 4th Sgt., 3rd Sgt., 2nd Sgt., 1st Sgt. Enl. 5/28/61, age 30. 4th Sgt. 7/11/61, 3rd Sgt. 12/21/61. 2nd Sgt. 2/1/62. Wounded at Sharpsburg while 1st Sgt. 9/17/62. At home (2/28/63). Still at home, Pvt. (10/31/63). Present on crutches from Sharpsburg wound 12/31/64. NFR. D. 11/11/08.

FREEMAN, JOHN ALFRED or ALFORD: Pvt. Enl. 2/26/64, Louisa Co. Clothes issued 3/14/64. Paroled at Lynchburg 4/15/65. Amherst Co. pensioner 1902.

FREEMAN, WILLIAM T.: Pvt. Enl. 2/26/64, Louisa Co. Paroled at Lynchburg 4/15/65. Amherst Co. Pensioner 1902. D. 8/30/15.

FRIEDHOFF, HARMAN A.: Pvt. Enl. 3/12/62, Lynchburg. CM for violation of the 21st article of war, G.O. #57, 4/18/63. Clothes issued 4th qtr./63, 2/20/64. Paroled at Lynchburg 4/13/65.

116

GADDESS, JOHN B.: 6th Sgt., QM Sgt., 2nd Lt. Enl. 7/10/62, 6th Sgt., QM Sgt. (10/31/63). Clothes issued 4th Qtr./63, 12/12/63. 2nd Lt. when paroled at Lynchburg 4/13/65.

GALVIN, JAMES: Postwar reference.

GALVIN, JOHN: Postwar reference.

GALVIN, SAMUEL: Postwar reference.

GILLIAM, JOHN M.: Pvt. Enl. 5/28/61, age 19. Clothes issued 3rd qtr./63, 2/20/64. Paroled at Appomattox. Amherst Co. pensioner 1888.

GOING or GOWIN, GEORGE: Pvt. Enl. 7/20/62, Lynchburg. Clothes 4th qtr./63, 2/22/64. Captured at Cedar Creek 10/19/64. NFR. Amherst Co. Pensioner 1888.

GOING or GOWIN, LOUIS: Pvt. Enl. 5/28/61, age 18. Wounded 7/11/61. Sick at Lynchburg G.H. (8/31/61). Present 12/31/61. Clothes issued 4th qtr./63, 2/20/64. CM per G.O. #57, violation of 21st Article of War, 4/18/63. Wounded 9/19/64, Winchester. Admitted to U.S.A. Field Hospital Winchester 9/19. GSW to the side and perforating abdomen and pancreas, hernia of pancreas. Simple dressing applied. D. 9/21/64.

GOOLSBY, ALEXANDER: Pvt., Cpl. Enl. 5/28/61, age 18. Clothes issued 4th qtr./63, 12/24/63. Captured 4/2/65, Petersburg. Sent to Ft. Delaware from City Point 4/4/65. Released 6/20/65; residence: Campbell Co., fair complexion, dark hair, brown eyes, 5'5".

GOOLSBY, JOSHUA W.: Pvt., 7th Cpl. Enl. 5/28/61, age 20. 7th Cpl. 10/31/63. Clothes issued 11/21/63, 12/23/63, 1/12/64, 2/6/64, 4th qtr./64.

GOOLSBY, LOUIS: Postwar reference.

GREEN, CHARLES W.: Pvt. Enl. 8/21/62, Lynchburg. In bttn. guardhouse under arrest 3/7/64. Violation of G.O. #17-10, disrespectful conduct. As of 12/31/64 "was at Staunton at time of Hunter's Raid undergoing GCM said to have made escape and piloted enemy to Lynchburg, now in Philadelphia, Pa."

GREEN, GEORGE WASHINGTON: Pvt. Enl. 5/28/61, age 16. Left at Camp Alleghany, to home sick (8/31/61). Present 12/31/61. Clothes issued 4th qtr./63, 12/24/63, 1/30/64. Paroled at Lynchburg 4/13/65.

GREEN, JOHN L.: Pvt., Cpl. Enl. 10/1/63. Clothes issued 12/12/63, 1/12/64, 2/22/64. Cpl. 10/1/64. Paroled at Appomattox. D. 9/9/09.

GRUBBS, RICHARD MORRIS: Pvt., Cpl. Bn. 2/26/35, Lynchburg. Enl. 3/3/62, Lynchburg. Clothes issued 5/16/63 (while at Pratt Hospital, Lynchburg), 4th qtr./63. Cpl. 10/1/64. Paroled at Lynchburg 4/13/65. D. 1890, Lynchburg.

GRUBBS, WILLIAM: Postwar reference.

GUNTER, EDMUND P.: Pvt. Enl. 12/11/63. Clothes issued 1/12/64. Paroled at Burkesville Junction, Va. by HQ 9th A.C. Provost Marshal's Office, between 4/14-4/17/65.

HARDWICKE, WILLIAM W.: Pvt., 2nd Lt., 1st Lt., Capt. Enl. 12/21/61. Assigned as 2nd Lt. by Gen. E. Johnson at Camp Alleghany 12/13/61. Absent detached 12/31/61. Again on recruiting duty 2/25/62-2/28/62. Leave taken per S.O. #229/5, 10/25/62. Junior 1st Lt. (2/28/63). Horse KIA 5/12/64, received $800 for horse, $10 for blanket, $30 for bridle. Promoted to Captain by S.O. #104, 6/8/64; to rank from 3/1/64 by virtue of G.O. #43. Paroled at Appomattox.

HARRINGTON, RICHMOND H.: Pvt. Enl. 5/28/61, age 22. Present to 1/30/64 when captured by Provost Marshal Cavalry Corps (rebel deserter). Committed to Old Capital Prison 2/2/64. Released on oath and sent to Philadelphia 3/15/64. Residence: Washington, D.C., light complexion, brown hair, blue eyes, 5'6".

HAW, THOMAS: Pvt. Enl. 5/28/61, age 36. AWOL 12/12/61. Present 2/28/62. Admitted to Charlottesville G.H. with confusio 6/26/62. Deserted near Rappahannock 7/2/62. NFR.

HILL, EDWARD: Pvt. Enl. 8/9/62, substitute for James D. Hawkins. Deserted at Lynchburg 8/17/62.

HUGHES, BENJAMIN W.: Pvt. Enl. 3/3/62. At Winder divisional hospital 10/9/62-11/11/62. Clothes issued 4th qtr./63. Paroled at Lynchburg 4/13/65.

HUGHES, JAMES: 2nd Lt. Postwar reference.

HUGHES, TIMOTHY: Pvt. Enl. 2/28/63. Deserted 6/6/63. Arrested and sent to Castle Thunder. Another reference shows POW at Harrisburg, Pa. Sent to Philadelphia 7/22/63. NFR.

HUGHES, WILLIAM HENRY: 2nd Lt. Bn. 9/9/26, Campbell Co. Elected 2nd Lt. Upon transfer from Shoemaker's Battery 6/11/64. Officially transferred per S.O. #148, 7/29/64. Horse (bay) KIA at Winchester 9/19, received $1,666.66. He was also wounded at same time and sent to Harrisonburg G.H. Paroled at Appomattox. See also, Portsmouth Artillery. D. 11/8/05, Danville, Va.

HYMAN, HENRY A.: Pvt. Enl. 7/25/62. Clothes issued 4th qtr./63. Captured 4/2/65, Petersburg. From City Pt. to Pt. Lookout. Released 6/27/65. Residence: Campbell Co., fair complexion, light hair, blue eyes, 5'8".

JOHNSON, CHARLES S.: Pvt. Enl. 5/28/61, age 26. Sick at Staunton G.H. (8/31/61). Present (12/31/61). Clothes issued 4th qtr./63, 11/21/63. Later on list of rebel deserters, surrendered in Dept. of W.Va. 3/65. Took amnesty and sent north 5/16/65 to Cumberland, Md.

JOHNSON, JOEL: Pvt. Enl. 2/9/63, Lynchburg. At Chimbo. #3 with debilitas 9/23/63. Clothes issued 2/22/64. On extra duty as a driver for the Bttn. (12/31/64). Captured 4/2/65 at Petersburg. From City Pt. to Pt. Lookout. Released 6/21/65; residence: Campbell Co., dark complexion, hair and eyes, 5'5".

JOHNSON, JOSEPH: Postwar reference.

JOHNSON, THOMAS E.: Pvt. Enl. 8/17/62. Deserted and apprehended ($30 paid for arresting him); confined in brigade guardhouse (2/28/63). CM per G.O. #57, 4/18/63. At Chimbo. #3 9/17/63-9/23/63. Present 10/31/63. Clothes issued 3rd qtr./63, 12/24/63. NFR.

JOHNSON, WILLIAM L.: 4th Sgt., Pvt., Cpl., Pvt. Enl. 5/28/61, age 25. 4th Sgt. until 7/11/61. 1st Cpl. 12/21/61. AWOL 8/17/62. Deserter 8/1/62. NFR.

KALLIHER, DENNIS: Pvt. Bn. Ireland. Enl. 5/28/61, age 30. Clothes issued 4th qtr./63, 12/12/63. MIA 7/12/64. Captured near Rockville, Md. 7/12/64. Gave up to some privates of the 6th Corps at Ft. Stevens who took him to General McCook. Sent to Old Capitol Prison and then to Elmira, N.Y. While there he gave a "statement. . .desirous to take oath." Claimed he voted against secession and had only resided in the county for 10 years. D. of pneumonia 12/24/64. Grave #1205.

KELLY, JOHN: Pvt. Enl. 7/29/62, substitute for Abraham P. Lark? Deserted 8/62, Lynchburg. NFR.

KERSEY, EDWARD H.: Pvt. Occupation: shoemaker. Enl. 5/28/61, age 31. Wounded and captured 7/11/61. At hospital in Beverly (8/31/61). Paroled (age 32, residence: Amherst Co., 5'11", dark complexion, black hair, dark eyes) and later discharged 10/9/61. Reenl. 2/14/63. Chimbo. #5 with hemorrhoids 5/25/64. Paroled 4/14/65, Lynchburg.

KERSEY, JAMES: Postwar reference (photo).

KERSEY, WILLIAM A.: Pvt. Enl. 5/28/61, age 30. At Chimbo. #1 with phthesis 11/5/62-4/22/63. Sick at home (2/28/63). Admitted to Chimbo. #1 with acute bronchitis 5/6/63. Transferred to Danville G.H. 6/11/63. Returned to duty 7/1/63. Clothes issued 7/20/63. Detailed as Bttn. teamster (10/31/63). Clothes issued 2/6/64, 2/22/64. Captured 10/19/64 at Cedar Creek. To Harper's Ferry and then to Pt. Lookout. Released 6/14/65; residence: Hanover Co., dark complexion, sandy hair, blue eyes, 6'3".

KINLOCK, WILLIAM: Pvt. Enl. 10/1/61. Sick at Staunton G.H. (8/2/28/62). Present 2/28/63. Severely wounded 7/2/63, Gettysburg. GSW of right arm near wrist shattering bones, and face burnt. Captured 7/3/63. Amputated arm (circular operation, below elbow) in field that day, 3rd flap method. Sent to DeCamp G.H. on David's Island, N.Y. Harbor. Paroled and back on duty by fall of 1863. Clothes issued 4th qtr./63, 12/24/63, 1/30/64, 2/20/64. Assigned to extra duty with the medical dept. Left with wounded at Winchester 9/19/64 and captured. Sent to West Buildings Hospital, Baltimore and then to Ft. McHenry where received 11/19/64. Transferred to Pt. Lookout 1/1/65. Sick and sent to U.S. G.H. Ward 12, noted age as 24, 1/28/65. Released 6/2/65. Entered Lee Camp Soldier's Home 8/12/86, age 47. Apparently deserted from there and went to Maryland Line Soldier's Home in Baltimore in 1894. Dismissed from R. E. Lee Camp Home for breaking arrest 3/27/03.

KIRBY, CHARLES: Pvt. Enl. 6/7/61. Sick in Staunton G.H. (8/31/61). Sick at Lynchburg G.H. (12/31/62), and still as of 2/28/62. NFR.

KNOLL, JOHN: Pvt. Enl. 5/28/61, age 22. Clothes issued 4th qtr./63, 12/12/63, 2/20/64, 2/22/64. Paroled 4/13/65, Lynchburg. NFR.

KOONTZ, JOHN: Pvt. Enl. 12/9/62, Camp Corbin. Clothes issued 4th qtr./63, 11/21/63, 2/20/64. Captured 9/22/64, Fisher's Hill. Sent to Harper's Ferry and then to Pt. Lookout 9/30/64. Joined U.S. Service 10/18/64.

LAMBDEN, JOSEPH: Pvt. Occupation: clerk. Enl. 5/28/61, age 24. Captured 7/11/61. Paroled and discharged 8/7/61; age 24, native of Baltimore Co., Md., 5'11", light complexion, auburn hair, grey eyes.

LANE, LEWIS: Pvt. Enl. 7/18/62. Clothes issued 11/21/63, 12/24/63, 1/30/64. At Chimbo. #1 with catarrh 5/1/64 (admitted 4/18/64). Transferred to Lynchburg 5/22. Sick at Lynchburg (12/31/64). Paroled 4/15/65, Lynchburg.

LAYNE, WILLIAM: Postwar reference.

LIPSCOMB, JOHN H.: Pvt. Enl. 7/20/62. Admitted to Richmond G.H. #21 with gonorrhea, 9/9/62. Returned to duty 10/1/62. At Lynchburg G.H. (2/28/63). Present 10/31/63. Clothes issued 4th qtr./63, 11/21/63. NFR.

LIPSCOMB, WILLIAM J.: Pvt. Occupation: painter. Enl. 5/28/61, age 24. Captured 7/11/61. Paroled and discharged 8/27/61; age 25, native of Prince Edward Co., 5'10", dark complexion, black hair, grey eyes. Reenl. 2/14/62. AWOL 2/28/63. Present 10/31/63. NFR.

LYNCH, JOHN: Pvt. Enl. 5/28/61. Notation of Co. K, 1st Regt. Va. Artillery. Admitted to Williamsburg (Episcopal Church) Hospital with chronic rheumatism 4/28/62. To Chimbo. #1 5/1/62. To Lynchburg G.H. 5/27/62. Still absent as of 10/63. NFR.

MADDEN, JOHN: Pvt. Bn. Ireland. Occupation: Carpenter. Enl. 5/28/61. Age 20. Severely wounded and captured 7/11/61. Paroled and discharged 10/9/61; age 20, native of Mullon Co., Ireland, 5'8", dark complexion and hair, blue eyes.

MANN, JOSIAH J.: Pvt. Enl. 3/17/62, Lynchburg. At Pratt Hospital in Lynchburg 5/14/63. At G.H. Liberty, Va. (May and June 1863). Clothes issued 4th qtr./63. NFR.

MANNING, JOHN: Postwar reference.

MARSH, CHARLES WILLIAM: Pvt. Bn. 8/17/43, Campbell Co. Former member of F3 Reserves. Enl. 5/28/61, age 18. AWOL 12/16/61. Present 2/28/62. Clothes issued 4th qtr./63, 12/12/63. Captured 6/24/64, Prince William Co., Va. Sent to Ft. Delaware 9/19/64. Released 5/3/65; residence: Charles Co., Va., dark complexion, black eyes and hair, 5'8". D. 1/6/30, Mitchells, Va.

MARSH, ROBERT B.: Pvt. Enl. 4/19/62. Confined in 2nd Brigade, 1st Division guardhouse charged with desertion (2/28/63). CM per G.O. #57, 4/18/63. Detailed as bttn. blacksmith (10/31/63). Clothes issued 4th qtr./63, 2/2/64. Deserted near Washington, D.C. 7/12/64.

MARSH, TILGHMAN A.: Pvt. Enl. 5/28/61, age 25. Present 2/28/62. Confined to 2nd brigade, 1st division guardhouse charged with desertion (2/28/63). CM per G.O. #57, 4/18/63. Wounded 5/3/63 at Chancellorsville, slightly in hand and arm. Present (10/31/63). Clothes issued 4th qtr./63, 2/22/64. Wounded 5/12/64, Spotsylvania C.H. Detailed as hospital guard at Lynchburg G.H. #1 (10/5/64). Paroled 4/13/65, Lynchburg.

MARTIN, WILLIAM: Pvt. Enl. 8/7/61, substitute for George M. Pitzer. AWOL 8/17/62.

MASSEY, JOHN ROBERTSON: 2nd Lt. Formerly a private in Turney's 1st regiment Tennessee Volunteers, Company K, Boon's Hill Minute Men, 5/9/61. Enl. with Lee Battery 6/7/61, elected 2nd Lt. Absent on sick leave 11/27/61, with chronic bronchitis and inflamation of the throat. At home in Fayetteville, Lincoln Co., Tennessee (2/28/62). Discharged 3/6/62. Killed by Union soldiers at his home, "brutally murdered, riddled with bullets" in 1864. Buried in Whitaker Cemetery, Fayetteville, Tn.

MAYS, JOHN J.: Pvt. Occupation: tobacconist. Enl. 5/28/61, age 49. Captured 7/11/61. Paroled and discharged 8/29/61. Age 49, native of Amherst Co., 6', dark complexion, light hair, blue eyes. NFR.

MAYS, ROBERT ALONZO: Pvt. Enl. 2/10/63. Clothes issued 4th qtr./63, 2/22/64, 3/14/64, 11/21/64. At Wayside Hospital assigned to duty 2/5/65. NFR.

MAYS, SAMUEL L.: Pvt. Enl. 5/28/61, age 41. AWOL 12/17/61. Present 2/28/62. Confined to 2nd Brigade, 1st Division guardhouse charged with desertion. CM per G.O. #57, 4/18/63. Restored to duty by presidential amnesty 5/27/63. Clothes issued 11/21/63, 4th qtr./63, 12/24/63. Admitted to Charlottesville G.H. with chronic diarrhea 9/1/64-9/22/64. NFR. Entered R. E. Lee Camp Soldier's Home 11/28/94, age 76. Sent to asylum 6/8/95.

McCORMICK, JAMES: Pvt. Enl. 3/3/62. Sick (10/31/63). Clothes issued 11/21/63, 12/2/63. Sick (10/31/63). Wounded 9/19/64 at Winchester. At Lynchburg G.H. (12/31/64).

MILSTEAD, FRANK DUNNINGTON, JR.: Pvt., 4th Sgt., 1st Sgt., Pvt. Bn. 1841, Campbell Co. M. Susan Anne Wade in 1859. Enl. 5/28/61, age 20. 4th Sgt. 2/1/61. Absent on recruiting duty 2/25/62. Present (2/28/63). 1st Sgt. (10/31/63). with artillery supply train near New Market, Va. 12/1/63-10/31/64. Clothes issued 1st qtr./64, as Pvt. detailed as Pvt. to commissary for 2nd Corps Artillery (12/31/64). Paroled at Appomattox. D. 11/12/00, Lynchburg.

MITCHELL, WILLIAM H.: Bugler. Enl. 4/23/61, Richmond? Clothes issued 4th qtr./63, 12/24/63, 1/12/64, 2/22/64. Wounded and captured 10/19/64, Cedar Creek. NFR.

MONIHAN, PATRICK: Pvt. Bn. Calais Co., Ireland. Occupation: merchant. Enl. 5/28/61, age 23. Sick at Lynchburg (2/28/63). Discharged 1/15/63, on account of disability; 5'5", blue eyes, brown hair.

MONROE, JOHN W.: Pvt. Enl. 5/28/61, age ? AWOL 6/7/61. Sick at Camp Alleghany Hospital (8/31/61). D. there 9/1/61.

MOODIE, ROBERT P.: Pvt., 2nd Sgt., Pvt. Enl. 5/28/61, age 22. 2nd Sgt. 12/21/61. Pvt. 2/1/62. Detailed by order of the Secretary of War to ordinance workshop Richmond (2/28/63). - 12/64? NFR.

MORIARTY, PATRICK: Pvt. Bn. Ireland. Enl. 5/28/61, age 22. AWOL 12/17/61. Present (2/28/62). Sent to Lynchburg G.H. sick. Robbed an officer, broke jaw, now at large (10/31/63). NFR.

MORTON, HENRY: Pvt. Enl. 7/26/62. AWOL (2/28/63). NFR.

MOSBY, HENRY B.: 4th Cpl., Pvt. Enl. 3/13/62, 4th Cpl. Issued clothing 4th qtr./63, 12/12/63, 2/12/64. Sent to Harrisonburg hospital sick 12/13/64. Then to Charlottesville G.H. with chronic rheumatism 12/20/64 and sent to Lynchburg G.H. 1/15/65. Pvt. (12/31/64). Captured 4/2/65, Petersburg. To Ft. Delaware from City Point 4/4/65. Released 6/20/65; residence: Campbell Co., light complexion, dark hair, grey eyes, 5'5".

MURPHY, TIMOTHY: Pvt. Enl. 5/28/61, age 50. AWOL 7/11/61. Discharged 9/27/61 by order Major H. L. Clay - a British subject.

NORTH, EDWARD A.: Pvt. Enl. 5/28/61, age 35. Deserted 9/23/61. D. from exposure about 12/1/61, Amherst Co.

NORTH, JOHN QUINCY ADAMS: Cpl., Pvt. Enl. 5/28/61, age 23, Cpl., Pvt. 7/11/61. AWOL 12/17/61. Present (2/28/62). Confined in guardhouse (2/28/63) for desertion. CM per G.O. #57, 4/18/63. Present (10/31/63). Clothes issued 4th qtr./63, 2/20/64. AWOL 11/25/64. Paroled 4/19/65, Winchester; age 24, 5'6", dark complexion and hair, grey eyes.

NORVELL, ANDREW JACKSON: Pvt. Enl. 8/21/62. Present 2/63. NFR.

NORVELL, GEORGE: Postwar reference.

NORVELL, MARION D.: Pvt. Enl. 5/28/61, age 18. AWOL 9/15/61. In confinement per GCM for violation of 21st Article of War. Sentenced to hard labor and stoppage of pay for one month (2/28/62). CM again for desertion, 4/18/63. Wounded in head, slightly 5/3/63, Chancellorsville. Clothing issued 4th qtr./63, 11/21/63, 12/24/63, 2/22/64. Paroled 4/15/65, Lynchburg.

O'CONNER, WILLIAM: Pvt. Enl. 5/28/61, age 32. AWOL 8/17/62. NFR.

OWEN, WADE N.: Pvt. Enl. 5/28/61, age 28. Sick at Lynchburg hospital (12/31/61-2/28/62). Admitted to G.H. #12 in Richmond 11/14/62-12/1/62. 2/28/63, in brig, charged with desertion. CM 4/18/63. NFR.

PAGE, ARWINE: Pvt. Enl. 8/15/63. AWOL 10/23/63. NFR.

PEARMAN, CHARLES R.: Pvt. Enl. 5/28/61, age 20. AWOL 12/16/61. Present 2/28/62. Clothes issued 4th qtr./63, 1/30/64, 2/22/64. AWOL 9/16/64. Paroled 4/15/65, Lynchburg.

PERDUE, BENJAMIN: Postwar reference.

PERDUE, ISAIAH: Pvt. Enl. 5/28/61, age 38. Clothes issued 4th qtr./63, 11/21/63, 12/12/63, 2/12/64. Paroled 4/14/65, Lynchburg.

PHELPS, WILLIAM W.: Pvt. Enl. 5/28/61, age 39. Clothes issued 4th qtr./63, 12/24/63, 11/21/64. Paroled 4/13/65, Lynchburg.

PLUMB, LOUIS: Postwar reference.

PROFFITT, A. M.: Pvt. Enl. 5/28/61. AWOL 6/7/61.

RAINE, CHARLES I.: 2nd Lt., Capt. Son of John (4/12/1795-4/17/51) and Eliza D. Raine (11/04/05-8/03/56). M.? had four children. Enl. 5/28/61, age 27. Elected 2nd Lt. Elected Captain 12/21/61. Leave taken per S.O. #256/2, 11/29/62. Detailed for court per G.O. #25/2, 2/21/63. Recommended for promotion by John B. Baldwin, 4/19/63. Recommended as Major for bttn. with endorsements for the officers of the other batteries of the bttn., 5/26/63. Recommended for Major to replace Major Latimer by General Pendleton, senior Captain of the Andrew's Bttn., 8/6/63. Also recommended by General Ewell. Took leave per S.O. #228/13, 9/11/63. Absent sick in Lynchburg Hospital (10/31/63). KIA 11/30/64, Mine Run. Buried in Raine family cemetery in Appomattox, Va. Across highway 24 from the Confederate cemetery. Stone gives the middle initial J. not I. As given in so many accounts and records.

RAINE, CHARLES JAMES: Pvt., Guidon, Cpl. Enl. 5/28/61. Age 18. Discharged at Richmond per S.O. #119, 8/9/61. Convalescent at Farmville G.H. 12/2/62-2/7/63. Present 2/28/63. Clothes issued 2/7/63, 4th qtr./63, 11/21/63, 2/6/64, 2/20/64. KIA 9/19/64, Winchester.

RAINE, JOHN Q.: Pvt. Enl. 9/1/63. Clothes issued 4th qtr./63, 11/21/63. Present 12/64. NFR.

RANSOME, JAMES M.: Pvt., Artificier. Enl. 3/3/62, age 31. Detailed to extra duty with the Bttn. ordinance officer as artificier through (10/31/63). "Seen at Lynchburg hospital" 12/31/64. Ordered to be retired as "unfit for duty", (2/17/64); age 34, employed as harness maker. Paroled 4/13/65, Lynchburg.

REYNOLDS, JOHN J.: Pvt. Enl. 5/28/61, age 49. Sick in Staunton hospital (8/31/61). Present (12/31/61). Discharged 2/18/62, on surgeon's certificate.

RICHEY, JAMES: Postwar reference.

RIDER, ISAIAH: Pvt. Enl. 5/28/61, age 39. KIA 7/11/61, Rich Mountain.

ROBERTSON, DAVID G.: Pvt. Enl. 9/1/63. Clothes issued 4th qtr./63, 2/20/64.

ROBERTSON, JAMES A.: Pvt. Enl. 7/28/62. Clothes issued 2/20/64. Assigned extra duty with commissary dept. (12/31/64). Paroled 4/14/65, Lynchburg.

ROBINSON, JAMES: Postwar reference.

ROBINSON, TURNER: Postwar reference.

ROCHE, JAMES: Pvt. Bn. Cork Co., Ireland. Occupation: laborer. Enl. 5/28/61, age 60. Absent sick in Staunton (8/31/61). Detailed to Huntersville afterwards and employed in QM Dept. Present 2/28/62. Discharged on surgeon's certificate due to sinusitis, 11/13/62; age 65, 5'10", ruddy complexion, blue eyes, light hair.

ROCK, JOHN J.: Pvt. Enl. 2/2/63. Clothes issued 4th qtr./63, 12/12/63. NFR.

ROCKE, GEORGE WILLIAM: Postwar reference. D. 10/9/78. Buried in range 3, lot 7, Presbyterian Cemetery, Lynchburg.

RULE, PETER H.: Pvt., Blacksmith. Enl. 5/28/61, age 23. Detailed as blacksmith (2/28/63). Clothes issued 4th qtr./63. Still as blacksmith as of 12/31/64. Paroled but no date, place.

SEAY, JAMES F.: Pvt. Enl. 3/27/62. Clothes issued 4th qtr./63, 12/12/63, 12/24/63, 1/12/64. Paroled 4/13/65, Lynchburg.

SHARP, HENRY: Postwar reference.

SHARP, WILLIAM: Postwar reference.

SHARPE, ROBERT J.: Pvt. Enl. 3/27/64, Louisa Co. Sent to hospital sick (12/31/64). NFR.

SHEEHAN, JAMES: Pvt. Enl. 7/26/62, substitute for W. B. Rees. AWOL 8/17/62.

SHEFFIELD, JAMES M.: Pvt. Enl. 12/13/63. Clothes issued 1/30/64, 2/22/64. Wounded and captured 9/19/64, Winchester. Gsw by one ball passing through fleshy part of arm. 2nd ball entered right side below clavicle and came out below the scapula. Noted as being in U.S.A. depot field hospital with gsw to right lung, applied simple dressing. Sent to Baltimore Hospital 11/23/64. Then to Pt. Lookout hospital 1/28/65. Age either 42, 43, or 45. Released 6/2/65.

SHEPHERD, RICHARD: Pvt. Enl. 5/28/61, age 26. Under arrest for mutiny (10/31/63) at Brandy Station. Clothes issued 4th qtr./63, 2/20/64. CM per G.O. #17-10, 3/7/64. Paroled at Appomattox.

SHEPPARD, JOSEPH B.: Pvt., 4th Cpl., Pvt. Enl. 5/28/61, age 30. 4th Cpl. 7/11/61. Pvt. 12/21/61. On furlough for 15 days as of 2/20/62. Present 2/28/62. Clothes issued 4th qtr./63. Present 12/64. NFR.

SMITH, JOHN: Pvt. Enl. 7/16/62, substitute for R. H. Watkins. AWOL 8/17/64.

SMITH, JOSEPH B.: Pvt. Bn. Danville, Va. occupation: salesman. Enl. 2/10/62, age 30. Clothes issued 12/12/63, 12/24/63, 1/12/64. At Chimbo. with hernia 3/7/64. At Lynchburg G.H. 7/23/64. Discharged 10/3/64; age 31, 6'2½", dark complexion, hair, and eyes.

SPROUTS, HENRY: Pvt. Enl. 5/28/61, age 19. Sick in camp with measles (8/31/61). AWOL 12/17/61. Present 2/28/62. Clothes issued 4th qtr./63, 2/20/64. KIA 9/19/64, Winchester.

SPROUTS, WILLIAM: Pvt. Enl. 5/28/61, age 22. Clothes issued 4th qtr./63, 11/21/63, 1/12/64. Paroled at Appomattox.

STANLEY, WILLIAM HENRY, SR.: Pvt. Bn. Lynchburg. M. Martha _____. Enl. 5/28/61, age 39. Wounded in right thigh 5/12/64, Spotsylvania C.H. Sent to Chimbo. #3 5/20-7/1/64. Paroled 4/15/65, Lynchburg. D. 9/15/72, Lynchburg.

STANLEY, WILLIAM HENRY, JR.: Pvt. Bn. 5/18/46, son of William and Martha. Occupation: student. Enl. 5/28/61, age 15. Claimed he caught Captain Raines as he fell from his horse in action at Mine Run. Clothes issued 1/30/64. MIA 7/30/64, Williamsport, Md. Supposed POW. NFR. M. Martha C. Moyer of St. Augustine, Pa. Moved to Birmingham, Alabama in 1885. D. 12/17/64.

STATHAM, CHARLES WESLEY: 1st Lt. Bn. 5/19/19. Enl. 5/28/61, age 42. Elected 1st Lt. Wounded in right hand, 7/11/61, Rich Mountain. Paroled and back with battery by 2/28/62. Detailed for court duty per S.O. #135/13, 5/19/63. On extra daily duty as bttn. officer of the day, (10/31/63). CM per G.O. #11-7, conduct unbecoming an officer, 1/30/64. Resigned 3/1/64, based on proven medical board examination. "Unfit for duty," by George M. Burtlett, asst. surgeon, Braxton's Bttn. Later Colonel of the Lynchburg local defense troops. D. 5/31/89, buried in the Presbyterian Cemetery, range 17, lot 5, Lynchburg, Va.

STEWART, JOHN F. R.: Pvt. Enl. 5/28/61. AWOL 6/7/61.

STEWART, WILLIAM WARWICK: Pvt. Bn. 1806, Campbell Co. Enl. 5/28/61, age 55. Severely wounded and taken prisoner 7/11/61. D. about 8/15/61.

STONE, JAMES T.: Pvt. Enl. 5/28/61. AWOL 6/7/61.

STRATTON, JOHN W.: Pvt. Enl. 5/28/61, age 50. Sent on detached service (12/31/61). Present (2/28/62). On extra duty as ambulance driver (10/31/63-12/31/64). Clothes issued 4th qtr./63, 12/12/63, 12/24/63. Paroled 4/13/65, Lynchburg.

SULLIVAN, THOMAS: Pvt. Enl. 7/28/62, substitute for William Wingfield. AWOL 8/17/62.

TAYLOR, JAMES: Postwar reference.

TAYLOR, JOHN A.: Pvt. Bn. Williamson Co., Mississippi. Occupation: printer. Enl. 5/28/61, age 22. Severely wounded and captured 7/11/61. Sent to Hart's Hospital, Rich Mountain; right thigh amputated. Paroled and discharged later on 10/3/61; age 21, 5'6", dark complexion, black hair, dark eyes.

THOMAS, WILLIAM G.: Pvt. Enl. 7/15/62, substitute for D. W. Kyle. AWOL 8/17/62.

THOMPSON, H. B.: Pvt. Enl. 12/11/63. CM per G.O. #17-12, 3/7/64; deserter. Sentenced to death; per S.O. #31 2/2/64. Sentence commuted per S.O. #68/3, 3/22/64. At Richmond G.H. #13, 4/6/64. Disease: anasanca? at Castle Thunder 5/2/64. Sent to C.S. Military Prison, Salisbury, N.C. to serve sentence of hard labor with ball and chain. In camp hospital with debility 9/64. D. 9/12/64.

TINDALL, JAMES: Pvt. Enl. 5/28/61, age 27. Sick at Staunton hospital (8/31/61). D. about 11/25/61.

TOLER, WILLIAM J.: Pvt. Enl. 8/21/62. Clothes issued 4th qtr./63, 11/21/63, 1st qtr./64, 2/20/64. Found to be deserter from Steptoe's 2nd Va. Cav. 4/64.

TRENT, BENJAMIN HUDSON: Pvt. Enl. 5/28/61, age 23. Present sick in camp (side hurt) (8/21/61). Sick at Richmond G.H. #21 with gravel? Furloughed 10/10/62, 40 days, age 23. Clothes issued 4th qtr./63, 12/24/63, 1/30/64, 2/19/64. On extra duty as bttn. teamster (10/31/63). Present 12/64 as bttn. driver. D. 2/2/16, age 76. Buried range N, lot 19, Presbyterian Cemetery, Lynchburg.

TURNER, WYTHE R.: Pvt., 2nd Sgt. Enl. 5/28/61, age 32. 2nd Sgt. 6/7/61. KIA 7/11/61, shot through both legs first immediately at the gun, and then through body. "A brave and gallant man." Lt. Statham saw the enemy bury him the next day. 1/2/62, #44 to his widow Landonia Turner.

TURPIN, WILLIAM RILEY: 1st Sgt., Pvt. Bn. Charlottesville, Va. Occupation: merchant clerk. Enl. 5/28/61, age 22, 1st Sgt. Pvt. (12/31/61). Sick (2/28/62). "Enlargement of his head with valvalas disease, frequent and violent attacks of rheumatism." Discharged 3/6/62; age 25, 5'9½", fair complexion, grey eyes, brown hair. NFR.

WALKER, HENRY TAYLOR: Pvt. Paroled at Appomattox.

WALKER, JOHN A.: Pvt. Enl. 5/28/61, age 18. Sick at Lynchburg hospital (2/28/63). At hospital in Buchanon, Va. 4/3/63. Detailed as bttn. butcher (10/31/63). Clothes issued 4th qtr./63, 12/24/63, 1/30/64, 2/20/64. Present (12/31/64). NFR.

WALKER, REESE W.: Pvt. Bn. Campbell Co. Occupation: tobacconist. Enl. 5/28/61, age 45. Captured 7/11/61. Paroled and later discharged 9/4/61; age 46, 5'10", dark complexion, brown hair, blue eyes.

WALKER, WILLIAM E.: Pvt. Enl. 5/28/61, age 19. At Richmond G.H. #21 with syphilis 9/6/62-10/2/62. Had transferred to Camp Winder 9/27/62. Sick in amp (2/28/63). Wounded and captured at Gettysburg 7/3/63. Paroled (10/31/63). Present 12/31/64. Paroled at Appomattox.

WATKINS, JAMES L.: Pvt., Cpl. Enl. 2/14/63. Clothes issued 4th qtr./63, 11/21/63, 2/6/64. Wounded 10/19/64, Cedar Creek. Later in Lynchburg Hospital. NFR.

WILSON, GEORGE: Pvt. Enl. 7/15/62, substitute for E. S. Hammond. AWOL 8/17/62.

WINGFIELD, JOHN WILSON: Postwar reference. Bn. 6/28/21. D. 1/2/01. Buried range 2, lot 6, Presbyterian Cemetery, Lynchburg.

WOOD, ANDREW JACKSON: Pvt. Enl. 7/29/61. Joined with party of men who had gone to Lynchburg after the evacuation of Camp Garnett. Sick with measles (8/31/61). AWOL 12/17/61. Present (2/28/62). Clothes issued 11/21/63, 1/12/64. Wounded 9/19/64 and captured, Winchester. Minie ball to right knee joint, "uninjured". Simple dressing at U.S.A. Depot Field Hospital Transferred 10/17 to Baltimore Hospital. To Pt. Lookout, exchanged 10/30/64. NFR.

WOOD, PATRICK: Postwar reference.

WOOD, THOMAS JEFFERSON I: Pvt., 4th Cpl., 3rd Cpl., Sgt. Brother of A. J. Enl. 5/28/61, age 29. 4th Cpl. 12/21/61. 3rd Cpl. (2/28/63). Sgt. (12/31/64). Clothes issued 4th qtr./63, 11/21/63, 1/12/64. Captured 4/2/65, Petersburg. Sent to Ft. Delaware. NFR.

WOOLDRIDGE, BEVERLY H.: Pvt. Enl. 3/7/62. Clothes issued 4th qtr./63, 12/24/63. Present until paroled at Appomattox.

WOOLDRIDGE, DANIEL F.: Pvt. Enl. 3/12/62. Admitted to Lynchburg Hospital #3 with chronic rheumatism 1/12/63-11/63. Detailed 12/9/63, per G.O. #302/18. Present 4/13/65, Lynchburg.

WOOLDRIDGE, LEWELLYN J.: Pvt. Bn. Campbell Co. Occupation: laborer. Enl. 5/28/61, age 21. Captured 7/11/61. Paroled and later discharged 8/7/61. Age 21, 5'11", dark complexion, brown hair, dark eyes. Under arrest for mutiny at Brandy Station (10/31/63). Clothes issued 12/12/63, 12/24/63, 1/12/64, 2/22/64. CM per G.O. #17-10, 3/7/64. AWOL 9/23/64. NFR.

WOOLDRIDGE, PETER: Postwar reference.

WOOLDRIDGE, RICHARD: Postwar reference.

WOOLDRIDGE, WILLIAM LORENZO: Pvt. Bn. Campbell Co. Occupation: shoemaker. Enl. 5/28/61, age 28. At Lynchburg #3 (8/31/61). Admitted to Charlottesville G.H. 6/29/62-7/5/62. Discharged 3/6/63, dyspepsia. Age 19, 5'8", fair complexion, dark hair and eyes.

WORLEY, ROBERT: Pvt. Enl. 5/28/61, age 19. Sick at Lynchburg hospital (8/31/61). AWOL 7/11/61. Deserter (10/31/63).

WORLEY, WILLIAM A.: Pvt. Bn. Campbell Co. Occupation: laborer. Enl. 5/28/61, age 27. Captured 7/11/61. Paroled and later discharged 9/3/61; age 25, 6', dark complexion, black hair, grey eyes. Reenl. 2/14/63. Clothes issued 4th qtr./63, 11/2/63, 11/21/63, 1/30/64, 2/6/64. Wounded and cpatured 9/19/64, Winchester. GSW to right hip passing through ilium, ball lodging in bladder? Simple dressing applied at U.S.A. depot field hospital. D. 9/28/64, peritonitis.

WRIGHT, STERLING C.: Pvt. Enl. 10/6/63. Clothes issued 12/12/63, 12/24/63. GCM, sentenced 6 months labor in Richmond. Escaped from provost guard on night of 10/19/64. At large (12/31/64). Paroled 4/15/65, Lynchburg.

WRIGHT, WILLIAM: Pvt. Enl. 5/28/61, age 21. Clothes issued 4th qtr./63, 11/21/63, 1/12/64, 1/30/64. Admitted to Chimbo. #3 with typhoid 6/13/64. Granted 30 day furlough, 7/7/64. KIA 10/19/64, Cedar Creek.

THE BEDFORD ARTILLERY
1861

The appeal of artillery or cavalry service far exceeded that of the life of an infantryman. Two companies of the 28th Virginia Infantry recognized that fact in the Summer of 1861 and made application for transfer to the artillery branch. One of the two companies, the Old Dominion Rifles (Company C), under the command of Captain Thomas Mickie Bowyer, received its wished-for conversion by late August.

Moving into Camp Pickens, not far from its old campsite near Centreville, the newly designated Bedford Artillery prepared itself to be properly equipped and officially recognized. On October 20, with armament of two 6-pounders and two 12-pounders, the battery was assigned to General Richard Taylor's Louisiana Brigade.

The officer structure of the company remained as it had been when organized as the "Old Dominion Rifles": Captain Thomas M. Bowyer, 1st Lieutenant Edmund Goode (who later left after appointment as colonel of the 58th Virginia Infantry), 1st Lieutenant John Richard Johnson, 2nd Lieutenants John M. Davis and Elias B. Poole. The acting, though uncommissioned, surgeon was James H. Bowyer. The sergeants were 1st Sergeant Newton H. Hazelwood, 2nd Sergeant John E. Mitchell, 3rd Sergeant Jesse L. Thomson, 4th Sergeants Joseph Snapp and Joseph S. Hardy, the 5th Sergeant William M. Burwell.

The company set to drilling daily in the gun manual and field maneuvers, but was not permitted to practice with cartridges. For the most part the company equippage was considered fair. The guns and horses were of good quality; however, the harness left something to be desired because it was poorly made. The Bedford County natives were also noted as "wanting in many stores." Captain Bowyer feared the onslaught of winter. Cold weather threatened the welfare of many of his men, who were without tents or shelters of any sort. The result was a large number of men on the sick rolls. In late November the company moved into winter quarters at Camp Carondelet, near Union Mills.

A Year of Disappointments
1862

In March the doldrums of winter quarters were interrupted when the battery accompanied Taylor's Brigade to the Rappahannock River. It remained there about a month, "constantly," as Lieutenant Johnson recollected after the war, "having small affairs with the enemy who were on the opposite bank." Between the "affairs" with the Federals, General Taylor ordered that Bowyer's battery be charged with training one company of men from each of the regiments of the brigade in the artillery manual. The sole purpose of this function was in case the brigade might at some point in a battle overrun an enemy battery, there would be several readily available men to turn the captured guns upon the Federals.

Here too the battery was reorganized. John R. Johnson was elected captain. Captain Bowyer went to the head of several of the Louisianans he had trained and helped to organize a new battery. The bad result for the Bedford Artillery in this fiasco was that Taylor ordered the Bedford company's guns and equipment turned over to the new Louisiana company, leaving the Virginians, to the disgust of Johnson, to march to Richmond and be rearmed.

By the time the company had been refitted with three pieces and made ready for active service again, the Seven Days Battles had concluded and Robert E. Lee's Army of Northern Virginia was en route to Gordonsville. Catching up to the Louisiana Brigade, now under Stafford, at Liberty Mills, the battery moved with "Stonewall" Jackson's Corps to Orange Court House. There the battery was switched over to Jubal A. Early's Brigade.

On August 9 a section of the battery, under Lieutenant Terry, moved along with Joseph W. Latimer's Battery and was placed in position on Cedar Mountain with Trimble's and Forno's Brigades, and under the direction of Major General R. S. Ewell. The guns opened with marked effect upon the enemy, drawing some enemy fire which otherwise would have been concentrated against the Confederate left wing. Lieutenant Terry's section was then moved near the foot of the mountain and opened on the enemy cavalry, as did some other pieces in front of General Beverly H. Robertson's headquarters. The enemy soon after responded with counterbattery fire, which only lasted a few minutes before the enemy withdrew. The only recorded loss for the day was Samuel Harris, hurt by a horse falling on his left ankle and crushing it.

123

From Cedar Mountain, after a brief pause in camp, the battery accompanied Jackson's Corps northward on August 20, crossing the Rapidan River at Somerville Ford, and bivouacking near Stevensburg that night. Pressing on again the following morning, the battery reached Cunningham's Ford on August 22.

On August 25, Johnson's battery continued on its trek to Henson's Mill above Waterloo Bridge, where it crossed the Rappahannock, and thence to Orleans, camping the night near Salem. From there the battery continued with the advance the following morning through Thoroughfare Gap and turning toward Manassas Junction, where it arrived on August 27.

Late on August 28 sharp firing could be heard near the village of Groveton and the Bedford Artillery was called up and posted on a ridge between Hays's and Early's Brigades. The battery remained unengaged as others on the left fired on the enemy column approaching from Warrenton Junction. Johnson recorded no casualties for the day.

On the following morning, under the direction of Brigadier General A. R. Lawton, the division moved up on a ridge perpendicular to the railroad track, leaving its right resting upon the turnpike facing Groveton. Early's and Hays's Brigades moved up the ridge west of the turnpike and tracks, under cover of the woods. Once skirmishers had been deployed, Johnson's battery was moved up. Just to the left the men could see Lindsay M. Shumaker's Battalion, where it had been placed earlier. The Bedford men, though eager to fight, saw relatively light action that day.

On August 30 the battery was once more engaged against a drove of Fitz John Porter's Federals as they pressed on Jackson's line holding in the railroad cut. Along with the massed guns of Shumaker's and S. D. Lee's battalions the Confederate artillery had a field day of execution, turning the ground to their front into a living hell for the enemy. Johnson in postwar years claimed to have charged the battery during the afternoon, quite possibly along with some of Shumaker's guns, to a higher elevation for more opportune fire. The only recorded loss for Manassas was M. P. Fergusson, killed.

On September 1, the Bedford Artillery followed Jackson to Chantilly, but was not engaged. From the events around Manassas, only one, Henry Arthur, was reported with a shoulder wound.

From Chantilly, the Bedford battery moved northwest through Leesburg and across the Potomac on September 5. Reaching Frederick, Maryland, on September 6, the battery remained for four days. During the unit's shuffling about, two new recruits who had recently fallen ill, Robert Burton and Frank Smith, were captured at Williamsport on the 9th. On September 11, the Bedford men were puzzled as they recrossed the

Potomac at Williamsport.

Soon all became clear; they found the destination to be Harper's Ferry. Lee's intention was to capture the garrison, thus keeping the Army of Northern Virginia free from any trouble in the rear as it moved into Maryland.

Onward from Martinsburg, the Bedford Artillery followed the corps to Halltown on September 12. From the little village, the battery was moved up to an elevated position with other batteries of the corps. The following day the mass of batteries ravaged the enemy position at Bolivar Heights, finally disengaging that night. Feeling that the garrison had been considerably softened, the batteries readied themselves for an infantry assault planned for the next day. However, before the charge was sounded on September 15, the garrison surrendered.

Recrossing the Potomac on September 16, Johnson's battery, now attached to Trimble's Brigade, pressed on with "Stonewall" toward Sharpsburg, where it arrived the same evening. Johnson's battery was placed, before dawn the next day, behind John B. Hood's Division, facing toward the Dunkard Church.

September 17 dawned with hard cannonading, but the Bedford men were not yet subjected to the brutal punishment being delivered by the enemy guns. The call did come in the afternoon when Johnson was ordered up to relieve Fry's Orange Artillery. Once the three guns had been put on line, the company suffered more than it ever had. Never before had the men been exposed to such an intense fire as they were now. It was indeed an "artillery hell." Before the day was over, and the battery withdrawn, one had fallen killed and ten were wounded, most severely. All the guns had been disabled and most of the horses killed or wounded. Lieutenant Poole narrowly escaped being wounded when his horse was shot from under him. Killed was a man referred to in postwar years only as West; among those wounded were Nat Thomson (incapacitating him and later after the war finally playing a role in his death), H. B. Elliott (by a shell in the foot — resulting in amputation), Jesse W. Wells (in the right hip), and J. W. Barbour.

The following day the Bedford Artillery limped back across the Potomac and into Virginia. Once at Opequon, Johnson reported to Colonel James A. Walker, now in command of the brigade. Upon seeing the state the company was in, the colonel made recommendation for the captain to be allowed to recruit the battery to its full quota and have it replenished, replacing the three disabled guns, and restocking the horses.

At Kernstown the recruiting began under the direction of Major Charles Richardson of Fredericksburg. Johnson learned from Richardson

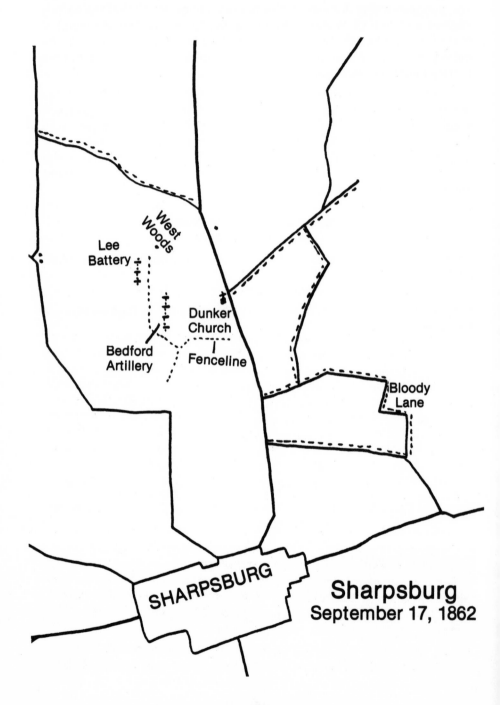

West Woods

Lee Battery

Dunker Church

Bedford Artillery

Fenceline

Bloody Lane

SHARPSBURG

Sharpsburg
September 17, 1862

that the plan was to have all the batteries that had been crippled from active service refitted by the captured stores from Harper's Ferry. Richardson suggested that Johnson make full requisition for all that the battery needed, and "not be modest." He requested 50 horses. The end result of that report and lengthy requisition list proved to be no extra favor for the battery, however. Within a short time, the captain received word that his battery might be disbanded.

In the hope of a strong recommendation from a general officer, Johnson turned to General Early, who, along with General Jackson, gave him support. Despite Johnson's best efforts, however, the battery was disbanded — along with many others that had done worthy service — by an order dated October 4, 1862. The men and horses were divided, some going to the Purcell Artillery, others to a unit from their home neighborhood, the Lynchburg Artillery.

Available Supply Data From
The Bedford Artillery

For period 10/9-12/9/61 at Camp Florida, for artillery horses, requisitioned by Captain Bowyer:
> ½ bushel salt

For period of four days, at Camp Florida, requisitioned by Captain Bowyer for 74 men, 4 women:
> 55 lbs. bacon
> 277 lbs. beef
> ? flour
> 4 lbs. 7 oz. coffee
> 35 lbs. 9 oz. sugar
> 5 lbs. 14 oz. soap
> 21 lbs. 3 oz. candles
> 2 gal. 7 qt. vinegar
> pepper
> potatoes

Forage at Camp Carondelet for 78 horses from 1/3-1/31/62, Capt. Bowyer:
> 936 lbs. corn
> 1092 lbs. hay

Same for 77 horses 1/30/62:
> 924 lbs. corn
> 1078 lbs. hay

Samuel R. Meade, Bedford Artillery

Jesse Ward Wells

129

William Henry Lafayatte Wells

APPENDIX

Tabulations From The Roster
Commissioned And Noncommissioned Officers
Of The Bedford Artillery

Bowyer, Thomas M., Captain
Johnson, John R., Captain
Goode, Edmonde, 1st Lt.
Cobb, John A., 1st Lt.
Davis, John M., 2nd Lt.
Poole, Elias B., 2nd Lt.
Hazelwood, Newton H., 2nd Lt.
Bowyer, James H., Surgeon
Holt, David S., 1st Sgt. (2nd)
Mitchell, John E., 2nd Sgt. (1st)
Holt, Joseph H., 2nd Sgt. (2nd)
Thomson, Jesse L., 3rd Sgt.

Snapp, Joseph, 4th Sgt.
Hardy, Joseph S., 4th Sgt.
Burwell, William M., 5th Sgt.
Campbell, Frederick M., 1st Cpl.
Hoffman, James R., 1st Cpl.
Noell, William T., 2nd Cpl.
Thomson, Nathaniel W., 4th Cpl.
McClintock, Richard D., 5th Cpl.
Elliott, Henry B., Cpl.
Goode, Breckinridge, Cpl.
Fellers, William, Treasurer
Fuqua, Walter M., Wagonmaster

Statistical Summary of Strengths and Losses

134 On Roster
__4 Postwar References
130 Actually Enrolled In Battery

Killed In Action	6	5%
Wounded In Action	10	8%
Captured	2	2%
Died Of Disease	2	2%
Died Of Unknown Causes	2	2%
Total Known War Dead	10	8%
Sick At Least Once	42	32%
Retired, Resigned, Discharged	10	8%
Transferred	5	4%
Detailed w/NFR	4	3%
NFR	6	5%
On Certificate for Johnson	63	48%
Remustered		
2/7/62	21	
2/10/62	6	
3/4/62	6	
3/7/62	1	
4/11/62	17	

Summary of Battery Strength (End Of Month)

As Extracted From The Information Provided In The Roster, Included Temporary Absences Due To Sickness And Wounds

9/61 - 97	1/62 - 90
10/61 - 87	2/62 - 88
11/61 - 87	3/62 - 114
12/61 - 91	4/62 - 118
	5/62 - 116
	6/62 - 114
	7/62 - 109
	8/62 - 108
	9/62 - 104
	10/62 - 101

Occupations At Enlistment

Farmer - 30
Carpenter - 7
Blacksmith - 3
Clerk - 3
Teacher - 3
Tobacconist - 3
Gentleman - 2
Planter - 2
Printer - 2
Salesman - 2
Student - 2

Bricklayer, Collector, Cooper, Druggist, Editor, Farm Manager, Farmer/Schoolteacher, Farmer/Tinner, Gambler, Laborer, Lawyer, Machinist/Cabinetmaker, Printer, Shoemaker, Teacher, Trader - one each

Ages At Enlistment

15 - 1 (N. Creasy)		
17 - 2	28 - 5	Percentage in teens - 22%
18 - 11	29 - 2	Percentage 20-29 - 54%
19 - 9	30 - 2	Percentage 30-39 - 15%
20 - 8	31 - 3	Percentage 40 + - 9%
21 - 5	32 - 6	
22 - 10	33 - 1	
23 - 8	34 - 2	
24 - 5	38 - 2	
25 - 7	40 - 3	48 - 2
26 - 4	44 - 1	50 - 1
27 - 2	46 - 1	56 - 1 (Moore)

Residences At Enlistment
Or
Counties of Birth if the
Former is Unavailable

Appomattox Co.	1	Nelson Co.	1
Bedford Co.	19	Pittsylvania Co.	1
Botetourt Co.	2	Prince Edward Co.	1
Buckingham Co.	1	Rockbridge Co.	1
Campbell Co.	2	Frederick Co., Md.	1
Fluvanna Co.	1	St. Paul, Minn.	1
Montgomery Co.	1		

Bedford Artillery

ADAMS, ALEXANDER H.: Pvt. For the election of J. R. Johnson 4/12/62 (hereafter referred to as "on certificate"). NFR.

ADAMS, SAMUEL W.: Pvt. Bn. Campbell Co. Son of Joel. M. Mary Dowdy 12/20/39. Occupation: farmer. Transferred from 28th Va. Inf. Present to 10/21/61 when abs. on surg. cert. G.H. Och (fever) furloughed to Holmes Co., Mississippi 10/61. Age 23, 6'2¼", dark complexion, dark hair, blue eyes. Remustered for the war 2/7/62. Reassigned to the Lynchburg Artillery.

ADAMS, WILLIAM HENRY: Pvt. B. 3/18/28, Campbell Co. Occupation: farmer. Enl. 3/7/62 at Liberty. Age 34. Reassigned to the Purcell Artillery. D. Amherst Co., 1906.

ARTHUR, HENRY S.: Pvt. Bn. Pittsylvania Co. Enl. 3/18/62 at Liberty. At Lynchburg Hospital 9/12/62 with shoulder wound. Reassigned to the Lynchburg Artillery.

ARTHUR, JAMES W. A. or W. H.: Pvt. Enl. 3/18/62 at Liberty. On certificate. Reassigned to Lynchburg Artillery.

AUNSPAUGH, JAMES S.: Pvt. Enl. 7/22/62, Liberty. Reassigned to the Lynchburg Artillery.

BARBOUR, JOHN W.: Pvt. Enl. 10/31/61 from Co. D, 28th Va. Inf. Admitted to G.H. #18, formerly, Greaner's Hospital, Richmond, with diarrhea 2/26/62. Transferred to Hugenot Springs 4/1/62. Res. Hendrick's Store, Bedford Co., Va. Notated on postwar roster as wounded.

BOHN, DABNEY: Pvt. Bn. Bedford Co. Occupation: Laborer/farmer. Transfer from Co. C, 28th Inf. on certificate. Age 20, 5'8", dark complexion, dark eyes, light hair. Reassigned to Purcell Artillery. Bedford pensioner in 1915.

BOOTHE, JOHN H.: Pvt. Enl. 3/17/62, Liberty, Va. Age 32.

BOWYER, JAMES H.: Asst. surgeon. "Not commissioned." Bn. 1835, Fincastle, Va. Student at UVa. '54-5. Joined by transfer from Co. C, 28th Va. Inf. 12/1/61. Present through 12/31/61. Detailed for attending sick prisoners 6/62. Detail terminated so that he might go before the medical board in Richmond 7/11/62. Reassigned to Lynchburg Artillery.

BOWYER, ROBERT H.: Pvt. Bn. Bedford Co. Absent on surgeon's certificate 9/15/61. Admitted to Charlottesville G.H. with typhoid fever 9/29/61. Transferred to Lynchburg G.H. 9/30/61. Present 12/61. Remustered 2/10/62. On certificate. Furloughed to Knoxville, Tennessee 2/9/62; age 26, 5'8", dark complexion, hair and eyes. Occupation: gambler.

BOWYER, THOMAS MICKIE: Captain. Bn. 2/22/30, Fincastle, Va. Student at UVa. '51. Graduated from Univ. of Pennsylvania. On certificate. Recommended for promotion to Major by Brig. Gen. Taylor 5/62. Admitted to Danville G.H. #1 6/14/62, sent to Richmond. Chief of Ordinance for Ewell's Division 5/27/63. Major in summer of 1863. Postwar M.D./Physician. Mayor of Liberty. D. 9/8/00, Battle Creek, Michigan. Buried Longwood Cemetery, Bedford Co.

BROWN, EDMUND: Enl. 3/22/62, Lynchburg. Age 50. On certificate. Reassigned to the Purcell Artillery.

BROWN, JAMES C.: Pvt. Enl. 3/17/62, Liberty. Age 32. On certificate.

BURKS, ALBERT SHERMAN: Pvt. Bn. 3/17/38, son of Martin. Attended New London Academy and Professor Winston's School near Lynchburg, "Westwood Academy." Finished under General Pendleton. Occupation: Farmer. From 28th Inf. Present through 12/31/61. Reassigned to Purcell Artillery, but provided Samuel Sprouse as a sub. M. 1) Virginia Catherine Rucker (dau. of James Monroe and Marinda McD. Rucker) 6/2/62. 2) Mary Emma McDaniel (dau. of Judge J. R. McDaniel of Campbell Co.) 4/84. D. 4/11/13.

BURKS, GEORGE WELLINGTON: Pvt. Bn. 4/4/40, son of Martin. Educated as above. From 28th Va. Inf. Absent on surgeon's certificate 9/15/61. Admitted to the Lynchburg G.H. 10/30/61, debility following typhoid and jaundice. Discharged 2/18/62. Married: Harriet Eliza Hopkins (dau. of Edward and Lucy Cheatwood Hopkins of Amherst Co.) 11/20/67. D. 9/5/12. Also served with 21st Va. Cavalry.

BURROUGHS, JOHN F.: Pvt. Enl. 3/7/62, Lynchburg. Age 18. Reassigned to Lynchburg Artillery.

BURTON, ROBERT: Pvt. Enl. 9/19/62? Captured by 54th Pennsylvania at Williamsport 9/9/62. Sent to Atheneum Prison, Wheeling, W.Va. Transferred to Cairo, Illinois 9/29/62. To Camp Chase; res. St. Louis, Missouri, age 31, 5'11", fair complexion, hazel eyes, dark hair.

BURWELL, WILLIAM M.: Pvt., 5th Sgt. From 28th Va. Inf. Promoted to 5th Sgt. 12/61.

CAMPBELL, ELCANAH M.: Pvt. Enl. 5/22/62, Liberty. NFR. Reassigned to the Lynchburg Artillery.

CAMPBELL, FREDERICK M.: 1st Cpl. From 28th Va. Inf. Occupation: student, age 19, light complexion, dark eyes, red hair. Absent on surgeon's certificate 10/15/61-12/31/61. Remustered 2/10/62. On certificate. Reassigned to Purcell Artillery.

CAMPBELL, ROBERT: Pvt. Age 18 and occupation: student in 1860, Bedford Co. From 28th Va. Inf. Absent on surgeon's certificate since 7/21/61. Present 11/61. Remustered 4/11/62. Reenl. 4/12/62. On certificate. On hospital musters at Liberty G.H. 7-12/62. Reassigned to Purcell Artillery. Entered the Lee Camp Soldier's Home 12/17/27, age 46(?) 61. Dropped.

COBB, JAMES HENRY: Pvt. Reassigned to Purcell Artillery.

COBB, JOHN A. JR.: Trumpeter, Lieutenant. Born Prince Edward County. Occupation: druggist. Hospital Steward at Culpeper 8/14/61. Rejoinee per S.O. #534-1, 11/19/61; age 23, 5'9", light complexion and hair, hazel eyes. Trumpeter. Remustered 2/7/62. On certificate. Lieutenant sometime late in 1862. Died 7/22/62. James F. Johnson, attorney, presented a claim 1/12/63. Per certificate #7850, $156.00 due.

COOPER, CHRISTOPHER J.: Pvt. Occupation: tobacconist. Enl. Bedford Co. Present through 12/31/61. Reassigned to Lynchburg Artillery.

CREASY, NATHANIEL G.: Pvt. Bn. Bedford Co. Enl. 3/14/62 at Liberty, age 17. Reassigned to the Purcell Artillery. Age 69 in 1915.

DAVIS, JOHN MICAJAH: 2nd Lieutenant, 1st 2nd Lieutenant. Bn. 6/24/43, son of Micajah and Sarah W. Sheldon (Seldon) Davis. Present through 12/31/61. M. 1866 to Virginia Finney Phillips of Memphis, Tn. D. 3/8/75. Buried in Longwood Cemetery, Roanoke Co.

DAVIS, SAMUEL PHILLIPS: Pvt. Bn. ca. 1838, Liberty, Va. Attended UVa. 1856, 58, 59. Detailed as QM Sgt. to Co. C, 28th Va. Inf. Relieved 12/31/61. NFR. Postwar editor/lawyer. D. 1/20/72, St. Louis, Mo.

EARLY, HENRY T.: Pvt. Bn. Bedford Co. Occupation: student. Present until discharged due to hernia, 10/30/61; age 19, 5'4", lt. complexion, brown eyes, light hair. Reassigned to Lynchburg Artillery. Noted as killed on a postwar roster.

EARLEY, JOEL N.: Pvt. Enl. 8/22/61 in Bedford Co. Present through 12/31/61. Remustered 3/4/62. On certificate. Furloughed 10/2/62. Treated for typhoid at Mr. J. Sudith's House. On report of sick and wounded at Jefferson Hospital, 10/26/62. Reassigned to Lynchburg Artillery.

ELAM, GEORGE P.: Postwar reference.

ELLIOTT, HENRY BELLFIELD: Pvt., Cpl. Occupation: Bricklayer. Present through 12/31/61. Remustered 2/7/62. On certificate. Cpl. in 1862. Wounded by a shell in the foot and leg amputated 9/17/62. On hospital muster at Liberty, Va. 9-10/62; age 28, 5'10", dark complexion, hair, and eyes. Reassigned to Lynchburg Artillery.

FARMER, ETHELBERT: Pvt. Bn. Bedford Co. Occupation: blacksmith. Present 12/31/61. Remustered 2/7/62. Age 20, 5'8", dark eyes and complexion, auburn hair. Reassigned to the Purcell Artillery.

FELLERS, WILLIAM: Treasurer. Occupation: clerk. Age 24. Transferred from Bowyer's Battery to Co. C, 28th Va. Infantry, 10/31/61. Detailed as office clerk for provost marshal, S.O. #472, 10/30/61.

FERGUSON, MARTIN P.: See Moore, Cannoneer, 120-21. Bn. 1830. Occupation: editor. Age 19. Absent on Surgeon's certificate 11/24/61. Remustered 4/11/62. On certificate. Noted as KIA 2nd Manassas, but reassigned to Lynchburg Artillery.

FOWLER, THOMAS C.: Pvt. Occupation: farmer. Age 20. Present through 12/31/61. Remustered 4/11/62. On certificate.

FREEMAN, EDWARD LAFAYETTE: Pvt. Bn. Bedford Co. Occupation: carpenter. Present through 12/31. Remustered 2/7/62. Convalescent 3/21/62. Returned to duty 4/22/62. Age 18, 5'9", light complexion and hair, blue eyes.

FUQUA, CHARLES E.: Pvt. Enl. 3/12/62 at Liberty by Nat Terry. On certificate.

FUQUA, CORNELIUS TYREE: Pvt. Bn. Bedford Co. Occupation: student/farmer. Age 18. Present through 12/31/61. Remustered 2/7/62. On certificate. Age 19, 6', dark complexion, light hair, hazel eyes. Reassigned to Purcell Artillery. D. of wounds received at Gettysburg. His mother, Sally, received the settlement of $133.27.

FUQUA, WALTER M.: Wagon master. Occupation: farmer. Age 21. Wagon master for battery effective 10/31/61. Remustered 4/11/62. On certificate.

FUQUA, WILLIAM H.: Pvt. Occupation: teacher. Present through 12/31/61. Discharged due to epileptic, 2/17/62; age 22, 6', dark complexion and hair, blue eyes.

GIBBS, DAVID C.: Pvt. Enl. 3/17/62, Liberty, Va. On certificate. Reassigned to Lynchburg Artillery.

GIBBS, PETER: Pvt. Bn. Bedford Co. Occupation: Carpenter. Enl. 3/13/62, Liberty. On certificate. Discharged due to hypertrophy of heart, 5/14/62. Age 29, 5'6", dark hair, eyes, and complexion.

GOODE, BRECKINRIDGE: Cpl. Bn. Bedford Co. Occupation: student/farmer. Present through 12/31/61. Remustered 2/7/62. On certificate. Age 18, 5'8", light complexion and eyes, red hair.

GOODE, EDMONDE: 1st Lt. Occupation: planter. Age 25 later colonel of 58th Va. Infantry. D. 3/62.

GORDON, JACOB: Pvt. Detailed per S.O. #45/11, 9/27/72 to furnace in Western Virginia (by order Gen. G. W. Smith).

HAMMOND, MAYBERRY: Pvt. Bn. Botetourt Co. Occupation: farmer/school teacher. Age 20. Present through 12/31/61. Remustered 2/7/62. On certificate. Reassigned to Purcell Artillery. Killed in Hunter's advance to Lynchburg.

HARDY, JOSEPH STODGEN: 4th Sgt. Bn. 2/17/23. Occupation: farmer. Present through 12/31/61. D. 4/91 in Bedford. Buried family cemetery.

HARRIS, SAMUEL H.: Pvt. Bn. Blacksburg, Montgomery Co., Va. Occupation: carpenter. Present through 12/31/61. Remustered 2/7/62. On certificate. Age 31, 6', light complexion, hair and eyes. Wounded at Cedar Mountain by a horse falling and crushing his left foot. Reassigned to Purcell Artillery. Buried in Longwood Cemetery, Bedford Co.

HAWKINS, JOHN H.: Pvt. Bn. Bedford Co. Occupation: farmer. Returned from hospital 9/17/61. Present through 12/31/61. On certificate. Age 20, 5'7", light hair, complexion, and eyes.

HAWKINS, JULIUS C.: Pvt. Absent on Surgeon's certificate 9/8/61. Admitted to Charlottesville G.H. with rheumatism, 10/7/61. Furloughed 30 days. Discharged 10/27/61. Present 12/31/61. Remustered 3/4/62. On certificate. Reassigned to Lynchburg Artillery.

HAWKINS, WILLIAM E.: Pvt. Enl. 3/15/62, Liberty. Entered R. E. Lee Camp Soldier's Home 9/18/07, age 74. Died 4/21/12. Buried Hollywood Cemetery, Richmond. Reassigned to Purcell Artillery. Resided in Bedford after the war.

HAZELWOOD, NEWTON H.: 1st Sgt., 2nd Lieutenant. Occupation: student. Absent on surgeon's certificate 10/10/61. Remustered 2/10/62. On certificate. Age 21, 5'10", light hair and complexion, hazel eyes.

HEWETT, WILLIAM L.: Pvt. Occupation: farmer. Age 17. Present through 12/31/61. Remustered 4/11/62. On certificate.

HOFFMAN, FRAZIER O.: Pvt. Enl. 3/11/62, Liberty. On certificate. Reassigned to the Purcell Artillery.

HOFFMAN, JAMES ROBERT: 1st Cpl. Exempted, reason not stated.

HOFFMAN, JOHN: Pvt. Occupation: Tobacconist. Age 40. Returned from hospital 9/8/61. Present through 12/31/61. Discharged in 1862.

HOLT, DAVID S.: Occupation: Gentleman. Age 25. 1st Sgt. Present through 12/31/61. Discharged 5/12/62. D. 1904. Buried Longwood Cemetery, Bedford Co.

HOLT, JOHN D.: Postwar reference. Bn. 5/19/26. D. 9/8/95. Buried Presbyterian Cemetery, Lynchburg.

HOLT, JOSEPH H.: 2nd Sgt. Occupation: Planter. Age 30.

HOPKINS, FRANCIS E.: Pvt. Enl. 3/13/62. On certificate.

HORTON, ACHILLES W.: Pvt. Occupation: clerk. Returned form hospital 9/14/61. Present 12/31/61. Discharged due to carditis 1/30/62.

HORTON, JAMES MADISON: Pvt. Bn. 12/29/37, Bedford Co. Occupation: farmer. Returned from hospital 9/10/61. Present through 12/31/61. Remustered 2/10/62. On certificate. Age 22, 5'6", fair complexion, light hair and eyes. See Purcell Artillery. D. 8/4/99. Buried Centenary Burial Association Amherst Co.

JETER, TINSLEY WHITE: Pvt. Bn. 5/4/39, Bedford Co. Son of Fielden Harris and Virginia Anne White (m. 1/4/37). Occupation: farmer. Present through 12/31/61. Remustered 2/7/62. On certificate. Age 22, 5'8", dark complexion, blue eyes, dark hair. D. 8/15/77, Cass Co., Missouri.

JOHNSON, CHARLES H.: Pvt. Enl. 4/7/62, Lynchburg. On certificate. At Winder Hospital and returned to duty 9/26/62. Reassigned to Purcell Artillery. Deserted and took oath.

JOHNSON, JAMES FOOTE, JR.: Pvt. Present through 12/31/61. Remustered 4/11/62. On certificate. Enl. in Purcell Artillery 3/1/64. Lived in Roanoke after the war. Member of the Pegram Bttn. Association.

JOHNSON, JOHN RICHARD: 1st, 2nd Lt., Lt., Captain. Occupation: Gentleman. Age 20. Present through 12/31/61. On certificate. After company was reassigned, he reported to Colonel Shields, in charge of the enrolling dept. Served until he felt he could do better service at the front, whereupon he enlisted as a private in the 2nd Va. Cavalry. Going home to procure a horse, his father reproached him for such a hasty action. Through the influence of Major John W. Reilly, an old college classmate, Johnson's resignation was withdrawn, and he was reinstated as Captain. Ordered to report to General Kemper, in charge of reserves, and by him sent to Staunton River Bridge to take charge of the artillery at that point and organize another company. Mustered in young men from the reserves, forming this new company, but saw little action. Usually held at the river, the company, along with other regular troops and reserves, were sent on several occasions into North Carolina to repel raids. Though Johnson reapplied for service at the front, he was always met with the reply that troops were needed at the point he was at. Remained there for the balance of the war. Postwar attorney at Christiansburg, Va.

JONES, ALBERT: Pvt. Occupation: teacher. Age 26. Present through 12/31/61.

JONES, HENRY B.: Pvt. Occupation: salesman. Age 18. Present through 12/31/61. Remustered 4/11/62. On certificate. Reassigned to Purcell Artillery.

JONES, WILLIAM B.: Pvt. Occupation: Salesman. Age 23. Absent on Surgeon's certificate 10/11/61. Present 12/31/61. Remustered 4/11/62. On certificate. Reassigned to the Purcell Artillery. Deserted 1864.

KEY, JOHN S.: Pvt. Occupation: farmer. Present through 12/31/61. Remustered 4/11/62. On certificate.

KIDD, WILLIAM A.: Pvt. Bn. Buckingham Co. Occupation: farmer. Enl. 3/8/62, Lynchburg, age 40. On certificate. Discharged 7/18/62; age 44, 5'8", shallow complexion, gray eyes, dark hair.

LATHAM, ALBERT: Pvt. Occupation: farmer. Present through 12/31/61. Remustered 3/4/62. On certificate.

LAWLESS, WILLIAM L: Present through 12/31/61.

LOGWOOD, JOHN C.: Pvt. Bn. 10/10/42, Bedford Co. Occupation: farmer. Absent on surgeon's certificate 10/21/61. Present 12/31/61. Remustered 2/7/62. On certificate. Age 18, blue eyes, light hair and complexion, 5'10". Reassigned to Purcell Artillery. WIA Fredericksburg. Captured at Petersburg 4/11/65.

LOWRY, C. L.: Postwar reference. Noted as killed.

LOWRY, GRANVILLE N.: Pvt. Occupation: farmer. Age 25. Present through 10/31/61. Absent on surgeon's certificate 11/17/61.

LOWRY, HAMES M.: Pvt. Occupation: wagondriver. Reassigned to Purcell Artillery.

LOWRY, HENRY CLAY: Pvt. Attended Emory and Henry. Occupation: farmer. Returned from hospital 10/8/61. Present through 12/31/61. Remustered 3/4/62. On certificate. D. 1917, age 78.

MARKHAM, JAMES M.: Pvt. Enl. 3/18/62, Liberty. At Chimbo. 7/12/62. To Lynchburg 7/24/62.

MARKHAM, PARSON W.: Pvt. Res. Bedford in 1860. Absent on surgeon's certificate 10/27/61. Present 12/31/61. Admitted to Chimbo. #5 with debility 3/15/62. Reassigned to Purcell Artillery. Captured 4/65, Petersburg. Light hair and complexion, hazel eyes, 5'8".

MARKHAM, URIAH M.: Pvt. Absent on surgeon's certificate 9/11/61. D. 11/18/61, of typhoid at Chimbo.

MARKHAM, WILLIAM T.: Pvt. Returned from hospital 9/20/61. D. 1/5/62, in camp. Claim filed 9/17/62, $51 due.

MAYO, JOSEPH ROBERT: Pvt. Bn. 1839, Fluvanna Co. Occupation: blacksmith. Present through 12/31/61. Remustered 3/7/62. On certificate. Age 22, 5'6", light complexion, dark eyes, red hair. D. 1914.

McCARY, JAMES C.: Pvt. Age 23, 1861. Discharged 10/3/61.

McCARY, CRAVEN P.: Pvt. Age 24, 1861. Occupation: Blacksmith and farmer. Returned from hospital 9/9/61. Remustered 4/11/62. On certificate.

McCARY, JAMES C.: Pvt. Age 23, 1861. Absent on surgeon's certificate 10/31-12/31/61. Detailed per S.O. #227/3 to make shoes, 11/18/61.

McCARY, THOMAS D.: Pvt. Occupation: saddler. Present through 12/31/61. Remustered 4/11/61. On certificate. KIA Petersburg.

McCLINTOCK, RICHARD DAVIS: Pvt., 5th Cpl. Bn. 10/7/37. Res. Bedford in 1860. Occupation: farmer/tinner. Age 28. Present through 12/31/61. Remustered 2/7/62. On certificate. Reassigned to Purcell Artillery. WIA Chancellorsville. Elected lieutenant. Captured at Petersburg 4/65. Fair complexion, light hair, hazel eyes, 5'8". After the war res. in Bedford as an agent for a fruit nursery. Alive in 1905, Roanoke, Va.

McDANIEL, ALEXANDER: Pvt. Enl. 3/12/62, Liberty. On certificate. Reassigned to Lynchburg Artillery.

McMILLAN, JAMES M.: Pvt. Present through 12/31/61.

MEAD, SAMUEL RICHARD: Pvt. Bn. 1/20/38, Bedford County. Occupation: farmer. Absent on surgeon's certificate 7/10/61, dated 10/31. Again since 11/24/61, dated 12/31. On hospital muster at Liberty G.H. Reassigned to Lynchburg Artillery. M. 1/7/68 to Bettie Hopkins of Amherst Co. D. 3/21/21.

MERRIMAN, GEORGE S.: Pvt. Occupation: farmer. Present through 12/31. Remustered 4/11/62. On certificate. Reassigned to Lynchburg Artillery.

MERRIMAN, JAMES A.: Pvt. Reassigned to ? KIA Petersburg.

MERRIMAN, HARVEY L.: Pvt. Occupation: farmer. Age 22. Returned from sick furlough 10/8/61. Present 12/31/61. NFR.

MERRIMAN, JOHN EDWARD: Pvt. Occupation: farmer. Age 26. Detailed as hospital steward. To Culpeper C.H. per S.O. #470, 10/31/61. Absent on surgeon's certificate 12/15/61. Remustered 4/11/62. On certificate. NFR.

MITCHELL, JOHN E.: 2nd Sgt. Bn. Bedford Co. Occupation: student. Age 18. Present through 12/31/61. Remustered 2/10/62. In Moore Hospital, Danville G.H. #1 with fever, 1/13/62. Sent to Orange. Age 19, 5'8", light complexion, hair, and eyes. Reassigned to Lynchburg Artillery.

MITCHELL, ROBERT B.: Pvt. Enl. 3/10/62. On certificate. Discharged per S.O. #187/3, 9/62. On roll of Co. A, 28th Inf. Later. Paroled at Appomattox.

MITCHELL, THOMAS FREDERICK: Pvt. Occupation: teacher. Age 19. Detailed for office clerk per order Genl. Johnston, 8/61. NFR.

MOORE, HIRAM: Pvt. Enl. 3/21/62, Lynchburg, age 56. On certificate. Reassigned to Lynchburg Artillery.

NOELL, WILLIAM TRIPP: 3rd, 2nd Cpl. Occupation: trader. Absent on surgeon's certificate 12/15/61.

OTEY, ALEXANDER W.: Pvt. Occupation: farm manager. Age 23. Returned from hospital 9/20/61. Present through 12/31/61. Remustered 4/11/62. On certificate. Reassigned to Purcell Artillery. WIA Fredericksburg, lost right arm, shot away at shoulder.

OTEY, JAMES W.: Pvt. Bn. Bedford Co. Occupation: carpenter. Age 27 or 33 in 1860. Returned from hospital 9/10/61. Present through 12/31/61. Remustered 2/7/62. Age 32, 5'4", light eyes, florid complexion, red hair. Reassigned to Purcell Artillery.

PAINTER, THAXTON B.: Pvt. Enl. 3/20/62, Liberty. NFR.

PARKER, LEWIS C.: Pvt. Occupation: Farmer. Age 18. Enl. 3/20/62, Liberty. Discharged on surgeon's certificate 10/15/62, officially dated 12/3/61; age 19. Apparently returned however and is on certificate. Reassigned to Lynchburg Artillery.

PEARSON, JOHN QUINCY ADAMS: Pvt. Bn. Henry Co. Occupation: farmer. Present through 12/31/61. Remustered 2/7/62. On certificate. Reassigned to Purcell Artillery. D. of typhoid age 21, 11/2/63. Dark eyes, brown hair, light complexion, 6'2".

PERRY, JOHN F. S.: Pvt. Bn. Rockbridge Co. Occupation: printer. Age 29. Returned from hospital 9/22/61. Absent on surgeon's certificate 11/17/61. Age 30, 5'6", dark complexion and hair, grey eyes.

PERRY, OLIVER HAZARD: Pvt. Occupation: farmer. Age 40. Absent detailed (dated 10/31), 12/31/61. NFR.

POOLE, ELIAS B.: 2nd Lt. Age 24. Present through 12/31/61. Remustered 4/11/62. On certificate. Horse KIA 9/17/62, due $275 by claim dated 12/8/62. Assigned per S.O. #193/6, 8/14/63 to duty at Camp Lee to parole and exchange prisoners. Lt. of Engineers in Pulaski Co. 1864. Paroled as Lt. in conscription dept. at Ashland, Va. 4/21/65.

PRESTON, JOHN S.: Pvt. Enl. 3/10/62, Liberty. On certificate. D. unknown date, claim filed 4/1/63.

REYNOLDS, WILLIAM J.: Pvt. Enl. 3/12/62, Liberty; age 46. Returned to Co. F, 28th Inf. WIA 8/30/62.

SALE, RICHARD CHANNING MOORE: Pvt. Present through 12/31/61. NFR.

SALE, RICHARD D. M.: Pvt. Bn. Bedford Co., son of Dr. Richard A. and Martha S. Sale. Occupation: student. Age 19. Present through 12/31/61. Remustered 2/7/62. On certificate. Furloughed 8/22/62 per S.O. #196/6. Transferred to Captain L. A. Sale's Co. Va. Arty. per S.O. #105/7. Age 20, 5'11", light complexion and hair, hazel eyes. Also in Purcell Artillery. WIA Fredericksburg. D. at private quarters 12/17/62.

SAUNDERS, ROBERT A. or H.: Pvt. Bn. Bedford Co. Transferred from Co. K, 28th Va. Inf. 9/1/61. Present through 12/31/61. Remustered 2/7/62. Age 32, 5'8", dark complexion and hair, hazel eyes.

SAUNDERS, WESLEY M. or W.: Pvt. Bn. 8/22/40. Present through 12/31/61. Remustered 2/10/62. On certificate. D. 8/6/25, Bedford.

SCRUGGS, CHARLES OTEY: Pvt. Occupation: farmer. Absent on surgeon's certificate 10/10/61. Reassigned to Lynchburg Artillery.

SHEPHERD, ALBERT N.: Pvt. Occupation: lawyer. Age 32. Transferred from this company back to Co. D, 28th Va. Inf., 10/31/61 per S.O. #472.

SIMMS, JAMES C.: Pvt. Enl. 3/20/62, Liberty. On list of sick and wounded at the Lovingston Hospital, Winchester 8/14/62. In the Farmville G.H., ward 13 with a diseased heart 10/1/62. Furloughed for 60 days 10/28/62. Reassigned to Purcell Artillery.

SIMMS, JOSHUA F.: Pvt. Enl. 3/20/61, Liberty. Reassigned to Purcell Artillery. Captured 4/65, Petersburg. Light complexion, brown hair, hazel eyes, 5'6".

SMITH, FRANK: Pvt. Captured by 54th Pennsylvania at Williamsport, Md. 9/9/62 "sick". Taken first to Cincinatti, Ohio then to Camp Chase 9/20/62. List of prisoners at Atheneum Prison; age 28; 5'11", dark complexion, grey eyes, brown hair, occupation: laborer. Residence: St. Paul, Minnesota. Exchanged 9/29/62.

SMITH, ISAAC B.: Pvt. Enl. 3/13/62, Liberty. On certificate. Reassigned to Lynchburg Artillery.

SMITH, SAMUEL H.: Pvt. Bn. Nelson Co. Occupation: carpenter. Present through 12/31/61. Remustered 2/7/62. On certificate. Age 22, 5'8", light eyes and hair, dark complexion. Reassigned to Lynchburg Artillery.

SNAPP, JOSEPH: 4th Sgt. Bn. Appomattox Co. Occupation: clerk/machinist/cabinetmaker. Age 25. Returned from hospital 9/25/61. Present through 12/31/61. Age 25, 5'10", light complexion, light hair and eyes. Reassigned to Purcell Artillery. WIA 10/64.

STONE, SAMUEL M.: Pvt. Bn. Campbell Co. Occupation: carpenter. Age 28. Present through 12/31/61. Artificier. Remustered 2/7/62. On certificate. Age 28, 6', light complexion and hair, blue eyes. Reassigned to Lynchburg Artillery.

TERRY, NATHANIEL: Pvt., 5th Sgt., 2nd Lt., 1st Lt., 2nd Lt. Occupation: tobacconist. Age 25. 11/6/61. Enrolling officer for Bedford Co., 8/2/63. Age 28, on list of employees enrolling duty in Smyth Co., Va. by authority of Col. Shields, 3/15/64.

TERRY, THOMAS J.: Pvt. Occupation: carpenter. Age 25. Absent on surgeon's certificate 10/27/61. Present through 12/31/61. Remustered 4/11/62. On certificate. Reassigned to Lynchburg Artillery. KIA.

THOMAS, WILLIAM PETER: Pvt. Age 38. Present through 12/31/61. "Gunner, accidentally wounded, discharged. NFR.

THOMSON, JESSE L.: 3rd Sgt. Occupation: collector. Age 20. Present through 12/31/61. Remustered 2/7/62. On certificate. NFR.

THOMSON, NATHANIEL WADDY: Pvt., 4th Cpl. Bn. Bedford Co., 12/7/29, son of Jesse L. and Rhoda Whorton Thomson. Occupation: farmer. M. Anne Logwood White (d. 1857). Member of St. Thomas Episcopal Church of Bedford City. Occupation: farmer. Present 10/31-12/31/61. To 4th Cpl. 11/61. Remustered 3/4/62. Incapacitated by wounds received at Sharpsburg. Physique of a "viking, splendid, strong, not unlike norsemen of old." To Purcell artillery and then back to 28th Inf. M. 2) Sarah Virginia Wharton of Bedford Co. 12/65. One daughter. D. ultimately from effects of wounds 2/10/18, at the home of his daughter, Mrs. Belle Foster.

WALDRON, BURWELL: Pvt. Occupation: cooper. Age 24. Absent on surgeon's certificate 10/15/61. Present through 12/31/61. Remustered 2/7/62. On certificate. Wounded by railway accident, "contusion." Admitted to Farmville G.H. 7/22/62. Returned to duty 8/9/62. Reassigned to Purcell Artillery. WIA Fredericksburg. D. of jaundice 7/8/64.

WALDRON, JACOB: Pvt. Occupation: shoemaker. Age 34. Present through 12/31/61. Remustered 2/7/62. Wounded by railway accident admitted to Farmville G.H. 7/22/62. Returned to duty 9/16/62. Reassigned to Purcell Artillery. Captured at Petersburg 4/65. Fair complexion, dark hair, blue eyes, 5'11".

WELLS, JESSE WARD: Pvt. B. 10/7/42. Absent on surgeon's certificate 10/21/61. Remustered 4/11/62. On certificate. At Orange C.H. G.H. with typhoid fever 10/21/62. Transferred to Lynchburg G.H. 10/29/62. Reassigned to Lynchburg Artillery. D. 8/27/42, Bunker Hill, Bedford Co.

WELLS, WILLIAM HENRY LAFAYETTE: Pvt. Bn. Bedford Co., 9/4/40. Returned from furlough 9/7/61. Present through 12/31/61. Remustered 3/4/62. On certificate. Reassigned to Lynchburg Artillery. D. 1/27/39, Plano, Texas.

WEST, _____: Pvt. Killed.

WHITTEN, BENJAMIN S.: Pvt. Occupation: farmer. Age 22. Transferred to Co. G, 28th Va. Inf., 9/5/61.

WILLIAMS, CHARLES McK.: Pvt. Postwar reference.

YOUNG, JOHN H.: Pvt. Bn. Frederick Co., Md. Occupation: farmer. Enl. 3/19/62, Liberty. On certificate. Discharged, "alcoholic," age 48, 5'8", blonde complexion, grey eyes and hair.

ZIMMERMAN, WILLIAM: Pvt. Enl. 3/62, Liberty. Age 48. Reassigned to Purcell Artillery.

BIBLIOGRAPHY

Manuscripts

Albemarle County Historical Society
    Memoirs of Leroy Wesley Cox
Charlottesville, Mr. J. Harvey Bailey
    Wilbur F. Davis Papers
Duke University
    P.G.T. Beauregard Papers
Fredericksburg and Spotsylvania National Military Park
    Henry Herbert Harris Diary (Copy)
    Jerry Malcolm Harris Letters (Copies)
Library of Congress
    Jedediah Hotchkiss Papers
National Archives
    Compiled Service Records of the Bedford and Charlottesville Artillery and the Lee Battery.
    Population Schedules of the Eighth Census of the United States, 1860.
United States Military Academy
    Register of Graduates and Former Cadets
University of Virginia
    John Warwick Daniel Papers
    Wilbur F. Davis Memoirs
    Fitzhugh Family Papers
    McCoy Family Papers
Tennessee State Library and Archives
    William Jasper Muse Memoirs
Virginia Military Institute
    Alumni Records
Virginia State Library
    Joseph V. Bidgood Papers, Unit Record Department, Adjutant Generals Office, Confederate Military Records.
Washington and Lee University
    Alumni Records
    W. B. Pettit Papers

Published Primary Sources

Alexander, Edward Porter. *Fighting for the Confederacy: The Personal Recollections of General Edward Porter Alexander.* Edited by Gary W. Gallagher. Chapel Hill, 1989.

Fonerden, Clarence Albert. *History of ... Carpenter's Battery* New Market, 1911.

Hotchkiss, Jedediah. *Make Me a Map of the Valley.* Dallas, 1973.

Moore, Edward Alexander. *Story of a Cannoneer Under Stonewall Jackson.* New York, 1907.

Poague, William Thomas. *Gunner with Stonewall.* Jackson, Tennessee, 1957.

Smith, Tunstall, ed. *Richard Snowden Andrews, A Memoir.* Baltimore, 1910.

Stiles, Robert. *Four Years Under Marse Robert.* New York, 1903. Reprint, Dayton, Ohio, 1977.

United States War Department. *War of the Rebellion: A Compilation of the Official Records of the Union and Confederate Armies.* 128 vols. Washington, D.C., 1880-1901.

Newspapers and Periodicals

Fredericksburg *Free Lance*
Fredericksburg *Star*
Richmond *Examiner*
Blue and Gray
Civil War Times Illustrated
Coffee County Historical Quarterly
Confederate Veteran, 1893-1932, 40 vols.
Southern Historical Society Papers, 1876-1953, 52 vols.

Secondary Sources

Bearss, Edwin C. and Chris Calkins, *The Battle of Five Forks.* Lynchburg, 1985.

Bohannon, Keith S. *The Giles, Alleghany and Jackson Artillery.* Lynchburgh, 1990.

Carmichael, Peter S. *The Purcell, Crenshaw and Letcher Artillery.* Lynchburg, 1990.

Chilton, Ann. *Remnants of War, 1861-1865: The Civil War Records of Bedford. . .* Signal Mountain, Tennessee, 1986.

Civil War Centenial Commission. *Tennesseans in the Civil War: A Military History of Confederate and Union Units with Available Rosters of Personnel.* 2 vols. Nashville, 1964-65.

Collier, Calvin L. *They'll Do to Tie To! The Story of the Third Regiment Arkansas Infantry, C.S.A.* Little Rock, 1959.

Dickey, Elaine Owens. *Lincoln County: A Tribute to Our Past.* Fayetteville, Tennessee, 1977.

Driver, Robert J., Jr. *The 1st and 2nd Rockbridge Artillery.* Lynchburg, 1987.

Early, R. H. *Campbell Chronicles and Family Sketches Embracing the History of Campbell County, Virginia.* Lynchburg, 1927.

Evans, Clement Anselm, ed. *Confederate Military History.* 12 vols. Atlanta, 1899.

Freeman, Douglas Southall. *Lee's Lieutenants.* 3 vols. New York, 1942-45.

Graham, Martin F. and George F. Skoch. *Mine Run: A Campaign of Lost Opportunities.* Lynchburg, 1987.

Hardesty's Historical and Geographical Encyclopedia. . . Special Virginia Edition. New York, 1884.

Hayden, Horace E. *Virginia Genealogies.* Washington, D.C., 1983.

Hennessy, John. *Troop Movements for the Second Battle of Manassas.* Denver, 1985.

Hogg, Anne M. *Virginia Cemeteries: A Guide to Resources.* Charlottesville, 1986.

Johnson, John Lipscomb. *The University Memorial: Biographical Sketches of Alumni of the University of Virginia Who Fell in the Confederate War.* Baltimore, 1871.

Johnson, Robert U. and C. C. Buell, editors. *Battles and Leaders of the Civil War.* 4 vols. New York, 1965.

Jordan, Ervin L., Jr. *Charlottesville and the University of Virginia in the Civil War.* Lynchburg, 1988.

Kemp, Vernon E. *The Alumni Directory and Service Record of Washington and Lee University.* Lexington, 1926.

Matter, William D. *If It Takes All Summer: The Battle of Spotsylvania.* Chapel Hill, 1988.

McMahon, Basil B. *Coffee County, Then and Now.* Nashville, 1983.

Morris, George and Susan Foutz. *Lynchburg in the Civil War: The City-The People-The Battle.* Lynchburg, 1984.

Pfanz, Harry W. *Gettysburg, The Second Day.* Chapel Hill, 1987.

Richey, Homer, ed. *Memorial History of the John Bowie Strange Camp, United Confederate Veterans.* Charlottesville, 1920.

Robertson, James I., Jr. *The Stonewall Brigade.* Baton Rouge, 1963.

Swank, Walbrook D. *Confederate Letters and Diaries, 1861-1865.* Charlottesville, 1988.

Tanner, Robert G. *Stonewall in the Valley.* New York, 1981.

University of Virginia. *Students of the University of Virginia, a Semi-Centennial Catalogue, with Brief Biographical Sketches.* Baltimore, 1878.

Virginia Military Institute. *Virginia Military Institute Register of Former Cadets.* Lexington, 1957.

Wainwright, Charles S. *A Diary of Battle: The Personal Journals of Charles S. Wainwright, 1861-1865.* Edited by Allan Nevins. New York, 1962.

Walker, Charles D. *Biographical Sketches of the Graduates and Eleves of the Virginia Military Institute. Philadelphia, 1875.*

Wallace, Lee A. *A Guide to Virginia Military Organizations*. Richmond, 1964.

Wise, Jennings C. *Long Arm of Lee*. 2 vols. Lynchburg, 1915.

Zinn, Jack. *R. E. Lee's Cheat Mountain Campaign*. Parsons, W.Va., 1974.